D0543181

ALL NEW 100 MATHS LESSONS

Licence

YEAR R

Ann Montague-Smith

Contents

Acknowledgements

Extracts from the National Numeracy Strategy Framework for Teaching Mathematics © Crown copyright. Reproduced under the terms of HMSO Guidance Note 8.
Qualifications and Curriculum Authority for the use of extras from the QCA/DfEE document Curriculum Guidance for the Foundation Stage © 2000 Qualification and Curriculum Authority.

Resources on CD-ROM

Karen King for 'Five Parcels' by Karen King © 2005, Karen King, previously unpublished.
Karen King for 'Sparky's Travels' by Karen King © 2005, Karen King, previously unpublished.
Neela Mann for 'Working Week' by Neela Mann © 2005, Neela Mann, previously unpublished.
Judith Nicholls for 'Giant's Breakfast' by Judith Nicholls from 'Scholastic Collections: Early Years Poems and Rhymes' compiled by Jill Bennett © 1993, Judith Nicholls (1993, Scholastic Ltd).
Brenda Williams for 'Ladybird Spots' by Brenda Williams © 2005, Brenda Williams, previously unpublished.
Brenda Williams for use of 'Four for Fun!' by Brenda Williams © 2005, Brenda Williams, previously unpublished.
Brenda Williams for the use of 'Ten Crafty Crocodiles" by Brenda Williams © 2005, Brenda Williams, previously unpublished.

Designed using Adobe Inc. InDesign™ v2.0.1

British Library Cataloguing-in-Publication Data
A catalogue record for this book is available from the British Library.
ISBN 0-439-98466-1
ISBN 978-0439-98466-9

Published by
Scholastic Ltd
Villiers House
Clarendon Avenue
Leamington Spa
Warks. CV32 5PR

© **Scholastic Ltd, 2005**
Text © Ann Montague-Smith, 2005
Printed by Bell & Bain
3 4 5 6 7 8 9   6 7 8 9 0 1 2 3 4

Series Consultant
Ann Montague-Smith

Author
Ann Montague-Smith

Editors
Joel Lane and Nancy Candlin

Assistant Editor
Charlotte Ronalds

Series Designer
Joy Monkhouse

Designers
Cath Mason, Micky Pledge and Andrea Lewis

Illustrations
Cathy Hughes and Baz Rowell
(Beehive Illustration)

CD development
CD developed in association with Footmark Media Ltd

Visit our website at
www.scholastic.co.uk

About the series

100 Maths Lessons is designed to enable you to provide clear teaching, with follow-up activities that are, in the main, practical activities for pairs of children to work on together. These activities are designed to encourage the children to use the mental strategies that they are learning and to check each other's calculations. Many of the activities are games that they will enjoy playing, and that encourage learning.

About the book

This book is divided into three termly sections. Each term begins with a Medium-term plan ('Termly planning grid') based on the National Numeracy Strategy's Medium-term plans and Framework for teaching mathematics. Each term's work is divided into a number of units of lessons on a specific topic.

Note: Because the units in this book follow the structure of the National Numeracy Strategy's Framework for teaching mathematics, the units in each term jump from Unit 5 to Unit 7. The Strategy suggests you put aside the time for Unit 6 for Assess and review.

Finding your way around the lesson units

Each term is comprised of 10 units. Each unit contains:
- a short-term planning grid
- up to five session plans
- photocopiable activity sheets.

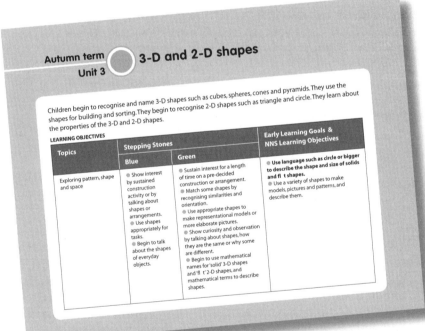

Autumn term
Unit 3
3-D and 2-D shapes

Children begin to recognise and name 3-D shapes such as cubes, spheres, cones and pyramids. They use the shapes for building and sorting. They begin to recognise 2-D shapes such as triangle and circle. They learn about the properties of the 3-D and 2-D shapes.

LEARNING OBJECTIVES

Topics	Stepping Stones		Early Learning Goals & NNS Learning Objectives
	Blue	Green	
Exploring pattern, shape and space	● Show interest by sustained construction activity or by talking about shapes or arrangements. ● Use shapes appropriately for tasks. ● Begin to talk about the shapes of everyday objects.	● Sustain interest for a length of time on a pre-decided construction or arrangement. ● Match some shapes by recognising similarities and orientation. ● Use appropriate shapes to make representational models or more elaborate pictures. ● Show curiosity and observation by talking about shapes, how they are the same or why some are different. ● Begin to use mathematical names for 'solid' 3-D shapes and 'fl t' 2-D shapes, and mathematical terms to describe shapes.	● **Use language such as circle or bigger to describe the shape and size of solids and fl t shapes.** ● Use a variety of shapes to make models, pictures and patterns, and describe them.

Short-term planning grids

The short-term planning grids ('Learning objectives') provide an overview of the objectives for each unit. The objectives come from the Medium-term plan and support clear progression through the year. Key objectives are shown in bold, as in the Yearly Teaching Programme in the NNS *Framework for teaching mathematics*.

Lesson plans

The lessons are structured on the basis of a daily maths lesson following the NNS's three-part lesson format: a ten-minute **Starter** of oral work and mental maths, a **Main teaching activities** session with interactive teaching time and/or group/individual work, and a **Plenary** round-up including **Assessment** opportunities.

However, this structure has not been rigidly applied. Where it is appropriate to concentrate on whole-class teaching, for example, the lesson plan may not include a group-work session at all. The overall organisation of the lesson plan varies from unit to unit depending on the lesson content. In some units all the plans are separate, though they provide different levels of detail. Elsewhere you may find a bank of activities that you can set up as a 'circus', or instruction and support for an extended investigation, either of which the children will work through over the course of several days. Most units of work are supported with activity pages provided in the book, which can also be found on the accompanying CD.

How ICT is used

Ideas for using ICT are suggested wherever appropriate in *100 Maths Lessons*. We have assumed that you will have access to basic office applications, such as word-processing, and can email and research using the Internet.

While some lessons use dataloggers or floor robots, we have avoided suggesting specific software, except for the games and interactive teaching programs (ITPs) provided by the NNS. If you do not already have them, these can be downloaded from the NNS website at:
http://www.standards.dfes.gov.uk/numeracy

How to use the CD-ROM

System requirements
Minimum specification:
- PC with a CD-ROM drive and at least 32 MB RAM
- Pentium 166 MHz processor
- Microsoft Windows 98, NT, 2000 or XP
- SVGA screen display with at least 64K colours at a screen resolution of 800 x 600 pixels

100 Maths Lessons **CD-ROMs are for PC use only.**

Setting up your computer for optimal use
On opening, the CD will alert you if changes are needed in order to operate the CD at its optimal use. There are two changes you may be advised to make:

Viewing resources at their maximum screen size
To see images at their maximum screen size, your screen display needs to be set to 800 x 600 pixels. In order to adjust your screen size you will first need to **Quit** the program.

If using a PC, select **Settings**, then **Control Panel** from the **Start** menu. Next, double click on the **Display** icon and then click on the **Settings** tab. Finally, adjust the **Screen area** scroll bar to 800 x 600 pixels. Click **OK** and then restart the program.

Adobe® Acrobat® Reader®
Acrobat® Reader® is required to view Portable Document Format (PDF) files. All of the unit resources are PDF files. It is not necessary to install Acrobat Reader on your PC. If you do not have it installed, the application will use a 'run-time' version for the CD, i.e. one which only works with the 100 Maths Lessons application.

However if you would like to install **Acrobat® Reader®**, the latest version (6) can be downloaded from the CD-ROM. To do this, right-click on the **Start** menu on your desktop and choose **Explore**. Click on the + sign to the left of the CD drive entitled '100 Maths Lessons' and open the folder called **Acrobat Reader Installer.** Run the program contained in this folder to install **Acrobat® Reader®.** If you experience any difficulties viewing the PDF files, try changing your **Acrobat® Reader®** preferences. Select **Edit**, then **Preferences**, within **Acrobat® Reader®**. You will then be able to change your viewing options. For further information about **Adobe® Acrobat® Reader®**, visit the **Adobe®** website at www.adobe.com

Getting started
The *100 Maths Lessons CD-ROM* program should auto run when you insert the CD-ROM into your CD drive. If it does not, use **My Computer** to browse the contents of the CD-ROM and click on the '100 Maths Lessons' icon.

From the start up screen there are three options: Click on **Credits** to view a list of acknowledgements. You must then read the **Terms and conditions**. If you agree to these terms then click **Next** to continue. **Continue** on the start up screen allows you to move to the Main menu.

Main menu

Each *100 Maths Lessons* CD contains:

- activity sheets – with answers, where appropriate, that can be toggled by pressing the 'on' and 'off' buttons on the left of the screen
- general resource sheets designed to support a number of activities.

You can access the printable pages on the CD by clicking:

- the chosen term ('Autumn', 'Spring' or 'Summer')
- the unit required (for example, 'Unit 2: Shape and space')
- the requisite activity page (for example, 'Counting on').

CD navigation

Back: click to return to the previous screen. Continue to move to the **Menu** or start up screens.

Quit: click **Quit** to close the menu program. You are then provided with options to return to the start up menu or to exit the CD.

Help: provides general background information and basic technical support. Click on the **Help** button to access. Click **Back** to return to the previous screen.

Printing

There are two print options:

- The **Print** button on the bottom left of each activity screen allows you to print directly from the CD program.
- If you press the **View** button above the **Print** option, the sheet will open as a read-only page in **Acrobat® Reader®**. To print the selected resource from **Acrobat® Reader®,** select **File** and then **Print**. Once you have printed the resource, minimise or close the **Adobe®** screen using _ or **x** in the top right-hand corner of the screen.

Viewing on an interactive whiteboard or data projector

The sheets can be viewed directly from the CD. To make viewing easier for a whole class, use a large monitor, data projector or interactive whiteboard.

About Reception Year

A formally structured daily maths lesson is not expected in this year. Children may start the year being able to count to at least five, recognise some shapes, and solve very simple practical problems. They are likely to have little concept of quantities beyond four or five, counting in ones beyond five or six in a meaningful way, recognising numerals, working out simple addition or subtraction, making simple patterns, describing and naming simple shapes, and using their mathematical ideas and methods to solve practical problems. These will be the key concepts learned this year.

	Topics	Stepping Stones		Early Learning Goals & NNS Learning Objectives
		Blue	**Green**	
1	Counting	● Use some number names accurately in play. ● Willingly attempt to count, with some numbers in the correct order.	● Show confidence with numbers by initiating or requesting number activities.	● **Say and use the number names in order in familiar contexts** such as number rhymes, songs, stories, counting games and activities (first to five, then ten, then twenty and beyond). ● Recite the number names in order, continuing the count forwards from a given number.
2	Counting	● Use some number names accurately in play. ● Willingly attempt to count, with some numbers in the correct order. ● Recognise groups with one, two or three objects.	● Show confidence with numbers by initiating or requesting number activities. ● Count up to three or four objects by saying one number name for each item.	● **Say and use the number names in order in familiar contexts** such as number rhymes, songs, stories, counting games and activities (first to five, then ten, then twenty and beyond). ● Recite number names in order, continuing the count forwards or backwards from a given number. ● **Count reliably up to 10 everyday objects** (first to five, then ten, then beyond), giving just one number name to each object.
3	Exploring pattern, shape and space	● Show interest by sustained construction activity or by talking about shapes or arrangements. ● Use shapes appropriately for tasks. ● Begin to talk about the shapes of everyday objects.	● Sustain interest for a length of time on a pre-decided construction or arrangement. ● Match some shapes by recognising similarities and orientation. ● Use appropriate shapes to make representational models or more elaborate pictures. ● Show curiosity and observation by talking about shapes, how they are the same or why some are different. ● Begin to use mathematical names for 'solid' 3-D shapes and 'flat' 2-D shapes, and mathematical terms to describe shapes.	● **Use language such as circle or bigger to describe the shape and size of solids and flat shapes.** ● Use a variety of shapes to make models, pictures and patterns, and describe them.
4	Counting Comparing and ordering measures	● Recognise groups with one, two or three objects.	● Count up to three or four objects by saying one number name for each item. ● Order two or three items by length. ● Adapt shapes or cut material to size.	● **Count reliably up to ten everyday objects** (first to five, then ten, then beyond), giving just one number name to each object. ● **Use language such as more or less, longer or shorter to compare two quantities**, then more than two, by making direct comparisons of lengths.
5	Counting Adding and subtracting	● Show curiosity about numbers by offering comments or asking questions. ● Show an interest in number problems.	● Show confidence with numbers by initiating or requesting number activities. ● Sometimes show confidence and offer solutions to problems. ● Find the total number of items in two groups by counting all of them. ● Use own methods to solve a problem. ● Say with confidence the number that is one more than a given number.	● Begin to recognise 'none' and 'zero' in stories, rhymes and when counting. ● **Find one more than a number from 1 to 10.**
6	Assess and review			

	Topics	Stepping Stones		Early Learning Goals & NNS Learning Objectives
		Blue	**Green**	
7	Counting	● Willingly attempt to count with some numbers in the correct order.	● Show confidence with numbers by initiating or requesting number activities.	● **Say and use the number names in order in familiar contexts** such as number rhymes, songs, stories, counting games and activities (first to five, then ten, then twenty and beyond). ● Recite the number names in order, continuing the count forwards or backwards from a given number.
	Comparing and ordering numbers	● Show an interest in number problems.	● Sometimes show confidence and offer solutions to problems. ● Use own methods to solve a problem.	● **Use language such as more or less, greater or smaller to compare two numbers** and say which is more or less.
8	Counting	● Use some number names accurately in play. ● Willingly attempt to count, with some numbers in the correct order.	● Show confidence with numbers by initiating or requesting number activities.	● Recite the number names in order, continuing the count forwards or backwards from a given number. ● **Count reliably up to 10 everyday objects** (first to 5, then 10, and beyond), giving just one number name to each object.
	Adding and subtracting	● Separate a group of three objects in different ways, starting to recognise that the total is still the same.	● Say with confidence the number that is one more than a given number. ● Say the number after any number up to 9.	● **Find one more or one less than a number from 1 to 10.**
9	Exploring pattern, shape and space	● Show interest by sustained construction activity or by talking about shapes or arrangements.	● Match some shapes by recognising similarities and orientation. ● Begin to use mathematical names for 'solid' 3-D shapes and mathematical terms to describe shapes.	● **Use language such as circle or bigger to describe the shape and size of solids and flat shapes.** ● Begin to name solids such as a cube, cone, sphere. ● Put sets of objects in order of size.
	Reasoning about numbers or shapes	● Use shapes appropriately for tasks. ● Begin to talk about the shapes of everyday objects.	● Use appropriate shapes to make representational models or pictures. ● Show curiosity and observation by talking about shapes, how they are the same or why some are different.	● **Talk about, recognise and recreate simple patterns**: for example, simple repeating or symmetrical patterns from different cultures.
10	Counting	● Recognise groups with one, two or three objects.	● Count up to three or four objects by saying one number name for each item.	● **Count reliably up to 10 everyday objects** (first to 5, then 10, then beyond), giving just one number name to each object.
	Comparing and ordering measures		● Order two items by weight.	● **Use language such as more or less, heavier or lighter to compare two quantities**, then more than two, by making direct comparisons of masses. ● Begin to understand and use the vocabulary of time. ● Sequence familiar events.
11	Counting	● Attempt to count, with some numbers in the correct order.	● Count actions or objects that cannot be moved.	● Count reliably in other contexts, such as clapping sounds or hopping movements.
	Problems involving 'real life' and money	● Show an interest in number problems.	● Sometimes show confidence and offer solutions to problems.	● Begin to understand and use the vocabulary related to money. Sort coins, including the £1 and £2 coins, and use them in role play to pay and give change. ● **Use developing mathematical ideas and methods to solve practical problems** involving counting and comparing in a real or role play context.
12	Assess and review			

Counting to five

Children recite the number names to five, then to ten, keeping a good pace to the count. They identify counting errors when listening to counting and correct these. They use counting rhymes and stories which include counting to five.

LEARNING OBJECTIVES

Topics	Stepping Stones		Early Learning Goals & NNS Learning Objectives
	Blue	**Green**	
Counting	● Use some number names accurately in play. ● Willingly attempt to count, with some numbers in the correct order.	● Show confidence with numbers by initiating or requesting number activities.	● **Say and use the number names in order in familiar contexts** such as number rhymes, songs, stories, counting games and activities (first to five, then ten, then twenty and beyond). ● Recite the number names in order, continuing the count forwards from a given number.

5 Sessions

Preparation

Place the listening centre and headphones, cassette recorder or CD player in a quiet area of the room. Make a display of counting books in the book area, or in a quiet area of the room with comfortable seating or cushions.

Learning objectives

Starter bank
ELGs/NNS
● **Say and use the number names in order in familiar contexts.**

Main teaching & group activities
Blue Stepping Stones
● Use some number names accurately in play.
● Willingly attempt to count, with some numbers in the correct order.
Green Stepping Stones
● Show confidence with numbers by initiating or requesting number activities.
ELGs/NNS
● **Say and use the number names in order in familiar contexts** such as number rhymes, songs, stories, counting games and activities (first to five, then ten, then twenty and beyond).
● Recite the number names in order, continuing the count forwards from a given number.

Vocabulary

one, two, three… ten, count, count on, count from, count to

You will need:
Photocopiable pages
'Counting on', for the teacher's/LSA's reference, see page 12.

CD pages
'Number rhymes for 1 and 2' and 'Number rhymes for 3' for the teacher's/LSA's reference (see General resources).

Equipment
Puppet or doll; listening centre with headphones, or cassette recorder or CD player; tape or CD of number rhymes or songs; counting books.

WHOLE CLASS TEACHING

Starter bank

Each day, choose number rhymes to sing or say from the following collection, which covers the numbers one, two and three (the words and actions are given on CD pages 'Number rhymes for 1 and 2' and 'Number rhymes for 3'):

● Hey diddle dumpling, my son John
● Hickory, dickory, dock
● Two little dicky birds sitting on a wall
● Three blind mice
● Three little ghosties

Invite the children to sing or say the words of one of the rhymes with you. Then demonstrate the actions and ask them to join in.

Discuss which numbers they can find in each rhyme. Ask questions such as: *How many mice were there? What numbers did you say? Now say the numbers one, two, three with me.*

Main teaching activity

Show the children the puppet or doll and explain that the puppet is going to count. Begin with: *One, two, three, four, five.* Ask the children to join in with the puppet as it counts. Repeat this several times. Now ask the children to count from *one* with the puppet, keeping a good pace to the count. The children may like to clap their hands in time with the count.

Ask the children to count quietly, saying *five* more loudly. Repeat this so that it becomes a repeating pattern of counting: *One, two, three, four, FIVE; one, two, three, four, FIVE.* Repeat this, emphasising different numbers in the count each time.

Ask the children to say the counting numbers 'in their heads'. Lightly clap your hands to keep the pace of the count clear. Ask the children to say *five* aloud each time. This can be repeated with the children saying any number you choose in the count, or by saying *One, two, three, four,* and not saying *five.*

When the children are confident with this, extend the count to ten. This may be developed over the course of the five sessions, so that the children gradually extend their recall of the counting numbers in order.

GROUP ACTIVITIES

Puppet counting errors

TEACHER DIRECTED

Learning objectives
Blue Stepping Stones:
● Use some number names accurately in play.
● Willingly attempt to count, with some numbers in the correct order.

Activity

Work with about six children. Hold up the puppet and ask the children to listen carefully to the puppet counting. Say, for example: *One, two, four, five.* Invite the children to tell you whether the puppet counted correctly, and to say what was missing. Ask them to say the count correctly all together. Repeat this for different counting errors:

● *One, two, three, five…* (missing number name)
● *One, two, four, three, five…* (number names in wrong order)
● *One, two, three, three, four…* (repeating a number name).

You can repeat this activity over time, extending the count to ten and beyond as the children become confident with numbers to ten.

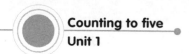
Plenary & assessment

Ask the children to listen carefully to the puppet counting. For example:
- *One, two, three, four, six…*
- *One, two, three, four, five, six, eight, seven…*
- *One, two, three, four, five, five…*

Each time, ask:
- *Did the puppet say the right counting words?*
- *What did the puppet do wrong?*
- *What should the puppet have said? Who can say this for me?*

Counting on

Learning objectives
Blue Stepping Stones:
- Use some number names accurately in play.
- Willingly attempt to count, with some numbers in the correct order.

ELGs/NNS:
- Recite the number names in order, continuing the count forwards from a given number.

Activity

This activity is provided in detail on CD page 'Counting on' for the adult's/LSA's reference. The page also provides the adult with a table in which to record the children's achievements and difficulties for feedback to the teacher.

Ask a group of about six children to sit in a circle with an LSA. The LSA asks the children to count on from a starting number until they say: *Stop!* For example, start with: *One, two…* When the children have said 'four' the LSA can say: *Stop!* The LSA could then ask:
- *What was the last number you said?*
- *What number comes next? And what number comes next after that?*

The LSA tells the children to repeat the count, stopping at three, four or five, and starting on one or two. Where children are confident with counting to ten, the LSA can extend the count and the stopping point to between six and ten.

Plenary & assessment

Ask the children to count with you: *One, two, three, four, five…*
Ask questions such as:
- *What was the last number that you said?*
- *What number comes next?*
- *And next?*

Now, ask the children to take turns to count on from one, two or three. Say the starting number and invite them to count on until you say: *Stop!* Then repeat the questions above. If the children seem confident, ask individuals to count on from the different starting numbers.

Where children are confident with counting to ten, repeat the counting and stopping activity for counts beyond five and up to ten.

Rhymes for one to five

Learning objectives
NNS:
- **Say and use the number names in order in familiar contexts** such as number rhymes, songs, stories, counting games and activities (first to five, then ten, then twenty and beyond).

Activity

Ask a group of about six children to sit in a circle with an LSA. The LSA will need CD pages 'Number

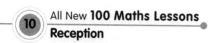

rhymes for 1 and 2' and 'Number rhymes for 3'. Choose one of the rhymes from the sheets and say or sing it and do the actions, encouraging the children to join in. Over time, this activity can be repeated for the other rhymes.

Plenary & assessment

Choose one of the rhymes and invite all of the children to say or sing it and to do the actions. Ask questions such as:

- *What number/s did you say in the rhyme?*
- *What number comes next after one/two/three?*
- *Who can count to five/ten for me?*

Invite children who are confident to count to three, four, five… ten. Praise them for their skill in counting. Children could count either as a group or individually.

Number rhyme tapes

Learning objectives

Green Stepping Stones:
- Show confidence with numbers by initiating or requesting number activities.

NNS:
- **Say and use the number names in order in familiar contexts** such as number rhymes, songs, stories, counting games and activities (first to five, then ten, then twenty and beyond).

Activity

Choose some tapes of number rhymes, or songs that include numbers or counts to about five. Ask a group of about four children to listen to the number rhymes or songs tape. They can 'sing along' to the tape and try to learn the rhymes.

Plenary & assessment

Play the rhymes or songs to the whole class. Ask all the children to join in with the songs. Ask questions such as:

- *Who would like to sing the song to the others?*
- *What numbers did you sing?*

Invite the children to sing other rhymes and songs that they know about numbers. Name a number and ask whether they can tell you a rhyme that has that number in it.

Counting books

Learning objectives

Green Stepping Stones:
- Show confidence with numbers by initiating or requesting number activities.

Activity

In the book area or a quiet area of the classroom, set out a variety of counting books. Children in pairs can share the books, or they could look at them individually. They will enjoy looking at the pictures and will become familiar with the books.

Plenary & assessment

In a group or as a class, choose one of the counting books and look at it together. Look at the pictures together and count as you point to each of the objects in turn. Ask, for example:

- *How many did we count?*
- *Say the numbers with me: One, two… What is the next number after…?*

Over time, this activity can be repeated for each of the counting books that you have selected.

Counting on

Work with a group of about six children. Ask them to sit in a circle beside you.

Explain that you will say a starting number (start with one, then two, and progress to numbers between one and five).

Ask the children to count on from that number until you say: *Stop!* For example, start: *One, two...* and then ask the children to continue. When they have said 'four', say: *Stop!* Ask:

- *What was the last number you said?*

- *What number comes next? And next?*

Repeat the activity, but this time starting on one or two and stopping them at three, four or five, like this:

- One... (to three). *Stop! What was the last number you said? What number comes next?*

- Record the children's achievements.

Child's name	What happened	What to do next time

Autumn term
Unit 2

Counting to ten

Children recite the number names to ten, keeping a good pace to the count. A circle of children take turns to say the next number in the count. They continue the count from a given starting number such as two… three… four… They count out up to five objects, synchronising the touch, move and count.

LEARNING OBJECTIVES

Topics	Stepping Stones		Early Learning Goals & NNS Learning Objectives
	Blue	**Green**	
Counting	● Use some number names accurately in play. ● Willingly attempt to count, with some numbers in the correct order. ● Recognise groups with one, two or three objects.	● Show confidence with numbers by initiating or requesting number activities. ● Count up to three or four objects by saying one number name for each item.	● **Say and use the number names in order in familiar contexts** such as number rhymes, songs, stories, counting games and activities (first to five, then ten, then twenty and beyond). ● Recite number names in order, continuing the count forwards or backwards from a given number. ● **Count reliably up to 10 everyday objects** (first to 5, then 10, then beyond), giving just one number name to each object.

2 Sessions

Learning objectives

Starter bank
ELGs/NNS
● **Say and use the number names in order in familiar contexts.**

Main teaching & group activities
Blue Stepping Stones
● Use some number names accurately in play.
● Willingly attempt to count, with some numbers in the correct order.
Green Stepping Stones
● Show confidence with numbers by initiating or requesting number activities.
ELGs/NNS
● **Say and use the number names in order in familiar contexts** such as number rhymes, songs, stories, counting games and activities (first to five, then ten then twenty and beyond).
● Recite number names in order, continuing the count forwards or backwards from a given number.

Vocabulary

one, two, three… ten, count, count on, count from, count to

You will need:
Photocopiable pages
'Round the circle counting' for the teacher's/LSA's reference, see page 18.

CD pages
'Number rhymes for 1 and 2', 'Number rhymes for 3' and 'Number rhymes for 4 and 5' for the teacher's/LSA's reference (see General resources).

Equipment
Puppet; doll or soft toy.

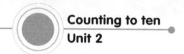
WHOLE CLASS TEACHING

Starter bank

Numbers one, two and three

Choose some number rhymes that cover the numbers one, two and three from CD pages 'Number rhymes for 1 and 2' and 'Number rhymes for 3'. With the children, say or sing the rhymes and do the actions. Ask questions such as: *How many ghosties were there? What numbers did you say? Now say the numbers one, two and three with me.*

Numbers four and five

Extend the children's number range by including some songs and rhymes that include the numbers four and five. The following examples can be found on CD page 'Number rhymes for 4 and 5':
- Ladybird spots
- Four for fun

Decide whether to include numbers up to four or to five, for each of these rhymes, as they can easily be adapted. Ask: *What numbers did you say? How many ladybirds were there at the end?*

Main teaching activity

Explain to the children that you would like them to count to ten with the puppet. Say the counting numbers, and invite the children to join in: *One, two, three… eight, nine, ten.* Repeat this several times, keeping a good, sharp pace to the counting. To help the children to keep the count rhythmical, encourage them to punch the air with one arm as they count.

Repeat the count, this time asking the children to whisper the numbers until they come to ten, which can be said in a normal voice. They might shout it, but don't worry about this.

Now explain that the puppet only wants to count to five/six/seven. Say the counting numbers together, stopping at the agreed number and starting again from one immediately: *One, two, three, four, five, six, one, two, three, four, five, six, one, two, three, four, five, six…*

The count can be extended beyond ten for those children who are confident with counting to ten.

Repeat the activity, this time counting backwards from five at first, then from up to ten.

GROUP ACTIVITIES

Round the circle counting

Learning objectives
Blue Stepping Stones:
- Use some numbers accurately in play.
- Willingly attempt to count, with some numbers in the correct order.

Green Stepping Stones:
- Show confidence with numbers by initiating or requesting number activities.

Activity

This activity is provided in detail on CD page 'Round the circle counting'. Ask the LSA to work with a group of between four and ten children sitting in a circle. The LSA will need a doll or soft toy. The LSA explains that they will give the doll to the child who begins the count. Each child, in turn, then says the next number in the count until everyone has had a turn. Repeat this for different stopping numbers.

If the group is large and you do not want to extend the count beyond four or five, the LSA could give another toy to the last child in the count to hold. Alternatively, with a small group, the children can count around the circle from the starting child until the LSA says: *Stop!*

Plenary & assessment

When the children are confident with counting to a specific number, ask them to take turns to count. Say, for example:

- *Jamil, count to five for me.*
- *What number did Jamil say to begin?*
- *What number did he say at the end?*

This activity can be repeated for other stopping numbers up to ten.

Counting forwards and backwards

TEACHER DIRECTED

Learning objectives

ELGs/NNS:

● **Say and use the number names in order in familiar contexts** such as number rhymes, songs, stories, counting games and activities (first to five, then ten, then twenty and beyond).

● Recite number names in order, continuing the count forwards or backwards from a given number.

Activity

Work with a group of about six to eight children. Say a number less than ten. Ask the children to count on from the number that you chose. Begin at one, then extend this to starting at two/five/three/six…

When the children are confident with this, suggest that they begin to count backwards from five/seven/ten. Say the counting numbers with the children.

Plenary & assessment

- *What number comes after one/two/five/nine?*
- *How do you know this? Count from one to show me.*
- *What number comes just before three/six/eight?*
- *How do you know this? Count back from nine to show me.*

3 Sessions

Preparation

Put the soft toys out in a row. Leave the sand resources in the damp sand tray.

Learning objectives

Starter bank

ELGs/NNS

● **Say and use the number names in order in familiar contexts.**

Main teaching & group activities

Blue Stepping Stones

● Recognise groups with one, two or three objects.

Green Stepping Stones

● Count up to three or four objects by saying one number name for each item.

ELGs/NNS

● **Count reliably up to 10 everyday objects** (first to 5, then 10, then beyond), giving just one number name to each object.

Vocabulary

one, two, three… to ten, how many…? count, how many…?

You will need:

Photocopiable pages
'Dressing up' for the teacher's /LSA's reference, see page 19.

CD pages
'Work mat' for each child (see General resources).

Equipment
Items for counting, such as five soft toys, large buttons or counters; dressing up clothes in a basket, with three of each item, such as hats, scarves, coats; damp sand in a tray, and buckets, spades, flags, stones, shells.

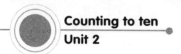

WHOLE CLASS TEACHING

Starter bank

Continue to use the material from the Starter bank for the first two sessions in this unit.

Main teaching activity

Ask the children to sit in front of you. Point to the soft toys and say: *We are going to count the toys to see how many there are.* Begin by touching each toy in turn, and then say the number name. Make sure that touching and saying the number name are done at the same time. Ask: *How many toys are there?* Check that the children recognise that 'how many' is given by the last number in the count. Repeat this for different quantities of soft toys, from two to five.

Invite children who are confident with counting to come out and touch the toys and say the number names. Ask the other children to say how many toys there are.

The count can be extended up to ten for the more confident children.

GROUP ACTIVITIES

Dressing up

Learning objectives
Blue Stepping Stones:
- Recognise groups with one, two or three objects.

Activity

The detail of this activity is provided on CD page 'Dressing up'. Ask the LSA to work with a group of four to six children. They ask the children to take turns to find the clothes that the LSA asks for.

For Green Stepping Stones, include up to four or five of each item. For ELGs/NNS, include up to ten of each item.

Plenary & assessment

Invite the children to choose one of the items of clothing and ask some of them to put them on. Ask questions about what the children have done. For example, for scarves:
- *Who is wearing a scarf?*
- *How many of you are wearing a scarf? Who will count them?*
- *So how many scarves are there?*

Sand pies

Learning objectives
Green Stepping Stones:
- Count up to three or four objects by saying one number name for each item.

Activity

Ask two or three children to work in the sand and to make sand pies. They decorate each sand pie with up to four items, for example three stones and one shell.

This activity can be adapted for children working to the Blue Stepping Stones by asking for up to three items on each sand pie. For children working to the ELGs/NNS, increase the number of items on a pie to ten.

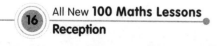

Plenary & assessment

As a group, look together at the sand pies that children have made. Invite each child to count how many items are on one of the sand pies. Encourage them to co-ordinate the touch and count and to say how many there are. Ask questions such as:

- *Count the flags on this sand pie. How many are there?*
- *Who can count all of the sand pies? How many sand pies are there?*

Counting out

TEACHER DIRECTED

Learning objectives

ELGs/NNS:

- **Count reliably up to 10 everyday objects** (first to 5, then 10, then beyond), giving just one number name to each object.

Activity

Work with a group of four to six children. Each child will need CD page 'Work mat' and some large buttons or counters. Ask them to count out the number of buttons that you say. Say, for example:

- *Count out five buttons onto your mat.*
- *Put them into a row. Count each button in turn: touch it, move it and say the number.*
- *What was the last number you said when you counted? So, how many are there in the count?*

Now ask the children to take a small handful of buttons, put them onto their mat in a line and count them, using the touch, move and count procedure.

This activity can be adapted for those working to the Green Stepping Stones by keeping the size of the count to no more than five each time.

Plenary & assessment

Put out a small handful of buttons onto a mat and invite a child to count them. Check that the counters are lined up, and that the touch, move and count procedure is used correctly. Ask:

- *What was the last number in your count? How many buttons are there?*
- *Put out another button. Count how many there are now.*

Round the circle counting

You will need a doll or soft toy.

Work with a group of four to ten children. Ask them to sit in a circle around you.

Explain that you will give the doll to the child who begins the count.
Each child in turn then says the next number in the count, until everyone has had a turn. Now repeat this for different stopping numbers. Explain that you would like the children to count in turn to three/five/eight.

If the group is larger and you do not want to extend the count beyond four or five, give another toy to the last child in the count to hold. Alternatively, with a small group, the children can count around the circle from the starting child until you say: *Stop!*

Ask some questions about their counting. For example:

- *Jamil, count to five for me.*
- *What number did Jamil say to begin?*
- *What number did he say at the end?*

This can be repeated for other finishing numbers, up to ten.

Record the children's achievements. It would be helpful to record which children count with confidence, and who can stop at a given number.

Child's name	What happened	What to do next time

Dressing up

You will need some dressing-up clothes in a basket, such as scarves, hats, and coats. There should be three of each item.

Work with a group of four to six children.

Show them the dressing-up clothes in the basket.

Ask the children to take turns to find the clothes that you ask for. For example:

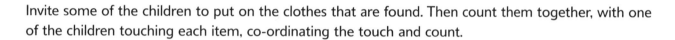

- *Dana, can you find me two scarves?*
- *Josh, can you find me three hats?*
- *Peter, how many hats did Josh find?*

Invite some of the children to put on the clothes that are found. Then count them together, with one of the children touching each item, co-ordinating the touch and count.

The children may enjoy asking each other to find a given quantity of items.

Record the children's achievements, especially those children who recognise one, two and three objects without needing to count them.

Child's name	What happened	What to do next time

3-D and 2-D shapes

Children begin to recognise and name 3-D shapes such as cubes, spheres, cones and pyramids. They use the shapes for building and sorting. They begin to recognise 2-D shapes such as triangle and circle. They learn about the properties of the 3-D and 2-D shapes.

LEARNING OBJECTIVES

Topics	Stepping Stones		Early Learning Goals & NNS Learning Objectives
	Blue	**Green**	
Exploring pattern, shape and space	● Show interest by sustained construction activity or by talking about shapes or arrangements. ● Use shapes appropriately for tasks. ● Begin to talk about the shapes of everyday objects.	● Sustain interest for a length of time on a pre-decided construction or arrangement. ● Match some shapes by recognising similarities and orientation. ● Use appropriate shapes to make representational models or more elaborate pictures. ● Show curiosity and observation by talking about shapes, how they are the same or why some are different. ● Begin to use mathematical names for 'solid' 3-D shapes and 'flat' 2-D shapes, and mathematical terms to describe shapes.	● **Use language such as circle or bigger to describe the shape and size of solids and flat shapes.** ● Use a variety of shapes to make models, pictures and patterns, and describe them.

6 Sessions

Preparation

Put the cones, pyramids, spheres and cubes into a basket.

Learning objectives

Starter bank
ELGs/NNS
- **Say and use the number names in order in familiar contexts** such as number rhymes, songs, stories, counting games and activities (first to five, then ten, then twenty and beyond).
- Recite number names in order, continuing the count forwards or backwards from a given number.
- **Count reliably up to 10 everyday objects** (first to five, then ten, then beyond), giving just one number name to each object.

Main teaching & group activities
Blue Stepping Stones
- Show interest by sustained construction activity or by talking about shapes or arrangements.
- Use shapes appropriately for tasks.
- Begin to talk about the shapes of everyday objects.
Green Stepping Stones
- Sustain interest for a length of time on a pre-decided construction or arrangement.
- Match some shapes by recognising similarities and orientation.
- Use appropriate shapes to make representational models or more elaborate pictures.
- Show curiosity and observation by talking about shapes, how they are the same or why some are different.
- Begin to use mathematical names for 'solid' 3-D shapes and 'flat' 2-D shapes, and mathematical terms to describe shapes.
ELGs/NNS
- **Use language such as circle or bigger to describe the shape and size of solids and flat shapes.**
- Use a variety of shapes to make models, pictures and patterns, and describe them.

Vocabulary

shape, pattern, flat, curved, straight, round, hollow, solid, corner, face, side, edge, end, sort, make, build, draw, cube, pyramid, sphere, cone, circle, triangle, square, rectangle, star

You will need:
Photocopiable pages
'Building' and 'Shape match' for the teacher's/LSA's reference, see pages 25–26, and 'Jigsaw', one copy for each child, see page 27.

CD pages
'Number rhymes for 1 and 2', 'Number rhymes for 3' and 'Number rhymes for 4 and 5' for the teacher's/LSA's reference (see General resources).

Equipment
Large toys, such as teddies; everyday objects such as balls, boxes, cones, pyramids, spheres, cubes; large opaque bag or 'feely box'; building blocks or construction kits; a tray of 2-D shape tiles of circles, triangles, squares, rectangles, stars; greetings cards; scissors; envelopes; basket; Plasticine.

WHOLE CLASS TEACHING

Starter bank

Number rhymes
Use the number rhymes on CD pages 'Number rhymes for 1 and 2', 'Number rhymes for 3' and 'Number rhymes for 4 and 5'. Say or sing the rhymes together, and do the actions. Ask questions such as:
- *What numbers did you say?*
- *Who can show four fingers?*

Count to and from ten
Ask the children to count with you up to ten. Keep the pace sharp, and invite the children to punch the air with an arm for each number said. Repeat this several times.

When the children are ready, count back from ten. You may have to say the numbers yourself to begin with, but the children will gradually gain in confidence and join in. Again, invite them to punch the air in order to help to keep the pace snappy.

Count out

Put out in front of the class some large toys to be counted, such as teddies. Begin with three teddies and invite a child to come out and touch and count the teddies. Ask the other children to point and count. Repeat this with different quantities of teddies, such as four, five and six.

Main teaching activity

You will need the basket of solid shapes. With the children, sit in a circle. Begin with the spheres. Pass some spheres around the circle of children for them to feel the shape. Discuss what they can see and feel. Say: *The sphere is round. What does it remind you of?* Children will probably say 'a ball'. Make a round shape with your hands hovering over the sphere.

Now repeat this with the cubes. Pass the cubes around the children and say: *The cube has flat sides.* Make your hand flat and move it above one of the faces of a cube. Ask: *What does the cube remind you of?* Children may refer to boxes.

Put the cubes and spheres into the bag or feely box and say that you would like the children to pass it around the circle. When you say *Stop!* ask the child holding the bag to take out a shape. Say: *Find me a shape that is round/has flat sides. What is this shape called?*

Over the unit, repeat this activity for the pyramid and cone. Children may notice that both have a 'point', and that the cone has a curved face, and the pyramid has triangles for its faces.

The activity can also be repeated using 2-D shape tiles.

GROUP ACTIVITIES

Building

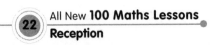

ADULT SUPPORTED

Learning objectives
Blue Stepping Stones:
- Show interest by sustained construction activity or by talking about shapes or arrangements.
- Use shapes appropriately for tasks.
- Begin to talk about the shapes of everyday objects.

ELGs/NNS:
- Use a variety of shapes to make models, pictures and patterns, and describe them.

Activity

The activity detail can be found on CD page 'Building'. Ask a group of up to six children to work in the construction area with the LSA. Provide some building blocks or a construction kit. The LSA can discuss with the children what they would like to make and then encourage them to plan their construction, giving them time to carry this out. As they build their models, the LSA asks:
- *Why is this a good shape to use here?*
- *Which shapes are round/have pointed ends/have flat faces?*
- *Which shapes can you name?*

Where this activity is used with more confident children, the LSA can encourage them to make a drawing of what they plan to do.

Plenary & assessment

Discuss with the children which shapes they found were good for building and why. Ask:
- *Which shapes did you use at the bottom? Why did you choose those shapes?*
- *Which shapes would not be good for building this…? Why do you think that?*

Praise the children for their constructions and, if possible, put them on display for others to see and talk about. For more confident children, ask:
- *Is your model like your drawing? How did you change it? Why was that?*
- *Which shapes worked well?*

Shape match

Learning objectives

Green Stepping Stones:

- Sustain interest for a length of time on a pre-decided construction or arrangement.
- Match some shapes by recognising similarities and orientation.
- Use appropriate shapes to make representational models or more elaborate pictures.
- Show curiosity and observation by talking about shapes, how they are the same or why some are different.
- Begin to use mathematical names for 'solid' 3-D shapes and 'flat' 2-D shapes, and mathematical terms to describe shapes.

Activity

The activity detail can be found on CD page 'Shape match'. Put some cubes, cones, spheres and pyramids into an opaque bag or feely box. Keep one of each shape in front of you. Ask four to six children to sit around a table with you. Explain that you will pass the box around the table and point to one of the shapes in front of you, then ask the child with the box to find that shape.

Encourage the children to explain how they found the shape by feeling in the box.

Plenary & assessment

Ask the children to describe each of the shapes in turn. Say, for example:

- *Which shapes have curves?*
- *Which shapes have flat faces?*
- *Which have edges?*
- *Who can tell me what this shape is called?*

Pass the box around the group again and invite each child to take a shape. Ask them to hide it in their hands so that the others cannot see, then to describe it. Invite the other children to guess which shape they have.

Shape sort

Learning objectives

ELGs/NNS:

- **Use language such as 'circle' or 'bigger' to describe the shape and size of solids and flat shapes.**

Activity

Ask four to six children to work with shapes. Put a selection of sizes of cubes, cones, pyramids and spheres on a tray on the table. Ask the children to sort out the shapes into sets of 'the same'. (Individual children can choose what 'the same' means.)

Plenary & assessment

Ask the children to show you the sets that they have made and to describe the shapes. Ask:

- *Which are the spheres/cones? How do you know?*
- *What is special about spheres/cones?*
- *What is the same about the spheres?*
- *Show me the big sphere. Show me the smaller spheres.*
- *How did you sort your shapes?*

Encourage the children to talk about the shapes and the sortings that they have made, describing the shapes by their properties and their size.

Making pictures and patterns

Learning objectives

ELGs/NNS:

- Use a variety of shapes to make models, pictures and patterns, and describe them.

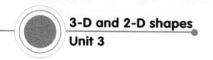

Activity

Provide some 2-D shape tiles in a tray. Ask the children to choose some of the shapes to make a picture. For example, they can combine a circle and triangles to make a simple animal face. As the children work, ask them about the shapes they use. Describe the shapes yourself in terms such as *It's round* or: *It has straight sides* so that the children hear the vocabulary of 2-D shape being used.

Plenary & assessment

Ask the children questions about the pictures and patterns that they have made, for example:
- *What shapes did you use?*
- *Which shapes are round?*
- *What sort of shape is this? Who can name this shape for me?*

Ask the children to make another picture or pattern and to describe the shapes as they work.

Making jigsaws

Learning objectives
ELGs/NNS:
- Use a variety of shapes to make models, pictures and patterns, and describe them.

Activity

Provide each child with a greetings card and ask them to cut it up into about four pieces. Then ask the children to muddle up their own pieces and rearrange them to make a jigsaw. Ask the more confident children to cut another picture into about eight pieces.

When the children are confident with this activity, provide CD page 'Jigsaw', which can be cut up and used in the same way to make a jigsaw.

Plenary & assessment

Ask the children some questions about how they produced their completed jigsaws. For example:
- *How did you know where this piece fitted?*
- *Try this jigsaw: which piece do you think will fit here? How can you tell?*

Encourage the children to use the vocabulary of shape to explain their thinking, for example:
I found the corners first.

Make a shape

Learning objectives
ELGs/NNS:
- Use a variety of shapes to make models, pictures and patterns, and describe them.

Activity

Ask a group of about four children to work with the LSA and to make Plasticine models of 3-D shapes. The LSA discusses with the children the shapes they make, such as: *It's round… flat…*

This activity can be repeated using a set of 2-D shape tiles to model circles, squares, and so on.

Plenary & assessment

Ask the children to describe the shapes that they have made. Encourage them to use vocabulary such as *round, flat, point…* Ask questions about their shapes such as:
- *Who made a cube/cone/circle/triangle?*
- *Which shapes are round/have flat faces?*
- *What is this shape called? Who can point to another shape like this one?*

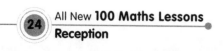

Building

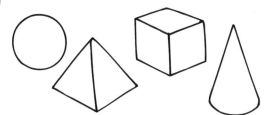

You will need some building blocks or a construction kit.

Work with a group of four to six children.

Ask the children what they would like to make. Encourage them to plan their construction. Now give them time to carry out their plan.

As they work, ask questions about the shapes they have chosen, such as:

- *Why is this a good shape to use?*
- *Which shapes are round/have pointed ends/have flat faces?*
- *Which shapes can you name?*

Record the children's achievements, especially the range of shape vocabulary that children use confidently.

Child's name	What happened	What to do next time

Shape match

You will need some cubes, cones, spheres and pyramids.

Put these into an opaque bag or feely box.

Keep one of each shape in front of you.

Ask four to six children to sit around the table with you.

Explain that you will pass the box around the table. Point to one of the shapes in front of you. Ask the child with the box to find that shape.

Encourage the children to explain how they found the shape by feeling in the box. Ask:

- *What can you feel?*
- *Which shape do you think that is?*
- *Is it this shape?*
- *How do you know that?*

Record the children's achievements, especially which shapes children recognise.

Child's name	What happened	What to do next time

Name	Date

Jigsaw

Cut out the pieces.

Make the jigsaw.

Children count by touching pictures and saying the counting number. They are encouraged to subitise for up to three or four objects. They make direct comparisons of two lengths then more than two.

LEARNING OBJECTIVES

Topics	Stepping Stones		Early Learning Goals & NNS Learning Objectives
	Blue	**Green**	
Counting	● Recognise groups with one, two or three objects.	● Count up to three or four objects by saying one number name for each item.	● **Count reliably up to 10 everyday objects** (first to 5, then 10, then beyond), giving just one number name to each object.
Comparing and ordering measures		● Order two or three items by length. ● Adapt shapes or cut material to size.	● **Use language such as more or less, longer or shorter to compare two quantities**, then more than two, by making direct comparisons of lengths.

2 Sessions

Preparation

Enlarge a copy of 'Rabbit count' to A3. Colour in three rabbits in grey, four in brown, and one in black. Put one, two, three or four counting objects into each box.

Learning objectives

Starter bank
ELGs/NNS
● **Count reliably up to 10 everyday objects** (first to 5, then 10, then beyond), giving just one number name to each object.
● **Use language such as circle or bigger to describe the shape and size of solids and flat shapes.**

Main teaching & group activities
Blue Stepping Stones
● Recognise groups with one, two or three objects.
Green Stepping Stones
● Count up to three or four objects by saying one number name for each item.
ELGs/NNS
● **Count reliably up to 10 everyday objects** (first to 5, then 10, then beyond), giving just one number name to each object.

Vocabulary

one, two, three… to ten, how many…? count, how many…?

You will need:

Photocopiable pages
'Rabbit count', one copy for each child and one enlarged to A3 for the teacher's/LSA's reference, see page 33.

Equipment
Up to ten small toys for counting; coins; transparent container; set of 3-D shapes; opaque bag; set of 2-D shape tiles; small counting items; small boxes; transparent containers; ten small counting rabbits or counters for each child.

WHOLE CLASS TEACHING

Starter bank

These Starter bank ideas can be used throughout the unit.

How many?

Put out a row of three toys and ask: *How many toys are there?* Invite a child to count them by co-ordinating the touch, move and count procedure. Now ask the children to count as you point to each toy. Say: *What was the last number you said? How many toys are there?* Over time, repeat this for up to ten toys.

Listen and count

Show the children the transparent container and explain that you will drop some coins into it. Ask the children to count each of the coins as it falls into the container. Begin with, say, two coins and, over time, extend the count range to ten. Ask: *What was the last number you said? How many coins are there in the container?* Tip out the coins, and invite a child to put them into a line and to count them, co-ordinating the touch, move and count procedure.

Guess my 3-D shape

You will need a set of 3-D shapes. Put these into the opaque bag in front of the children. Say the shape name for each shape as you drop it into the bag. Feel inside the bag for a shape. Describe the shape that you can feel. For example, for a sphere you might say: *It is round. It is curved all over.*

Invite the children to say what the shape is. When there is a correct guess, show the shape. Some of the less mature children may use everyday names such as 'ball' and 'box' for cube. Accept this, and encourage the others to give mathematical names. Repeat for other shapes.

Guess my 2-D shape

This works in the same way as 'Guess my 3-D shape'.

Main teaching activity

Show the children the enlarged picture from CD page 'Rabbit count'. Ask them to look carefully at the rabbits. Invite a child to point to the white rabbits. As the child points, encourage the others to count the rabbits. Ask: *What was the last number you said? How many white rabbits are there?* Repeat this for the grey rabbits, then the brown rabbits. Ask: *How many black rabbits can you see?*

Now ask the children to count different combinations of rabbits. For each count, invite a child to point by touching the rabbits as the other children count.

Note the following combinations of rabbits to make all quantities from one to ten:

Black:	1	Grey & black:	4	Brown & white:	6	Grey, brown & white:	9
White:	2	Brown:	4	Brown & grey:	7	All the rabbits:	10
Grey:	3	Brown & black:	5	Grey, brown & black:	8		

GROUP ACTIVITIES

Rabbit count

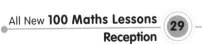

Learning objectives

ELGs/NNS:

● **Count reliably up to 10 everyday objects** (first to 5, then 10, then beyond), giving just one number name to each object.

Activity

Provide each child with their own copy of CD page 'Rabbit count', and ten counting rabbits or counters. Ask the children to count out four counters. Now ask them to place the four counters over

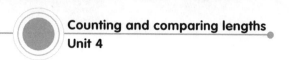
rabbits so that four rabbits are covered. Ask the children to touch each counter, but not move it, to count the rabbits covered again. Repeat for other quantities of rabbits, from four to ten.

Plenary & assessment

Use the A3 version of 'Rabbit count' and ask the children to take turns to touch and count the rabbits that you say. Use the combinations of rabbits given in the main activity, for example:

- *Count all the brown rabbits. What was the last number you said? How many brown rabbits are there?*
- *Count all of the rabbits. How many rabbits are there in the picture?*

Number boxes

ADULT SUPPORTED

Learning objectives
Blue Stepping Stones:
- Recognise groups with one, two or three objects.

Green Stepping Stones:
- Count up to three or four objects by saying one number name for each item.

Activity

For those working to Blue Stepping Stones, use the boxes with up to three objects inside. For those working to Green Stepping Stones, use the boxes with up to four objects inside.

Blue Stepping Stones: encourage the children to look and say whether there are one, two or three things in each box. If they are not sure, ask the children to put the items on the table and to count them one by one by the touch, move and count procedure.

Green Stepping Stones: encourage the children to look and say (or, for four, to count out) how many there are. If children manage this easily, put five, then six objects into a box for counting.

Plenary & assessment

Ask the children to demonstrate their counting. They can open boxes of small quantities of objects (up to three) and say, by looking, how many there are. Ask:

- *What was the last number you said?*
- *How many are in the box? How do you know?*

3 Sessions

Learning objectives
Main teaching & group activities
Green Stepping Stones
- Order two or three items by length.

ELGs/NNS
- **Use language such as more or less, longer or shorter to compare two quantities,** then more than two, by making direct comparisons of lengths.

Vocabulary

length, width, height, long, short, tall, high, low, wide, narrow, thick, thin, longer, shorter, taller, higher... and so on, longest, shortest, tallest, highest... and so on

You will need:
Photocopiable pages
'Hand prints' and 'Thicker and thinner' for the teacher's/LSA's reference:, see pages 34–35.

Equipment
Three teddies of clearly different sizes; large sheets of paper; paints; scissors; Plasticine and modelling tools; dry sand in a large sand tray.

WHOLE CLASS TEACHING

Main teaching activity

Choose two of the teddies that are clearly different in height and width, and ask the children what they can tell you about their sizes. They may comment that one is bigger than the other. Put the teddies, standing up, side by side, so that their feet are on the same level, and ask:

● *Which teddy is taller/shorter? How can you tell?*

If the children are unsure about 'taller' then use your hands to show the heights of each teddy. Repeat this for their width by standing the wider teddy behind the narrower one. Ask:

● *Which teddy is wider/narrower? How can you tell?*

Now lie the teddies down on a table top, with their heads at the edge of the table, and ask:

● *Which teddy is longer/shorter? How can you tell?*

During this unit, extend this to include three teddies using the superlatives of longest, shortest, widest, narrowest and tallest.

GROUP ACTIVITIES

Who is taller?

Learning objectives

Green Stepping Stones:
● Order two or three items by length.
● Adapt shapes or cut material to size.

ELGs/NNS:
● **Use language such as more or less, longer or shorter to compare two quantities**, then more than two, by making direct comparisons of lengths.

Activity

Work with two or three children at a time, depending upon whether they can order by two or three lengths at this stage. Ask the children to stand back to back and compare themselves for height. If they can use a full-length mirror, then they can see who is taller/shorter or tallest/shortest. Ask:

● *Who is tallest/shortest? Who is taller/shorter than…?*

Now ask the children to take turns to lie on a large sheet of paper while you draw around them. Ask the children to paint themselves onto their outline. When these are dry they can be cut out. Ask: *Is this about the same height as you are?* Over time, all the children in the class can produce their 'image' and these can be pinned onto a wall, with the feet of each 'image' just touching the floor so that the children can check how much they have grown during the year.

Plenary & assessment

When all of the children have completed the activity, ask them to look at the finished pictures and to find their own. Invite children to answer questions like these:

● *Who is taller/shorter than Jake? Who is the tallest?*

And for those children working to ELGs/NNS:

● *Who is taller than Paul but shorter than Nadeen?*

Hand prints

Learning objectives

Green Stepping Stones:
● Order two or three items by length.

ELGs/NNS:
● **Use language such as more or less, longer or shorter to compare two quantities**, then more than two, by making direct comparisons of lengths.

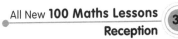

Activity

This activity is provided in detail on CD page 'Hand prints'. Ask the LSA to work with two or three children. The children make hand prints in the sand tray and compare them. The LSA asks:

- *Who has the longer/shorter hand? How do you know?*

Plenary & assessment

Ask two children each to hold up one hand, and to put their hands side by side so that the others can see them in order to make a direct comparison of length and width. Ask:

- *Who has the longer/shorter hand? How can you tell?*
- *Who has the wider/narrower hand? How can you tell?*

Extend this to comparing three hands to find the longest, shortest, widest and narrowest hand. For those working towards the ELGs/NNS, ask:

- *Whose hand is longer/wider than Paul's but shorter/narrower than Hilary's? How can you tell?*

Thicker and thinner

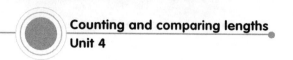

Learning objectives

ELGs/NNS:

- **Use language such as more or less, longer or shorter to compare two quantities**, then more than two, by making direct comparisons of lengths.

Activity

This activity is provided in detail on CD page 'Thicker and thinner'. Work with a group of four to six children with Plasticine, modelling tools and boards. Ask the children to make a Plasticine worm each. Invite pairs of children to compare their worms and to say which is thicker and which is thinner. If they are not sure about this vocabulary, show them what you mean by making two worms of the same length but clearly differing thicknesses. Ask of each pair of children's worms: *Who has made a thick/thin worm? How can you tell?* Keep the worms that the children make at the end of the activity to use during the Plenary.

Plenary & assessment

Choose two worms, clearly of different thicknesses but about the same lengths, and ask:

- *Which worm is thicker/thinner? How can you tell?*

Now choose two worms which are of different sizes and ask:

- *Which worm is thicker/thinner? How can you tell?*
- *Which worm is longer/shorter? How can you tell?*

Choose three clearly differently-sized worms and invite those working towards the ELGs/NNS to say:

- *Which worm is thicker than this one but thinner than that one? How can you tell?*
- *Which worm is shorter than this one, but longer than that one? How can you tell?*

Name	Date

Rabbit count

Hand prints

You will need a sand tray with dry sand.

Work with two or three children. Ask them to make hand prints in the sand tray. Encourage them to put their hand prints side by side so that a direct comparison can be made.

Ask:

- *Who has the longer hand? How do you know?*
- *Who has the shorter hand? How do you know?*

Record the children's achievements. It would be helpful to write down which children can use the language of 'longer' and 'shorter'.

Child's name	What happened	What to do next time

Thicker and thinner

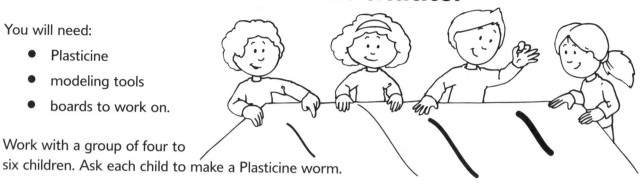

You will need:

- Plasticine
- modeling tools
- boards to work on.

Work with a group of four to six children. Ask each child to make a Plasticine worm.

Ask children to find a partner. Invite each pair of children to compare their worms and to say which is thick and which is thin. If they are not sure about this vocabulary, show them what you mean by making two worms that are the same length but are clearly of differing thicknesses.

Ask of each pair of children's worms:

- *Who has made a thick/thin worm? How can you tell?*

The children can use the tools to make faces on their worms, and designs along them.

Keep the worms that the children make at the end of the activity to use during the Plenary.

Record the children's achievements. It would be helpful to record who recognises 'thick' and 'thin' and can use that language in a sentence.

Child's name	What happened	What to do next time

Zero and one more

Through stories and rhymes, children begin to recognise and understand zero and none. Through counting objects then putting one more and re-counting they begin to understand 'one more than'.

LEARNING OBJECTIVES

Topics	Stepping Stones		Early Learning Goals & NNS Learning Objectives
	Blue	Green	
Counting	● Show curiosity about numbers by offering comments or asking questions.	● Show confidence with numbers by initiating or requesting number activities.	● Begin to recognise 'none' and 'zero' in stories, rhymes and when counting.
Adding and subtracting	● Show an interest in number problems.	● Sometimes show confidence and offer solutions to problems. ● Find the total number of items in two groups by counting all of them. ● Use own methods to solve a problem. ● Say with confidence the number that is one more than a given number.	● **Find one more than a number from 1 to 10.**

2 Sessions

Preparation

Enlarge a copy of CD page 'Touch and count' to A3. Colour in one clown yellow, two clowns in red, three in blue and four in green.

Put one, two, three, four or five treasures inside each small box, and also leave some boxes empty.

Learning objectives

Starter
ELGs/NNS
● **Count reliably up to 10 everyday objects** (first to 5, then 10, then beyond), giving just one number name to each object.

Main teaching activity
Blue Stepping Stones
● Show curiosity about numbers by offering comments or asking questions.
Green Stepping Stones
● Show confidence with numbers by initiating or requesting number activities.
ELGs/NNS
● Begin to recognise 'none' and 'zero' in stories, rhymes and when counting.

Vocabulary

zero, one, two, three… ten

You will need:

Photocopiable pages
'Hidden treasures' for the teacher's/LSA's reference, see page 41.

CD pages
'Touch and count', enlarged to A3, and 'Five parcels' for the teacher's/LSA's reference; and 'Work mat' for each child (see General resources).

Equipment
Small boxes with lids; 'treasures' such as pretty pebbles, shells, large beads…; up to ten counting items such as small toys for each child.

WHOLE CLASS TEACHING

Starter bank

These Starter bank ideas can be used throughout the unit.

Touch and count

Pin up the enlarged version of CD page 'Touch and count'. Ask the children to look at the picture and invite them to describe what they can see. Invite various children to come out and to touch and count the clowns that you say. The other children can join in with the count. Combinations include:

Yellow:	1	Green:	4	Blue & green :	7	All the clowns:	10
Red:	2	Red & blue:	5	Blue, green & yellow:	8		
Blue:	3	Red & green:	6	Red, blue & green:	9		

Begin with asking children to touch and count one, two and three clowns. Then extend this to four, five, six… Over time, extend the count to ten.

Show me finger count

Explain to the children that you will say a number. Ask them to hold up that number of fingers. Keep the quantity to one to five to begin with so that children can touch their fingers with the other hand in order to check how many. Over time, extend this to ten.

Five green bottles

Say the rhyme 'Ten green bottles' but start with five bottles. Invite five children to come to the front to mime the number rhyme. Touch each of the children and invite the other children to count with you. Then ask a child to come to the front and touch and count the five children. Say the first verse of the rhyme. Ask a child to come to count how many bottles are left by touching and counting, with the other children joining in the count. Repeat this until all the bottles have gone.

Other rhymes can be used in the same way, with a child touching and counting, and the other children joining in the count.

Main teaching activity

Ask the children to listen carefully to the story that you will read to them, from 'Five parcels'. Invite five children to come to the front to help to act out the story, and another child to touch and count each time one child disappears from the story. When there are no children left, ask: *How many children are there now? Yes, there are no children. Nobody is left.*

Invite the children to count back with you from, say, five, down to zero: *Five, four, three, two, one, zero.* Explain that zero means 'nothing', or 'nothing left'.

GROUP ACTIVITIES

Hidden treasures

Learning objectives:
Blue Stepping Stones:
- Show curiosity about numbers by offering comments or asking questions.

Green Stepping Stones:
- Show confidence with numbers by initiating or requesting number activities.

Activity

This activity can be found on CD page 'Hidden treasures'. Ask the children to look inside the boxes and to say how many are in each box. Encourage the children to look and say how many are in the boxes with zero, one, two or three items. For four and five objects they will probably want to tip the items out and count them, using the touch and count procedure, or touch, move and count method.

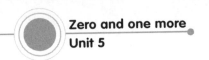

Plenary & assessment

Put some of the boxes in front of the children. Take each box in turn and show the children what is inside. Ask:

● *How many buttons are there in this box? How did you work that out?*

Praise the children who 'just know' how many there are, as these children have probably recognised the quantity without needing to count.

Count out game

TEACHER DIRECTED

Learning objectives:

Blue Stepping Stones:

● Show curiosity about numbers by offering comments or asking questions.

Green Stepping Stones:

● Show confidence with numbers by initiating or requesting number activities.

ELGs/NNS:

● Begin to recognise 'none' and 'zero' in stories, rhymes and when counting.

Activity

Play a count it out game with the children. Give each child CD page 'Work mat'. Ask a group of four to six children to put out counting items onto their work mat when you say how many. Say:

● *Count out three/four/seven/ten toys. Check by counting again.*

● *How did you count your toys?*

● *Put out no toys. How many is that?*

Ask the children to show you how they counted. Encourage those working to the ELGs/NNS to use touch and count for checking. Other children may need to touch, move and count at this stage.

Plenary & assessment

Show the children some toys on a work mat. Ask:

● *How many toys can you see?*

● *Who would like to come and check how many by counting?*

● *Shut your eyes. Now open them. How many toys can you see now?*

Include no toys, or zero, in what is on the mat.

3 Sessions

Preparation

Photocopy 'Find the card' on to card and cut out the cards.

Learning objectives

Main teaching activity

Blue Stepping Stones

● Show an interest in number problems.

Green Stepping Stones

● Sometimes show confidence and offer solutions to problems.

● Find the total number of items in two groups by counting all of them.

● Use own methods to solve a problem.

● Say with confidence the number that is one more than a given number.

ELGs/NNS

● **Find one more than a number from 1 to 10.**

Vocabulary

zero, one, two, three… to about ten, more

You will need:

Photocopiable pages
'Find the card', one copy for each child, photocopied onto card, see page 42.

CD pages
'Work mat' for each child (see General resources).

Equipment
Ten counting toys for each child; dolls and a dolls' house.

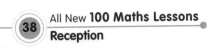

WHOLE CLASS TEACHING

Main teaching activity

Ask one child to stand in front of the group. Say: *How many are standing here?* Agree that there is one child. Now ask: *How many would there be if one more of you came out here? Yes, there would be two.* Invite a child to come out to stand next to the first child, and then count both by coordinating the touch and count, encouraging the children to join in with the count. Continue with this until there are ten children standing at the front. Ask the children to sit down again.

Now say:
- *Show me three fingers. Good. How many would one more than three be?*
- *Show me one finger. What is one more than one?*

Continue in this way, using at first the counting numbers to five, and, over time, extend this to one more than nine.

GROUP ACTIVITIES

Make it one more

Learning objectives
Blue Stepping Stones:
- Show an interest in number problems.

Green Stepping Stones:
- Sometimes show confidence and offer solutions to problems.
- Find the total number of items in two groups by counting all of them.
- Use own methods to solve a problem.
- Say with confidence the number that is one more than a given number.

ELGs/NNS:
- **Find one more than a number from 1 to 10.**

Activity
Work with a group of four to six children. Each child will need a CD page 'Work mat' and some counting items. Ask the children to count out three items onto the mat. Say:
- *How many do you have? How do you know that?*
- *How many would there be if you put one more?*
- *Check by putting one more and counting them.*

Repeat this for different quantities, keeping the quantities for the Blue Stepping Stones to about four or five, Green Stepping Stones to five or six, and the ELG/NNS group to up to ten.

Plenary & assessment
Ask the children some oral questions which involve calculating one more, encouraging the children to use their fingers to model the questions if they are unsure.
- *Show me three fingers. How many would one more be?* Check by putting up one more finger and counting.
- *There are two people on the bus. One more gets on. How many are on the bus now?*
- *There are four children building a tower. One more comes to join them. How many are there now?*
Choose numbers in the range one to ten for these oral word problems.

Dolls' house

Learning objectives:
Blue Stepping Stones:
● Show an interest in number problems.
Green Stepping Stones:
● Sometimes show confidence and offer solutions to problems.
● Find the total number of items in two groups by counting all of them.
● Use own methods to solve a problem.
● Say with confidence the number that is one more than a given number.

Activity
Set the dolls' house up with between one and four dolls in each room and a selection of more dolls beside the house. Suggest to a group of two or three children that they put one more doll in each room. Encourage them to count how many dolls are already in the room, and how many there will be when one more has been added.

Extend the activity for children working towards the Green Stepping Stones by increasing the quantities to up to about seven.

Plenary & assessment
Ask a child to take the dolls from one of the rooms and to place these in front of the house. Ask:
● *How many dolls are there? Let's count together.* (Touch each one in turn, and count, with the children joining in.)
● *How many would there be if we put one more there? Now let's check by counting.*
Repeat this activity for other quantities of dolls, keeping the quantity each time to between one and five. Extend the Plenary for Green Stepping Stones by increasing the quantities to up to about seven.

Find the card

Learning objectives:
ELGs/NNS:
● **Find one more than a number from 1 to 10.**

Activity
Provide each child with a set of cards cut from 'Find the card'. Ask the children to look carefully at each card and to count how many are on each one. Now say:
● *Find the card that shows four balloons. Show me.*
● *Find the card that shows one more than four balloons. Show me.*
● *Find the card that shows three balloons. Show me.*
● *Find the card that shows one more than four balloons. Show me.*

Plenary & assessment
Ask the children to show you the card with, say, six balloons and the card with one more than six balloons. Ask:
● *How did you work out which card you needed?*
● *So what is one more than six?*
● *Who can tell me what one more than seven is?*

Hidden treasures

You will need:

- small boxes with lids
- treasures, such as large beads, shells, pretty pebbles or similar.

Put one, two, three, four or five treasures into each box and shut the lid.

Keep some boxes empty.

Work with a group of up to four children.

Ask the children to look inside the boxes and to say how many are in each box. Some boxes will include zero, so talk about how there is nothing in the box.

Encourage the children to look and say how many for the boxes with zero, one, two or three items inside.

When working with four and five, children will probably want to tip the items out and count them, using the touch and count (or touch, move and count) method.

Record the children's achievements. It would be helpful to record who recognises zero, and who understands that zero means 'nothing'.

Child's name	What happened	What to do next time

Name	Date

Find the card

Photocopy onto card and cut out.

Counting forwards and backwards from a given number

Children count forwards and back again to ten. Then they begin on a small number, such as one… two… three…, and repeat this, stopping at the start number. They compare two quantities, and say which has more and which has fewer.

LEARNING OBJECTIVES

Topics	Stepping Stones		Early Learning Goals & NNS Learning Objectives
	Blue	**Green**	
Counting	● Willingly attempt to count with some numbers in the correct order.	● Show confidence with numbers by initiating or requesting number activities.	● **Say and use the number names in order in familiar contexts** such as number rhymes, songs, stories, counting games and activities (first to five, then ten, then twenty and beyond). ● Recite the number names in order, continuing the count forwards or backwards from a given number.
Comparing and ordering numbers	● Show an interest in number problems.	● Sometimes show confidence and offer solutions to problems. ● Use own methods to solve a problem.	● **Use language such as more or less, greater or smaller to compare two numbers** and say which is more or less.

2 Sessions

Preparation

Enlarge a copy of 'Touch and count' to A3, and colour the clowns: one blue; two red; three yellow; four green. Set up a listening area where children can use the headphones.

Learning objectives

Starter bank
ELGs/NNS
● **Find one more or one less than a number from 1 to 10.**
● **Count reliably up to 10 everyday objects.**

Main teaching & group activities
Blue Stepping Stones
● Willingly attempt to count with some numbers in the correct order.
Green Stepping Stones
● Show confidence with numbers by initiating or requesting number activities.
ELGs/NNS
● **Say and use the number names in order in familiar contexts** such as number rhymes, songs, stories, counting games and activities (first to five, then ten, twenty and beyond).
● Recite the number names in order, continuing the count forwards or backwards from a given number.

Vocabulary

zero, one, two, three… to ten

You will need:
Photocopiable pages
'Counting to and from five' for the teacher's/LSA's reference, see page 48.

CD pages
'Touch and count', photocopied to A3, for the teacher's/LSA's reference, and 'Five parcels', one for each child (see General resources).

Equipment
Commercially available cassette tape or CD of number rhymes; cassette recorder or CD player and headphones or a listening centre.

WHOLE CLASS TEACHING

Starter bank
These Starter bank ideas can be used throughout the unit.

One more than
Ask the children to use their fingers to help them to answer some questions. Explain that you will say a number. Ask them to show you one more than that number on their fingers. Begin with small numbers such as one, two, three. Gradually, and over time, extend the numbers used up to ten. Say:
● *Show me the number that is one more than two/one/three… How many is that? How did you work that out?*

Touch and count
Pin up the enlarged CD page 'Touch and count'. Explain that you will invite children to come out to count clowns, by co-ordinating the touch and count. Ask a child to start counting and encourage the others to check that all the clowns named have been counted. Say:
● *Count all the yellow clowns. How many are there?*
● *Count all the blue and red clowns. How many is that?*

Finger count
Explain to the children that you will say a number. Ask them to show you that number with their fingers. Begin with quantities from one to five and extend to ten. Say, for example:
● *Show me three/four/five fingers. Now show me nothing. How many is that?*

Main teaching activity
Explain that today you would like the children to say the counting numbers with you, forwards to ten and back again. Begin by counting from zero to five and then back. Repeat the count, this time counting to and from ten. Now ask the children to begin on another number (such as one, two or three) and count to ten, and then back to the start number. Initially they may find it more difficult to stop at the start number. Confident children may like to count forwards and backwards out loud.

GROUP ACTIVITIES

Number rhymes

Learning objectives
Blue Stepping Stones:
● Willingly attempt to count with some numbers in the correct order.
Green Stepping Stones:
● Show confidence with numbers by initiating or requesting number activities.
ELGs/NNS:
● **Say and use the number names in order in familiar contexts** such as number rhymes, songs, stories, counting games and activities (first to five, then ten, then twenty and beyond).

Activity
Read CD page 'Five parcels' with the children to introduce the concept of zero or nothing. Then ask four children to work in the listening area. They can listen to, and join in with, the number rhymes on the tapes or CDs.

Plenary & assessment
Ask the children to say or sing their favourite number rhymes, with actions where appropriate. Say:
● *Which numbers did you say? Show me one more than four on your fingers. How many is that?*

Counting to and from five

Learning objectives

Blue Stepping Stones:
- Willingly attempt to count with some numbers in the correct order.

Green Stepping Stones:
- Show confidence with numbers by initiating or requesting number activities.

ELGs/NNS:
- Recite the number names in order, continuing the count forwards or backwards from a given number.

Activity

This activity is provided in detail on CD page 'Counting to and from five' for the LSA's reference. Four to six children count with the LSA from zero to five on their fingers. Having counted forwards, they count back. Then they are asked to count without using their fingers to help them.

Plenary & assessment

Ask the children to count with you to five, and back again to three, and up to five, and so on. Say:
- *Count to four. Who can tell me the next number after four? Let's count together to five and back again.*

3 Sessions

Learning objectives

Main teaching & group activities

Blue Stepping Stones
- Show an interest in number problems.

Green Stepping Stones
- Sometimes show confidence and offer solutions to problems.
- Use own methods to solve a problem.

ELGs/NNS
- **Use language such as more or less, greater or smaller to compare two numbers** and say which is more or less.

Vocabulary

the same number as, as many as, more, larger, bigger, greater, fewer, smaller, less, most, biggest, largest, greatest, fewest, smallest, least

You will need:
Photocopiable pages
'One-penny shop', for the teacher's/LSA's reference, see page 49.

CD pages
'Partitioned work mat' for each child (see General resources).

Equipment
Twelve bricks of a uniform shape and size; items for a class shop; 1p coins; items for counting such as large buttons and so on; beads of the same shape and size; laces; safety mirror.

WHOLE CLASS TEACHING

Main teaching activity

Put out the bricks where the children can see them.
Explain that you will begin to make a staircase.
Make a two-stair pattern like this.

Ask the children: *How many bricks are in this* (the first) *stair? And in this?* (pointing to the second stair). *So which stair has more bricks? Which stair has fewer bricks?* If the children are unsure about 'more' and 'fewer', demonstrate with two piles of bricks, one with two and the other with about five, and ask: *Which has more? Which has fewer?* Now continue to build the staircase until all the bricks are used up, each time asking: *Which has more/fewer?*

Count the bricks in each stair. Agree with the children that each stair going up has one more

brick than the previous stair. When the children are confident with this, count the stairs back from the stair with four bricks. Agree that, working back, each stair has one fewer than the one before.

Take the staircase apart, and invite a child to make the first stair with one brick, then another child to make the second, and so on. Ask the children: *How many will there be in the next step? And the next? How did you work that out?*

GROUP ACTIVITIES

One-penny shop

Learning objectives
Blue Stepping Stones:
- Show an interest in number problems.

Green Stepping Stones:
- Sometimes show confidence and offer solutions to problems.
- Use own methods to solve a problem.

ELGs/NNS:
- **Use language such as more or less, greater or smaller to compare two numbers** and say which is more or less.

Activity
This activity is provided in detail on CD page 'One-penny shop' for the LSA's reference and so they can record the children's achievements and difficulties for use during feedback. Ask a group of about four children to work with the LSA in the 'shop' and provide each child with about five penny coins.

The LSA explains to the children that anything they choose will cost 1p. The LSA invites each child to choose something, saying: *How much is that?* The LSA takes the 1p coin from each child.

Next, the LSA asks the children to buy two things and says: *How many things did you buy? Which costs more, one thing or two things?*

Finally, the LSA can invite one of the children to act as shopkeeper and allow the children time to act as customer or shopkeeper.

Plenary & assessment
Ask the children to show you what they have bought. Invite the children working towards the Blue and Green Stepping Stones to say how many things they have and to count them out, by co-ordinating the touch and count. Invite the children working towards the ELGs/NNS to count how many things they have bought and then to answer questions like these:
- *Who bought more than one/two things? How many did you buy?*
- *Who bought fewer than five things? Who bought most things? How many?*
- *Who bought the smallest/least number of things? How many was that?*
- *Who bought the same number as Rajan?*

Threading beads

Learning objectives
Blue Stepping Stones:
- Show an interest in number problems.

Green Stepping Stones:
- Sometimes show confidence and offer solutions to problems.
- Use own methods to solve a problem.

ELGs/NNS:
- **Use language such as more or less, greater or smaller to compare two numbers** and say which is more or less.

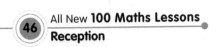

Activity

Suggest to four children that they make a necklace or bracelet by threading beads onto a lace. If a safety mirror is provided, they can admire what they have made. As the children work, ask:

- *How many beads has Jon threaded? Who has threaded more than that?*
- *Who has threaded fewer than Jon? How many have you threaded?*

Plenary & assessment

Admire the children's finished necklaces and bracelets. Ask the children to take a fresh lace each and to thread a few beads. Ask:

- *How many beads has Ashley threaded? Who has threaded more than Ashley?*
- *Who has threaded fewer than Ashley? How many have you threaded?*

Of those working towards the ELGs/NNS, ask:

- *Who has threaded most? How many is that?*
- *Who has threaded fewest? How many is that?*

Counting sets

Learning objectives

ELGs/NNS:

- **Use language such as more or less, greater or smaller to compare two numbers** and say which is more or less.

Activity

Work with four to six children. Each child will need a copy of CD page 'Partitioned work mat', and some items for counting. Ask the children to count out four items onto one section of their work mat. Now ask them to put out more than that onto the other section. Say: *How many have you counted out? Is that more than four?* Repeat this for other quantities for both sides of the mat.

When the children are confident with 'more', ask them to count out five things and put them onto one section of their work mat. Now ask them to put out fewer onto the other section of the mat. Ask: *How many did you count? Is that fewer than five?* Repeat for other quantities for both sides of the mat.

Plenary & assessment

Ask each child to count out some items onto their work mat. (They can decide how many to put out.) Now ask questions, such as:

- *Who has more than three/five/nine? Who has fewer than six?*
- *How many have you counted, Shereen? Who has more than Shereen? How many have you?*
- *Who has fewer than Shereen? How many have you?*
- *Has anyone counted out the same number as Shereen?*

Counting to and from 5

Work with a group of four to six children.

Ask the children to count with you from zero to five.

Encourage them to show you each number on their fingers,
putting up one more each time.

Now count back and ask the children to put one finger down each
time. Repeat this several times, keeping a good pace to the count.

Now ask the children to count forwards and backwards,
showing their fingers again. Then ask them to count without
using their fingers to help them.

Now ask them to start at two and count to four, and back again.

This can be extended for children working towards the ELGs/NNS by asking them to use both hands
to show fingers to up to ten.

Record the children's achievements. It would be helpful to record which children count with
confidence, forward and back.

Child's name	What happened	What to do next time

One-penny shop

You will need:

- some things to sell in a shop
- at least twenty 1p coins.

Work with a group of about four children in the shop.

Provide each child with about five 1p coins.

Explain to the children that anything they choose will cost 1p. Invite the children to choose something to buy. Say: *How much is that?* Take the 1p coin from each child.

Now ask the children to buy two things and ask: *How many things did you buy? Which costs more, one thing or two things?*

Invite one of the children to act as shopkeeper and give the children time to act as customer or shopkeeper.

Record the children's achievements. It would be helpful to record which children count how many things they have with confidence, and who can use the language of 'more' appropriately.

Child's name	What happened	What to do next time

Counting objects and one more and one less

Children count to ten, keeping a good pace. They repeat the count beginning on a small number and stopping before ten. They count up to ten objects in a picture by synchronising the point and count. They find one more and one fewer than a given quantity.

LEARNING OBJECTIVES

Topics	Stepping Stones		Early Learning Goals & NNS Learning Objectives
	Blue	**Green**	
Counting	● Use some number names accurately in play. ● Willingly attempt to count, with some numbers in the correct order.	● Show confidence with numbers by initiating or requesting number activities.	● Recite the number names in order, continuing the count forwards or backwards from a given number. ● **Count reliably up to 10 everyday objects** (first to 5, then 10, and beyond), giving just one number name to each object.
Adding and subtracting	● Separate a group of three/four objects in different ways, starting to recognise that the total is still the same.	● Say with confidence the number that is one more than a given number. ● Say the number after any number up to nine.	● **Find one more or one less than a number from 1 to 10.**

1 Session

Learning objectives

Starter bank
ELGs/NNS
● Recite the number names in order, continuing the count forwards or backwards from a given number.

Main teaching & group activities
Blue Stepping Stones
● Use some number names accurately in play.
Green Stepping Stones
● Show confidence with numbers by initiating or requesting number activities.
ELGs/NNS
● Recite the number names in order, continuing the count forwards or backwards from a given number.

Vocabulary

zero, one, two, three… to ten, count, count (up) to, count on (from, to), count back (from, to)

You will need:

Equipment
Commercially available cassette tape or CD of number rhymes; cassette recorder or CD player and headphones or a listening centre.

WHOLE CLASS TEACHING

Starter bank

These Starter bank ideas can be used throughout the unit.

Count to ten

Explain to the children that you would like them to count together, from zero to ten and back again. Count with the children, keeping the pace sharp. To help them keep the counting rhythm going, children can punch the air with their arms as they say each number. Repeat this several times.

When children are confident, count back from ten to zero. You may find that you need to do much of this counting yourself but, with practice and over time, the children will begin to join in.

Count up to...

Explain that you will say a starting number and a finishing number. Tell the children to count together from the starting number, and that the last number they say must be the finishing number. Say, for example:

- *Count up from two to six. Count up from three to nine.*

Count back to

This is similar to the 'Count up to...' activity above, except that the count is back. Say, for example:
- *Count back from five to one. Count back from eight to two.*

Main teaching activity

Ask the children to count to ten with you, encouraging them to keep a good pace. Now ask the children to count from two and continue to eight. Again, keep the pace sharp. Ask questions such as: *What number comes next after five/seven/eight? How did you work that out?*

Now ask the children to count around a circle. Say: *Ouni, you begin with one.* The next child says two, and so on, to ten. If there are more than ten children, begin again with one until everyone has said a counting number. Repeat this several times, starting with a different child each time.

When the children are confident with this, invite them to count around the circle starting from a number that is neither zero or one, such as two/three/five.

Finally, ask the children to count together. Suggest that they use their fingers to help them. Say:
- *Count on three numbers from two. Count on four, starting with six.*

GROUP ACTIVITIES

Count together

Learning objectives
Blue Stepping Stones:
- Use some number names accurately in play.

Green Stepping Stones:
- Show confidence with numbers by initiating or requesting number activities.

ELGs/NNS:
- Recite the number names in order, continuing the count forwards or backwards from a given number.

Activity

Ask the children to work in groups of about six. Explain that you would like them to count together, from one to ten. Repeat this several times. Now ask the children to count around the circle, from one to ten. This means that some children will say two numbers. Encourage the children to listen very carefully to the numbers that are said, and to be ready for their turn so that the pace remains sharp. At first it may be helpful to say quietly the number name with the individual child. When the children have all had several goes at this, ask them to begin counting at two, five, six, up to ten.

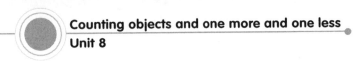
The activity can be adapted for children working towards the Blue or Green Stepping Stones by beginning the count on two or three, and counting to five.

Plenary & assessment

Invite the children to sit in a circle. Ask them to begin by counting from one to ten, at a good pace, and to repeat this several times. Now ask the children to count around the circle, from one to ten, then one to ten again, until everyone has had a turn. Ask the children to begin counting on, say, two/three up to six/eight/ten. Ask questions such as:

- *What number comes after three/five/eight?*
- *How did you work that out?*

4 Sessions

Preparation

Enlarge 'Garden scene' to A3.

Learning objectives

Main teaching & group activities

Blue Stepping Stones
- Separate a group of three/four objects in different ways, starting to recognise that the total is still the same.

Green Stepping Stones
- Say with confidence the number that is one more than a given number.
- Say the number after any number up to 9.

ELGs/NNS
- **Count reliably up to 10 everyday objects** (first to 5, then 10, and beyond), giving just one number name to each object.
- **Find one more or one less than a number from 1 to 10.**

Vocabulary

more, larger, bigger, greater, fewer, smaller, less, most, biggest, largest, greatest, fewest, smallest, least, one more, one less, how many?

You will need:

Photocopiable pages
'Sorting' and 'One more, one less', for the teacher's/ LSA's reference, see pages 55–56.

CD pages
'Garden scene', photocopied to A3, 'Work mat', one for each child and 'Partitioned work mat', one for each pair (see General resources).

Equipment
Ten counting toys for each child in a group of four to six; pegboards and pegs for a group of about four children.

WHOLE CLASS TEACHING

Main teaching activity

Ask the children to look at the garden scene on the enlarged version of CD page 'Garden scene'. Explain that today you would like them to count the things in the picture by pointing to each in turn. Say:

- *Count all the cats/dogs/birds. How many are there?*
- *Has Rania counted all of the birds? How do you know?*

Repeat this for other items in the picture. Put items together to be counted, for example:

- *Count the dogs and the flowers. How many is that?*

Now ask the children to count two sets each time. Say, for example:

- *How many trees are there? How many cats?*
- *Are there more trees or more cats? How many more cats are there?*
- *Are there fewer trees or fewer cats? How many fewer trees are there?*

Check that the children understand the idea of one fewer/less than. Repeat this for other sets from the picture with a difference of one, such as cats and dogs; dogs and rabbits; rabbits and birds; birds and squirrels; squirrels and flowers.

GROUP ACTIVITIES

Sorting

Learning objectives
Blue Stepping Stones:
- Separate a group of three/four objects in different ways, starting to recognise that the total is still the same.

Activity
This activity is provided in detail on CD page 'Sorting' for the LSA's reference. Ask a group of about four to six children to work with the LSA. Provide each child with a copy of CD page 'Partitioned work mat' and four counting toys. Children count a number of toys, split the toys into groups and check that the total is still the same.

Plenary & assessment
Put out four counting toys onto a copy of 'Partitioned work mat'. Ask: *How many toys are there?* Invite a child to count the toys and check that they co-ordinate the touch, move and count. Now ask another child to put one of the toys into the other area on the work mat. Ask:
- *How many are here? And here? How many are there altogether?*
- *But you have moved some of them. Are there still four?*
Repeat this for different partitions (separations) of the four toys.

One more, one less

Learning objectives
Green Stepping Stones:
- Say with confidence the number that is one more than a given number.
- Say the number after any number up to 9.

ELGs/NNS:
- **Find one more or one less than a number from 1 to 10.**

Activity
This activity is provided in detail on CD page 'One more, one less' for the LSA's reference and so they can record the children's performance for use during feedback. Ask four to six children to sit in a circle with the LSA. Children count to a number and say what the next number will be.

Plenary & assessment
Ask the children to count together for you, from one to ten. Repeat this, asking the children to count around the circle from one to ten. Ask: *What number comes after one/four/six/eight/nine?*

Extend this for the children working towards ELGs/NNS by asking:
What number comes before three/seven/ten?

Make it more or fewer

TEACHER DIRECTED

Learning objectives
Green Stepping Stones:
- Say with confidence the number that is one more than a given number.
- Say the number after any number up to 9.

ELGs/NNS:
- **Count reliably up to 10 everyday objects** (first to 5, then 10, and beyond), giving just one number name to each object.
- **Find one more or one less than a number from 1 to 10.**

Activity
Work with a group of four to six children in pairs. Each pair will need a copy of CD page 'Work mat' and ten counting toys. Ask the children to take turns to put out the number of toys you say, from one to nine. Ask their partner to count these to check, then to say how many one more would be. Say:
- *Put out four toys. How many is one more than four?*
- *Now check by putting one more and counting all of them.*

Repeat this for several different starting quantities, until each child has had four or five turns.
    For the children working towards ELGs/NNS, ask 'one fewer than' questions too, from one to ten.

Plenary & assessment
Invite children to say what is one more than any number from one to nine. Say, for example:
- *What is one more than four? What is one more than seven? How did you work this out?*

For the children working towards ELGs/NNS, ask 'one fewer than' questions too, such as:
- *What is one fewer than nine? How did you work this out?*

Pegboard count

STRUCTURED PLAY

Learning objectives
Green Stepping Stones:
- Say with confidence the number that is one more than a given number.
- Say the number after any number up to nine.

ELGs/NNS:
- **Count reliably up to 10 everyday objects** (first to 5, then 10, and beyond), giving just one number name to each object.
- **Find one more or one less than a number from 1 to 10.**

Activity
Put out some pegboards and pegs. Suggest to four children that they make staircase patterns of 'one more than' for each step. If the children are unsure about this, suggest that they begin by putting one peg in the first column, two in the next, and so on.

Plenary & assessment
Ask the children to show you their finished pegboard patterns. Talk about what they notice about the stair pattern – in particular, that each stair has one more peg than the last. Say, for example:
- *How many more/fewer pegs are there here… than here?* (pointing to two adjacent columns)
- *How many pegs are there in this* (the last) *stair? How many pegs would I need to make the next line?*

Sorting

You will need:

- 'Partitioned work mat' for each child
- four counting toys for each child.

Work with a group of about four to six children.

Ask the children to put three counting toys onto their work mat and to count them.
Check that they count by co-ordinating the touch, move and count.

Now ask the children to put their three toys into the two areas of their mat. They could put one and two, two and one, three and zero or zero and three.

Ask:

- *How many are here... and here?*
- *How many have you altogether?*

Check that the children are clear that there are still three toys.

Repeat this for four toys.

Record the children's achievements. It would be helpful to record whether the children recognise that splitting a set into two groups does not alter how many there are altogether.

Child's name	What happened	What to do next time

One more, one less

Ask four to six children to sit in a circle.

Explain that you will ask them to count around the circle. Say: *Jodie, start at one.*

When the children have counted around the circle to five, say: *Stop!* Ask:

- *What was the last number you said?*
- *What number comes after five?*

Repeat this for other stop numbers between three and nine.

Extend this for the children working towards ELGs/NNS by asking:

- *What number comes before...?*

Record the children's achievements. It would be helpful to record whether the children understand and can respond to the vocabulary of 'one more', and, for those working towards ELGs/NNS, 'one less'.

Child's name	What happened	What to do next time

Shapes and patterns

Children begin to name solid shapes and to recognise some of their properties. They order them for size. A group of children make repeating patterns such as 'hands up, hands down, hands up…'. They use shape tiles to make repeating patterns and say what comes next in the pattern.

LEARNING OBJECTIVES

Topics	Stepping Stones		Early Learning Goals & NNS Learning Objectives
	Blue	**Green**	
Exploring pattern, shape and space	● Show interest by sustained construction activity or by talking about shapes or arrangements.	● Match some shapes by recognising similarities and orientation. ● Begin to use mathematical names for 'solid' 3-D shapes and mathematical terms to describe shapes.	● **Use language such as circle or bigger to describe the shape and size of solids and flat shapes.** ● Begin to name solids such as a cube, cone, sphere. ● Put sets of objects in order of size.
Reasoning about numbers or shapes	● Use shapes appropriately for tasks. ● Begin to talk about the shapes of everyday objects.	● Use appropriate shapes to make representational models or pictures. ● Show curiosity and observation by talking about shapes, how they are the same or why some are different.	● **Talk about, recognise and recreate simple patterns**: for example, simple repeating or symmetrical patterns from different cultures.

4 Sessions

Learning objectives

Starter bank
ELGs/NNS
● **Count reliably up to 10 everyday objects** (first to 5, then 10, and beyond), giving just one number name to each object.
● **Find one more or one less than a number from 1 to 10.**

Main teaching & group activities
Blue Stepping Stones
● Show interest by sustained construction activity or by talking about shapes or arrangements.
Green Stepping Stones
● Match some shapes by recognising similarities and orientation.
● Begin to use mathematical names for 'solid' 3-D shapes and mathematical terms to describe shapes.
ELGs/NNS
● **Use language such as circle or bigger to describe the shape and size of solids and flat shapes.**
● Begin to name solids such as a cube, cone, sphere.
● Put sets of objects in order of size.

Vocabulary

cube, pyramid, sphere, cone, circle, triangle, square, rectangle, flat, curved, straight, round, hollow, solid, corner, face, side, edge, end, sort, size, star

You will need:
Photocopiable pages
'The three bears', for the teacher's/LSA's reference, see pages 62–63.

Equipment
Teaching set of a cube, sphere, pyramid and cone; sets of cubes, spheres, pyramids and cones of different sizes; sets of three teddies, beds, chairs, bowls, spoons, dolls and so on of different sizes; feely box; items for printing including paint, sponges and brushes; large sheets of paper.

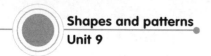

WHOLE CLASS TEACHING

Starter bank
These Starter bank ideas can be used throughout the unit.

Count the children
Ask five children to stand at the front. Invite the other children to count them, by pointing and saying the counting word. To help less able children, walk along the line of children and point to each one in turn as the children do their point and count. Ask: *What was the last number you said? How many children are there?* Repeat this for other quantities of children, from about three to ten.

Show me fingers
Explain to the children that you will say a number. Ask them to hold up that number of fingers. Begin with one, two, and then extend to up to ten, taking the number names out of counting order.

One more, one less
Explain to the children that you will say a number. Ask them to hold up that number of fingers, as in 'Show me fingers'. Now ask questions such as:
- *How many is one more than that? How do you know?*
- *How many is one less than that? How do you know?*

Repeat this, keeping the number of fingers between one and nine. Also, ask questions that are out of counting order.

Main teaching activity
Have in front of you one each of a cube, pyramid, sphere and cone. Begin with the cube and say: *What sort of shape is this?* Children may respond that it is like a box. Remind them that it is called a cube. Pass some cubes around for the children to touch and explore with their hands. Ask: *What can you tell me about the faces of a cube?* Point to each face, then run the flat of your hand across the face. If necessary, give the sentence: *A cube has flat faces.* Now ask: *Are all the faces of a cube the same or different?* Agree that the faces are the same. For the more able or older children, offer the sentence: *Each face is square.*

Ask the children to look at the set of cubes, which are of differing sizes. Ask: *What shape are these? Are they the same shape? Are they all the same size?* Invite three children each to choose a cube and to show these to the other children. Now invite them to put their cubes in order of size, beginning with the smallest. Discuss how the shape is the same, but the sizes are different.

Repeat this for the other shapes, either now, or during the week. Check that the children begin to name the solid shapes, and can identify curved faces. Introduce the word 'circle' for the flat face of a cone, and 'triangle' for the side faces of a pyramid for the more able children.

GROUP ACTIVITIES

Order by size

Learning objectives
Blue Stepping Stones:
- Show interest by sustained construction activity or by talking about shapes or arrangements.

Green Stepping Stones:
- Match some shapes by recognising similarities and orientation.

ELGs/NNS:
- Put sets of objects in order of size.

Activity
Put out three teddies and three cups of different sizes. Working with a group of about four children, ask them to put three teddies in a row. Say: *Are all the teddies the same size? Which is the biggest*

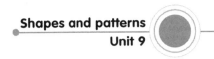
teddy? How can you tell? Which is the smallest teddy? How can you tell?

Then ask the children to sort the teddies so that the smallest is first and the biggest last. Repeat this, this time asking the children to put the largest teddy first. Repeat this with the cups.

Plenary & assessment
Show the children the three dolls and say:
- *Which is the biggest doll? Which is the smallest doll? How do you know?*
- *Can you put these dolls in order, starting with the smallest/biggest?*

The three bears

Learning objectives
Blue Stepping Stones:
- Show interest by sustained construction activity or by talking about shapes or arrangements.

Green Stepping Stones:
- Match some shapes by recognising similarities and orientation.

ELGs/NNS:
- Put sets of objects in order of size.

Activity
Put out three of each of the following in small, medium and large sizes: dolls, beds, chairs, bowls, spoons and bears. Ask the LSA to read the story of the three bears (from CD page 'The three bears') to the children. The LSA can invite the children to act out the story as they read it and encourage them to say which bowl/bed/spoon/chair belongs to which bear.

Plenary & assessment
Invite the children to retell the story of 'The three bears' and to act it out as they do. Ask:
- *Whose is this bowl? How did you decide that?*
- *Which chair will this bear need? How did you decide that?*

What is it?

Learning objectives
Blue Stepping Stones:
- Show interest by sustained construction activity or by talking about shapes or arrangements.

Green Stepping Stones:
- Match some shapes by recognising similarities and orientation.
- Begin to use mathematical names for 'solid' 3-D shapes and mathematical terms to describe shapes.

ELGs/NNS:
- **Use language such as circle or bigger to describe the shape and size of solids and flat shapes.**
- Begin to name solids such as a cube, cone, sphere.

Activity
Put one each of a cube, sphere, cone and pyramid into the feely box. Invite four to six children to sit in a circle and to take turns to feel for a shape in the feely box. Ask the child with the shape some questions, such as:
- *Is the shape round?*
- *Does it have flat/curved faces?*
- *Does it have a circle for a face?*

Encourage the other children to guess which shape it is. For those working towards Blue and Green Stepping Stones, provide some shapes to which they can point to show which one they think it is.

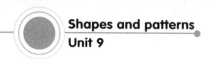

For those working towards ELGs/NNS, encourage them to name the shape.

Plenary & assessment

Invite each child to choose a solid shape and to hold it in their hands. Explain that you will describe a shape. Ask them to hold up their shape if they think they have the shape you describe. Say:

- *I am thinking of a shape that has flat faces. All the faces are squares.* (cube)
- *I am thinking of a shape with a circle face. It has a point.* (cone)
- *I am thinking of a shape with a square face. It has some triangle faces.* (pyramid)
- *I am thinking of a shape that has no flat faces. It is round.* (sphere)

Shape print

STRUCTURED PLAY

Learning objectives

Blue Stepping Stones:

- Show interest by sustained construction activity or by talking about shapes or arrangements.

Green Stepping Stones:

- Match some shapes by recognising similarities and orientation.

ELGs/NNS:

- **Use language such as circle or bigger to describe the shape and size of solids and flat shapes.**
- Begin to name solids such as a cube, cone, sphere.

Activity

Ask four children to work in the painting area, at a table. Provide paint, sponge, and shapes for printing of cubes, cones, spheres and pyramids. Ask the children to use the shapes to print each face. Remind them that they can also print with the 'points' of shapes.

Plenary & assessment

Invite the children to show you their finished prints. Ask questions about the prints such as:

- *Which shape did you use to make this print? Which part of the shape did you use?*
- *Who can remember what this shape is called?*

1 Session

Learning objectives

Main teaching & group activities

Blue Stepping Stones

- Use shapes appropriately for tasks.
- Begin to talk about the shapes of everyday objects.

Green Stepping Stones

- Use appropriate shapes to make representational models or pictures.
- Show curiosity and observation by talking about shapes, how they are the same or why some are different.

ELGs/NNS

- **Talk about, recognise and recreate simple patterns**: for example, simple repeating or symmetrical patterns from different cultures.

Vocabulary

pattern, shape, make, build, draw

You will need:

Photocopiable pages
'Make a pattern', for the teacher's/LSA's reference, see page 64.

Equipment
Gummed paper shapes; sheets of paper.

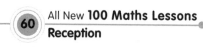

WHOLE CLASS TEACHING

Main teaching activity

Ask six children to stand at the front of the group. Ask the children to stand so that they alternate hands in the air, hands down, hands in the air. Ask: *What can you see?* Encourage the other children to describe the pattern that they see. Introduce the word 'pattern'. Repeat this for other patterns such as boy, girl, boy, girl; stand up, sit down, stand up. Each time ask the children to 'say' the pattern.

GROUP ACTIVITIES

Make a pattern

Learning objectives

Blue Stepping Stones:
- Use shapes appropriately for tasks
- Begin to talk about the shapes of everyday objects.

Green Stepping Stones:
- Use appropriate shapes to make representational models or more elaborate pictures.
- Show curiosity and observation by talking about shapes, how they are the same or why some are different.

ELGs/NNS:
- **Talk about, recognise and recreate simple patterns**: for example, simple repeating or symmetrical patterns from different cultures.

Activity

This activity is provided in detail on CD page 'Make a pattern' for the LSA's reference. Ask a group of about four children to work with the LSA. The LSA asks children to make a line pattern of repeating shapes and 'say' their pattern.

Plenary & assessment

Talk about the patterns that the children have made. Invite them to describe their patterns. Ask questions such as:
- *Who can say their pattern for me? Who can tell me what would come next in this pattern?*
- *What about this pattern? What comes next? And next?*
- *What would come before the first shape?*

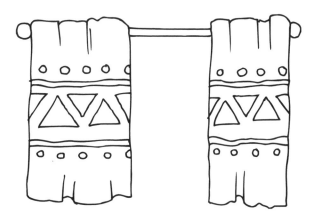

The three bears

Once upon a time, there were three bears who lived in a little house right in the middle of the forest.

There was great big Father Bear, and medium-sized Mother Bear, and little tiny Baby Bear.

One morning, Mother Bear made a big pot of porridge and put it into three bowls for breakfast. But the porridge was much too hot to eat.

'We will leave it to cool while we go for our early morning walk,' said Father Bear. 'When we come back, it will be just right.'

So off they went into the forest.

Nearby there lived a very naughty, mischievous little girl. She was called Goldilocks because she had long, golden hair.

That morning, as she was passing the three bears' house, Goldilocks saw that the front door was open.

'I'll just have a little peep inside,' she said to herself.

As soon as she saw the porridge, naughty Goldilocks rushed over to taste it.

'I do feel rather hungry,' she said.

But the porridge in Father Bear's big bowl was still too hot. And the porridge in Mother Bear's medium-sized bowl was lumpy.

At last Goldilocks tried Baby Bear's porridge. It was just right, so she ate up every spoonful!

After that, Goldilocks decided that she would like to sit down. But Father Bear's big chair was much too high.

Next she sat in Mother Bear's medium-sized chair. 'This one is much too hard!' she grumbled.

At last she found Baby Bear's tiny chair. It wasn't too high. It wasn't too hard. It was just right!

Goldilocks leaned back happily in Baby Bear's chair. But she was far too heavy. With a creak and a crack, the chair fell to pieces.

Bump! Goldilocks landed in a heap on the floor. 'Well, really!' she said crossly. 'I've had such a shock, I shall have to lie down.'

So Goldilocks went upstairs. She tried Father Bear's big bed, but that was far too hard.

And Mother Bear's medium-sized bed was far too soft! 'Now this is comfortable,' sighed Goldilocks, settling into Baby Bear's little bed. And she fell fast asleep!

Before long, the three bears arrived home from their walk.

'I'm ready for my breakfast right now,' said Father Bear. But when he got to the table he cried out in surprise, 'Someone's been eating my porridge!'

'And someone's been eating my porridge,' said Mother Bear. 'I wonder why they didn't like it?'

'They must have liked mine!' cried Baby Bear, holding his empty bowl. 'Someone's been eating my porridge, and they've eaten it all up!'
'Look!' said Father Bear. 'Someone's

been sitting in my chair!'

'And someone's been sitting in my chair,' said Mother Bear.
'Someone's been sitting in my chair,' sobbed poor little Baby Bear, 'and they've broken it to pieces!'

The three bears began to search the house. Upstairs, Father Bear looked around.

'Someone's been sleeping in my bed!' he said.

'And someone's been sleeping in my bed!' cried Mother Bear.

'Oh!' squeaked Baby Bear. 'Someone's been sleeping in my bed, and she's still here!'

At the sound of Baby Bear's voice, Goldilocks woke up. The first thing she saw was Father Bear looking very cross.

Goldilocks jumped up in fright. She ran down the stairs and out of the house as fast as she could.

'I don't think she'll trouble us again,' said Father Bear, smiling.
And she never did.

Make a pattern

You will need:

- gummed paper shapes
- a sheet of paper for each child.

Work with a group of about four children.

Ask the children to make a pattern with the gummed paper shapes. When they are happy with their pattern, ask them to stick the pattern onto the paper.

Ask the children to 'say' their pattern, such as: 'My pattern has a square, then two circles, then a square and two more circles.'

If children find making repeating patterns difficult, suggest to them that they 'say' their pattern as they make it. Suggest to the children that they begin with simple ABAB... patterns, such as square, circle, square, circle...

The children can develop more complex patterns when they are confident with these, such as ABCABC... or AABAAB... patterns.

Over time, this activity can be repeated using different materials for making patterns, such as solid shapes, 2-D shape tiles, mosaic shapes, or pegs and pegboards.

Record the children's achievements. It would be helpful to record whether the children can 'say' their pattern and predict what would come next if the pattern was continued.

Child's name	What happened	What to do next time

Counting ten objects, comparing weight and sequencing events

Children count out some toys, put some more, then count to say how many there are altogether. They coordinate the point and count and recognise that the last number said determines how many there are in the count. They compare two then three parcels for weight and check this with a balance. They sequence events of the day and in a story.

LEARNING OBJECTIVES

Topics	Stepping Stones		Early Learning Goals & NNS Learning Objectives
	Blue	**Green**	
Counting	● Recognise groups with one, two or three objects.	● Count up to three or four objects by saying one number name for each item.	● **Count reliably up to 10 everyday objects** (first to 5, then 10, then beyond), giving just one number name to each object.
Comparing and ordering measures		● Order two items by weight.	● **Use language such as more or less, heavier or lighter to compare two quantities,** then more than two, by making direct comparisons of masses. ● Begin to understand and use the vocabulary of time. ● Sequence familiar events.

1 Session

Learning objectives

Starter bank
ELGs/NNS
● Put sets of objects in order of size.
● **Count reliably up to 10 everyday objects** (first to 5, then 10, then beyond), giving just one number name to each object.

Main teaching & group activities
Blue Stepping Stones
● Recognise groups with one, two or three objects.
Green Stepping Stones
● Count up to three or four objects by saying one number name for each item.
ELGs/NNS
● **Count reliably up to 10 everyday objects** (first to 5, then 10, then beyond), giving just one number name to each object.

Vocabulary

count, one, two, three… to ten

You will need
Photocopiable pages
'The three bears', see pages 62–63, and 'Counting' for the teacher's/LSA's reference, see page 70.

CD pages
'Work mat' for each child in a group of four to six (see General resources).

Equipment
In small, medium and large sizes: beds, chairs, bowls and spoons; ten toys for counting; ten small counting toys for each child in a group of four to six.

WHOLE CLASS TEACHING

Starter bank

These Starter bank ideas can be used throughout the unit.

The three bears

Have ready the three beds, chairs, bowls and spoons. Read the story from the CD page 'The three bears' to the children and invite some children to act out the story as you read it. Encourage the other children to join in with the bears' speech. Ask questions such as:

- *Whose bowl/spoon is this?*
- *How do you know that?*
- *Which bear sits in this chair?*

Count the sounds

Sit so that you can hide a tambourine from the children's view. Ask the children to listen carefully to the taps of the tambourine. Begin with one, two or three taps. Encourage the children to listen very carefully and to count each tap. At first they may count the taps aloud. With further experience they will begin to be able to count silently. Extend the count to up to ten.

Clapping

Explain to the children that you will say a number and that you would like them to make that number of claps. Do this with the children, saying the counting numbers aloud and keeping a steady rhythm. Begin with one, two, three and then over time extend to up to ten.

Main teaching activity

Have the ten toys for counting beside you. Ask a child to pick out four toys and put them in a straight line for the others to see. This could be on a table top or on the floor, if the children sit in a circle. Invite another child to count the toys by co-ordinating the touch and count. Now ask a child to put out two more toys. Invite another child to count the toys. Encourage all the children to point and count, too. Say: *What was the last number that you said? How many toys are there?* Repeat this for other quantities of toys between three and ten.

GROUP ACTIVITIES

Counting

Learning objectives
Blue Stepping Stones:
- Recognise groups with one, two or three objects.

Green Stepping Stones:
- Count up to three or four objects by saying one number name for each item.

ELGs/NNS:
- **Count reliably up to 10 everyday objects** (first to 5, then 10, then beyond), giving just one number name to each object.

Activity

This activity is provided in detail on CD page 'Counting' for the LSA's reference. Ask a group of four to six children to sit with the LSA at a table. Provide each child with a copy of CD page 'Work mat' in front of them, and ten small counting toys. The LSA says a number and the children count out that number of toys.

Plenary & assessment

Ask the children to count some toys that you put out in front of you. Ask them to point to the toys. Check that they count each one. Ask: *What was the last number you said? How many toys are there?*

3 Sessions

Preparation

Make up some parcels for balancing; these should be of different weights and sizes and include a heavy small parcel, and a light large parcel. Put some items on to a tray, too.

Learning objectives

Main teaching & group activities
Green Stepping Stones
- Order two items by weight.

ELGs/NNS
- **Use language such as more or less, heavier or lighter to compare two quantities,** then more than two, by making direct comparisons of masses.

Vocabulary

weigh, weighs, balances, heavy/light, heavier/lighter, heaviest/lightest, weight, balance, scales, compare, guess, estimate

You will need:
Photocopiable pages
'Heavier and lighter' for the teacher's/LSA's reference, see page 71.

Equipment
Parcels of different sizes; bucket balances; items of varying masses and sizes for balancing, such as teddies, parcels, brushes and so on; tray.

Main teaching activity

Begin by asking the children to look at, for example, two parcels that are of different sizes. Pass these parcels around the group and ask each child to hold them, and to decide which is lighter and which is heavier. Then, explain that it is possible to check the guess, or estimate, by putting one parcel in each bucket of the balance. Talk about how to tell which is lighter and which is heavier by looking at the position of the buckets. Discuss how the heavier parcel makes the bucket 'go down' and the lighter bucket 'goes up' as a result. Repeat this for other items. Say: *The lighter/heavier parcel is this one. This parcel is heavier/lighter than that one.*

Over time, extend this to comparing three parcels and introduce the language of heaviest and lightest by ordering the three parcels by weight. Say: *The teddy is heavier than the brush. The blue parcel is heavier than the teddy. So the blue parcel is the heaviest, and the brush is the lightest.*

GROUP ACTIVITIES

Find something lighter

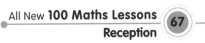

STRUCTURED PLAY

Learning objectives
Green Stepping Stones:
- Order two items by weight.

ELGs/NNS:
- **Use language such as more or less, heavier or lighter to compare two quantities,** by making direct comparisons of masses.

Activity

Put out a tray of items for weighing, two parcels and two bucket balances. Ask four children, working in pairs, to decide which items are lighter than the parcel they choose. Challenge them to find all the lighter things. Check that the children estimate by using their hands before checking with the bucket balance. This can be repeated for finding things that are heavier.

Plenary & assessment

Invite the children to show you which things they thought were lighter. Ask:
- *How did you find out? Who used their hands to estimate/guess first?*
- *How did you use the bucket balance to check? Show me.*

Heavier and lighter

ADULT SUPPORTED

Learning objectives

Green Stepping Stones:
- Order two items by weight.

ELGs/NNS:
- **Use language such as more or less, heavier or lighter to compare two quantities,** by making direct comparisons of masses.

Activity

This activity is provided in detail on CD page 'Heavier and lighter' for the LSA's reference. The LSA works with four to six children. Provide a bucket balance for each pair of children and some things to compare for mass. Children compare masses by holding and by using balances.

Plenary & assessment

Choose two parcels. Pass the parcels around the group. Ask the children to compare by holding and to estimate which is heavier and which is lighter. Say:
- *Which do you think is heavier/lighter? Why do you think that?*
- *Check with the bucket balance. Who made a good guess/estimate?*

Heaviest and lightest

STRUCTURED PLAY

Learning objectives

ELGs/NNS:
- **Use language such as more or less, heavier or lighter to compare two quantities,** then more than two, by making direct comparisons of masses.

Activity

The children need to have successfully completed activity 'Heavier and lighter' above before this.

Ask four to six children, working in pairs, to choose three things to compare and to order them from heaviest to lightest. Children estimate by holding and check their estimates by balancing.

Plenary & assessment

Pass three parcels around the group. Say:
- *Which do you think is heaviest/ lightest? Why do you think that?*
- *Check with the bucket balance. Who made a good guess/estimate?*

1 Session

Preparation

Enlarge a copy of 'Story sequencing' to A3. Cut out the pictures. Stick these, out of sequence, to a flip chart.

Learning objectives

Main teaching & group activities

ELGs/NNS
- Begin to understand and use the vocabulary of time.
- Sequence familiar events.

Vocabulary

morning, afternoon, evening, night, bedtime, dinnertime, playtime, today, yesterday, tomorrow, before, after, next, last, now

You will need:

Photocopiable pages
'Story sequencing', one copy for each child and one enlarged to A3, see page 72.

CD pages
'Time story', for the teacher's/LSA's reference (see General resources).

Equipment
Flip chart or board; scissors for each child; Blu-Tack; sheets of A4 paper.

WHOLE CLASS TEACHING

Main teaching activity

Invite the children to talk about their day so far. Ask questions such as:
- *What do you do when you wake up in the morning? What do you do next?*
- *Who does something different?*
- *What do you do before playtime/after dinnertime?*
- *What did we do before this today? What do you think we shall do next?*
- *What do you do at lunchtime? Did you do that yesterday? Will you do it tomorrow?*

When the children are confident with the vocabulary of sequencing time, read them the story on CD page 'Time story'. Now invite the children to help to retell the story. Ask, for example:
- *What happened first? Then what happened?*
- *What happened next?*

GROUP ACTIVITIES

Time story

Learning objectives

ELGs/NNS:
- Begin to understand and use the vocabulary of time.
- Sequence familiar events.

Activity

Work with four to six children. Reread the story 'Time story' and encourage the children to join in. Provide them with a copy each of 'Story sequencing'. Ask the children to cut out the pictures and place them in front of them. Explain that these pictures come from the story that they all listened to together. Ask the children to look at the pictures and to put them into order so that they help to tell the story. When children have done this, they can stick down the pieces of paper.

Plenary & assessment

Invite the children to look carefully at the pictures and to explain what each one shows, so that the children, between them, retell the story in sequence. Ask questions such as: *What happened first of all? What happened next?* Encourage the children to use the vocabulary of sequencing time, modelling sentences if necessary.

Counting

You will need:

- 'Work mat' for each child
- ten small counting toys for each child.

Ask a group of four to six children to sit at a table, with a copy of CD page 'Work mat' in front of each of them, and ten small counting toys.

Explain that you will say a number and that you would like the children to count out that number of toys.

Ask the children to check their count by co-ordinating the touch and count. Say:

- *What was the last number you said in your count?*
- *How many toys are there?*

Begin with smaller quantities, such as three and four. Extend over time to up to ten.

When the children are confident with counting by touching, ask them to co-ordinate pointing and counting.

Record the children's achievements. It would be helpful to record whether the children can count by co-ordinating the point and count.

Child's name	What happened	What to do next time

Heavier and lighter

You will need:

- bucket balance for each pair
- items to compare for mass, such as teddies, parcels, brushes, scissors.

Work with four to six children.

Invite the children to take two items, and estimate (by holding) which is heavier and which is lighter.

Ask the children to check their estimate by comparing the two items on the bucket balance. Ask:

- *Which do you think is heavier/lighter?*
- *Why do you think that?*
- *Check with the bucket balance. Did you make a good guess?*

Ask the children to carry out the comparison activity for several pairs of items.

Record the children's achievements. It would be helpful to record whether the children can make a reasonable estimate of 'heavier' and 'lighter' and understand which side of the bucket balance is demonstrating heavier or lighter.

Child's name	What happened	What to do next time

Name	Date

Story sequencing

Solving problems

Children count in a range of contexts, including their own movements. They learn the names of the coins and how to recognise the differences in appearance between them. They solve problems whilst shopping in the class shop, choosing the correct number of pennies for their chosen items. They respond to simple word problems using penny coins to model the problems.

LEARNING OBJECTIVES

Topics	Stepping Stones		Early Learning Goals & NNS Learning Objectives
	Blue	**Green**	
Counting	● Attempt to count, with some numbers in the correct order.	● Count actions or objects that cannot be moved.	● Count reliably in other contexts, such as clapping sounds or hopping movements.
Problems involving 'real life' or money	● Show an interest in number problems.	● Sometimes show confidence and offer solutions to problems.	● Begin to understand and use the vocabulary related to money. Sort coins, including the £1 and £2 coins, and use them in role play to pay and give change. ● **Use developing mathematical ideas and methods to solve practical problems** involving counting and comparing in a real or role play context.

2 Sessions

Preparation

Place items onto each tray so that the items do not make a set. Make sure that each tray contains between four and ten things of various sizes, and has a different quantity.

Learning objectives

Starter bank
ELGs/NNS
● **Count reliably up to 10 everyday objects** (first to 5, then 10, then beyond), giving just one number name to each object.

Main teaching & group activities
Blue Stepping Stones
● Attempt to count, with some numbers in the correct order.
Green Stepping Stones
● Count actions or objects that cannot be moved.
ELGs/NNS
● Count reliably in other contexts, such as clapping sounds or hopping movements.

Vocabulary

one, two, three… to ten; count

You will need:
Photocopiable pages
'Counting things', for the teacher's/LSA's reference, see page 78.

Equipment
Seven trays; a selection of different items for counting that are in various sizes; ten animal counting tiles for each child in a group of six to eight.

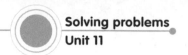
WHOLE CLASS TEACHING

Starter bank
These Starter bank ideas can be used throughout the unit.

Counting fingers
Explain to the children that you will say a number. Ask them to hold up that number of fingers. Begin with one to five, then extend this to up to ten and include zero.

One more
Repeat the activity 'Counting fingers', above. This time, ask the children to say how many there would be if they held up one more finger. Say, for example:
- *Show me four fingers. How many would there be if you held up one more?*
- *Check; hold up another finger and count again. Did you make a good guess?*

One fewer
Repeat the activity 'Counting fingers', above. This time, ask the children to say how many there would be if they put one finger down. Say, for example:
- *Show me four fingers. How many would there be if you put one finger down?*
- *Check; put a finger down and count again. Did you make a good guess?*

Main teaching activity
Work with the children in a large space, such as the hall, or outside. Say, for example:
- *Move across the hall/playground by making giant steps. Count the steps. Stop when I say 'stop!'.*
- *Move by jumping. Count the jumps until I say 'stop'.*
- *Use a skipping rope. Count the skips. Bounce a ball. Count the bounces.*
Continue like this, inviting children to count how many each time, then ask questions such as:
- *Who counted five/one more than five/one fewer than five? How many did you count, Claudette?*
Finish the activity by asking the children to look at something that is out of their reach, such as the panes in the window or the trees around the playground. Ask the children to count these by co-ordinating the point and count. Ask: *How many did you count?*

GROUP ACTIVITIES

Counting things

Learning objectives
Blue Stepping Stones:
- Attempt to count, with some numbers in the correct order.

Green Stepping Stones:
- Count actions or objects that cannot be moved.

ELGs/NNS:
- Count reliably in other contexts, such as clapping sounds or hopping movements.

Activity
This activity is provided in detail on CD page 'Counting things' for the LSA's reference. Ask a group of four to six children to work with the LSA. The LSA asks the children to count the items on a tray. One child can count by touching and counting, then the other child checks by counting again.

Plenary & assessment
Invite a child to show how they counted the items on a tray by touching and counting. Ask:
- *What was the last number you said? How many things are on the tray?*

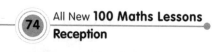

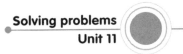

Animal count

Learning objectives
ELGs/NNS:
- Count reliably in other contexts, such as clapping sounds or hopping movements.

Activity
Work with a group of four to six children. They will each need ten animal counting tiles. Ask the children to put out five of their animal tiles, such as horse, cow, cat, dog and sheep. Say:
- *Count the animals. Start with the cat. How many have you?*
- *Now count them again. This time start with the dog/sheep/cow. How many are there?*

Repeat this for different quantities of tiles, at first up to about six. Over time extend to about ten.

Plenary & assessment
Ask: *How many animals? Does it matter which animal tile you begin with when you count? Why not?*

3 Sessions

Learning objectives

Main teaching & group activities
Blue Stepping Stones
- Show an interest in number problems.

Green Stepping Stones
- Sometimes show confidence and offer solutions to problems.

ELGs/NNS
- Begin to understand and use the vocabulary related to money. Sort coins, including the £1 and £2 coins, and use them in role play to pay and give change.
- **Use developing mathematical ideas and methods to solve practical problems** involving counting and comparing in a real or role play context.

Vocabulary

money, coin, penny, pence, pound, price, cost, buy, sell, spend, spent, pay, puzzle, count, sort, group, set, match. What could we try next? How did you work it out?

You will need:
Photocopiable pages
'Coin sort' for the teacher's/ LSA's reference, see page 79.

CD pages
'Money box mat' for each child (see General resources).

Equipment
Class shop: till; 1p, 2p, 5p, 10p, 20p, 50p, £1, £2 coins; sorting tray; pots for money.

WHOLE CLASS TEACHING

Main teaching activity
Pass around the group some 1p coins and name these as one penny coins. Repeat this for 2p coins. Ask the children to work at their tables, with each table having a pot of some 1p and 2p coins. Invite the children to sort the coins into 1p and 2p piles. Now ask: *How can you tell the difference between 1p and 2p coins?* Children may refer to the size or the pictures on the coins.

Repeat this for 5p, 10p and 20p coins.

Using just the 1p coins, invite a child to count out enough coins to pay 5p. Say: *How many 1p coins will Jasmine need to pay 5p? Yes, five. Let's count them together: one, two, three, four, five. That's 5p.*

Repeat this for other values between 2p and 6p, using just 1p coins, then extend to 10p.

Over time, introduce the 50p, £1 and £2 coins and ask the children to explain how they recognise each coin.

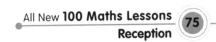

GROUP ACTIVITIES

Coin sort

Learning objectives

Blue Stepping Stones:
- Show an interest in number problems.

Green Stepping Stones:
- Sometimes show confidence and offer solutions to problems.

ELGs/NNS:
- Begin to understand and use the vocabulary related to money. Sort coins, including the £1 and £2 coins, and use them in role play to pay and give change.
- **Use developing mathematical ideas and methods to solve practical problems** involving counting and comparing in a real or role play context.

Activity

This activity is provided in detail on CD page 'Coin sort' for the LSA's reference and so they can record the children's achievements and difficulties for use during feedback. Ask four children to work together. Provide them with some coins to sort by value, and a sorting tray. For those working towards the Blue and Green Stepping Stones, provide 1p and 2p coins. For those working towards the ELGs/NNS, include silver coins.

Over time, include 50p, £1 and £2 coins for children working towards the ELGs/NNS.

Plenary & assessment

Check that the children have sorted the coins correctly, then show them some more coins. Ask:
- *What coin is this? How can you tell?*
- *Where should I put this coin? Why does it belong there?*

In the shop

Learning objectives

Blue Stepping Stones:
- Show an interest in number problems.

Green Stepping Stones:
- Sometimes show confidence and offer solutions to problems.

ELGs/NNS:
- Begin to understand and use the vocabulary related to money. Sort coins, including the £1 and £2 coins, and use them in role play to pay and give change.
- **Use developing mathematical ideas and methods to solve practical problems** involving counting and comparing in a real or role-play context.

Activity

Invite four children to work with the LSA in the class shop. For children working towards the Blue and Green Stepping Stones, the LSA can explain that everything in the shop costs 1p. Initially, the LSA is the shopkeeper and invites the children to choose something to buy, and to give the shopkeeper a penny for the item, for example: *That costs one penny.* When the children are confident, the LSA can ask them to buy one/two/three things and to count out the correct number of pennies.

For children working towards the ELGs/NNS, explain that items in the shop cost 2p/5p/10p. At first, ask the children to give you the correct coin for the price. When they are confident, say: *How many pennies do you need to give me for this, which costs 2p/5p/10p?*

When the children understand the role play, let them take turns to be the shopkeeper.

Plenary & assessment

Act as the shopkeeper. Ask the children to count out the penny coins for the price that you give. Say, for example:

- *How many penny coins for this tin, which costs 2p/5p/10p?*
- *Which coin could you give me for 2p/5p/10p?*

Money stories

TEACHER DIRECTED

Learning objectives

ELGs/NNS:

- Begin to understand and use the vocabulary related to money. Sort coins, including the £1 and £2 coins, and use them in role play to pay and give change.
- **Use developing mathematical ideas and methods to solve practical problems** involving counting and comparing in a real or role-play context.

Activity

Put out some pots of 1p coins. Work with six to eight children who will each need a copy of CD page 'Money box mat'.

Explain to the children that you will tell them a money story. Ask them to use the coins to help them to find the solution. Use stories such as:

- *Tom has 1p. Sam gives him another 1p. How much does Tom have now?*
- *Peter has four penny coins. He spends one penny. How much does he have left?*
- *How much altogether is 1p and 1p and 1p and 1p?*

Encourage the children to act out each story, using their coins to demonstrate the amounts.

Plenary & assessment

Ask the children to put out coins for this story:

- *Gemma has six 1p coins. Then she spends 1p. How much does she have left?*
- *Granny gives her another 1p. Grandpa gives her another 1p! Now how much does she have?*

Check that the children count out the correct number of 1p coins and can follow the money story.

Counting things

You will need:

- seven trays
- a selection of different items for counting which are in various sizes.

Put four things on one tray, five on the next, and so on.

Work with a group of four to six children.

Provide each pair of children with a tray of items and ask them to count the items on their tray. One child can count by touching and counting, then the other child checks by counting again.

Repeat this by asking the children to count the items on another tray.

For children working towards Blue Stepping Stones, you may want to limit the size of the count initially to about six.

For children working towards Green Stepping Stones, provide trays with up to seven or eight items at first. Ask:

- *What was the last number you said?*
- *How many things are on your tray?*

Record the children's achievements. It would be helpful to record which children can count by co-ordinating the touch and count.

Child's name	What happened	What to do next time

Coin sort

You will need:

- 1p and 2p coins for those working towards the Blue and Green Stepping Stones
- 1p, 2p, 5p, 10p and 20p coins for those working towards the ELGs/NNS
- a sorting tray.

Ask four children to work together.

Invite the children to sort their coins into the sorting tray. They should sort them so that the same value coins are placed together.

Ask:

- *What coin is this? How can you tell?*
- *Where should I put this coin? Why does it belong there?*

Record the children's achievements. It would be helpful to record which coins the children recognise and can name.

Child's name	What happened	What to do next time

	Topics	Stepping Stones **Green**	Early Learning Goals & NNS Learning Objectives
1	Counting	● Show confidence with numbers by initiating or requesting number activities.	● **Say and use the number names in order in familiar contexts** such as number rhymes, songs, stories, counting games and activities (first to five, then ten, then twenty and beyond). ● Recite the number names in order, continuing the count forwards or backwards from a given number.
	Comparing and ordering numbers		● Order a given set of numbers, for example, the set of numbers 1 to 6 given in random order.
2	Counting	● Count out up to six objects from a larger group.	● **Count reliably up to 10 everyday objects** (first to 5, then 10, then beyond), giving just one number name to each object.
	Adding and subtracting	● Find the total number of items in two groups by counting all of them.	● **Begin to use the vocabulary involved in adding and subtracting.** ● **Begin to relate addition to combining two groups of objects**, counting all the objects. ● Separate (partition) a given number of objects into two groups.
3	Exploring pattern, shape and space	● Begin to use mathematical names for 'solid' 3-D shapes and 'flat' 2-D shapes and mathematical terms to describe shapes.	● Begin to name solids such as a cube, cone, sphere and flat shapes such as circle, triangle, square, rectangle. Use a variety of shapes to make models, pictures and patterns, and describe them.
	Reasoning about numbers or shapes	● Choose suitable components to make a particular model.	● Solve simple problems or puzzles in a practical context, and respond to 'What could we try next?' ● Sort and match objects, pictures or children themselves, justifying the decisions made.
4	Counting	● Begin to count beyond 10.	● Recite the number names in order, continuing the count forwards or backwards from a given number.
	Comparing and ordering measures	● Order two items by capacity	● Use language such as more or less, greater or smaller to compare two capacities, then more than two, by filling and emptying containers.
5	Counting	● Count out up to six objects from a larger group.	● **Count reliably up to 10 everyday objects** (first to 5, then 10, then beyond), giving just one number name to each object. ● Count reliably in other contexts such as clapping or hopping movements.
	Adding and subtracting	● Count actions or objects that cannot be moved.	● **Begin to use the vocabulary involved in adding and subtracting.** ● **Begin to relate subtraction to 'taking away'** and counting how many are left.
	Problems involving 'real life' or money	● Sometimes show confidence and offer solutions to problems.	● Begin to understand and use vocabulary related to money. Sort coins, including the £1 and £2 coins, and use them in role play to pay and give change.
6	Assess and review		

	Topics	Stepping Stones	Early Learning Goals & NNS Learning Objectives
		Green	
7	Counting	● Begin to count beyond 10.	● **Say and use the number names in order in familiar contexts** such as number rhymes, songs, stories, counting games and activities (first to five, then ten, then twenty and beyond).
	Reading and writing numbers	● Recognise numerals 1 to 5, then 1 to 9.	● **Recognise numerals 1 to 9,** then 0 to 10, and beyond 10.
	Comparing and ordering numbers.	● **Say with confidence the number that is 1 more than a given number.**	● **Use language such as more or less, greater or smaller, to compare two numbers** and say which is more or less, and say a number that lies between two given numbers.
8	Counting	● Count out up to six objects from a larger group.	● **Count reliably up to 10 everyday objects** (first to 5, then 10, then beyond) giving just one number name to each object.
	Reading and writing numbers	● Recognise numerals 1 to 5, then 1 to 9.	● **Recognise numerals 1 to 9,** then 0 to 10, and beyond 10.
	Adding and subtracting	● Find the total number of items in two groups by counting all of them.	● **Begin to relate addition to combining two groups of objects**, counting all the objects. ● Begin to relate addition to counting on.
9	Reasoning about numbers or shapes	● Show awareness of symmetry.	● **Talk about, recognise and recreate patterns**: for example, simple repeating or symmetrical patterns in the environment.
	Exploring pattern, shape and space	● Find items from positional/directional clues. ● Describe a simple journey. ● Instruct a programmable toy.	● **Use everyday words to describe position**: for example, follow and give instructions about positions, directions and movements in PE and other activities.
10	Counting	● Begin to count beyond 10.	● **Recite the number names in order**, continiuing the count forwards and backwards from a given number.
	Reading and writing numbers	● Recognise numerals 1 to 5, then 1 to 9.	● **Recognise numerals 1 to 9,** then 0 to 10, and beyond 10.
	Comparing and ordering numbers	● **Say with confidence the number that is 1 more than a given number.**	● **Use language such as more or less, greater or smaller, to compare two numbers** and say which is more or less, and say a number that lies between two given numbers.
	Days of the week		● Begin to know the days of the week in order.
11	Counting	● Count an irregular arrangement of up to 10 objects.	● **Count reliably up to 10 everyday objects** (first to 5, then 10, then beyond), giving just one number name to each object.
	Reading and writing numbers	● Recognise numerals 1 to 5, the 1 to 9.	● **Recognise numerals 1 to 9**, then 0 to 10, then beyond 10.
	Adding and subtracting	● Sometimes show confidence and offer solutions to problems.	● Begin to relate addition to counting on.
	Problems involving real-life and money	● Match some shapes by recognising similarities and orientation.	● Begin to understand and use the vocabulary related to money. Sort coins, including the £1 and £2 coins, and use them in role play to pay and give change.
	Reasoning about numbers or shapes		● Sort and match objects, pictures or children themselves, justifying the decisions made.
12	Assess and review		

Counting and ordering numbers

Children recite the number words to 20. They count on from a small number to a given number. They order a set of numbers given in random order in practical situations.

LEARNING OBJECTIVES

Topics	Stepping Stones Green	Early Learning Goals & NNS Learning Objectives
Counting	● Show confidence with numbers by initiating or requesting number activities.	● **Say and use the number names in order in familiar contexts** such as number rhymes, songs, stories, counting games and activities (first to five, then ten, then twenty and beyond). ● Recite the number names in order, continuing the count forwards or backwards from a given number.
Comparing and ordering numbers		● Order a given set of numbers, for example, the set of numbers 1 to 6 given in random order.

3 Sessions

Learning objectives

Starter
ELGs/NNS
● **Say and use the number names in order in familiar contexts,** such as number rhymes, songs, stories, counting games and activities (first to five, then ten, then twenty and beyond).
● Recite the number names in order, continuing the count forwards or backwards from a given number.

Main teaching activity
Green Stepping Stones
● Show confidence with numbers by initiating or requesting number activities.
ELGs/NNS
● **Say and use the number names in order in familiar contexts** such as number rhymes, songs, stories, counting games and activities (first to five, then ten, then twenty and beyond).
● Recite the number names in order, continuing the count forwards or backwards from a given number.

Vocabulary

zero, one, two, three… to twenty, count, count (up) to, count on (from, to)

You will need:
Photocopiable pages
'One, two, buckle my shoe', for the teacher's/LSA's reference, see page 87.

CD pages
'Counting record', for the teacher's/LSA's reference (see General resources).

Equipment
Hand puppet.

WHOLE CLASS TEACHING

Starter bank

These Starter bank ideas can be used throughout the unit.

Start and stop counting

Ask the children to sit in a circle with you. Explain that you will ask someone to start counting from zero. When you say *Stop!*, the next child takes up the count from where the previous child stopped. Ask the children to count from zero to ten, then back from ten to zero. Do this several times until all the children have had at least three turns at some counting. Encourage them to keep the pace sharp. Stop counting at, for example, three, five or eight, and similarly when counting back.

What comes next?

Ask the children to begin a count from zero to ten. When you say: *Stop!* they stop counting. Ask questions such as:
- *What was the last number you said?*
- *What would the next number be?*

Repeat this several times, stopping at different numbers.

Puppet count

You will need a hand puppet for this activity. Ask the children to listen to the puppet counting and to put up their hands if they think the puppet counted wrongly. Say, for example:
- *Zero, one, two, three, five, six…*
- *Ten, nine, eight, six, five…*

Ask:
- *What was wrong? What should the count be?*

Do this several times, with a different error each time.

Main teaching activity

Explain to the children that today they will be counting beyond ten. Ask them to join in with you: *One, two, three… 10, 11, 12, 13… 20.* At first, the children are likely to count with you to ten, then stop and listen to you counting. Do not worry about this. Instead, repeat the count several times, and the children will begin to join in.

Now ask the children to count from a number that you say. Say, for example: *Start counting from three/five/six.* Then ask them to count on from a given number, and to stop at another given number. Say, for example: *Count from three and on to eight.* Ask the children to count aloud at first. When they are confident with this, ask them to count silently. They may find it helpful to use their fingers.

GROUP ACTIVITIES

One, two, buckle my shoe

ADULT SUPPORTED

Learning objectives
Green Stepping Stones:
- Show confidence with numbers by initiating or requesting number activities.

ELGs/NNS:
- **Say and use number names in order in familiar contexts** such as number rhymes, songs, stories, counting games and activities (first to 5, then 10, then 20 and beyond).

Activity

Ask the children to count with the LSA, from zero to 20. At first, children may not be sure about the count from 11 on, so repeat this several times, keeping the pace sharp and saying the number names clearly so that the children will begin to join in.

Now the LSA can teach the children the rhyme 'One, two, buckle my shoe', which can be found on CD page 'One, two, buckle my shoe'. The LSA can show the children the actions as they say the rhyme with you.

Plenary & assessment
Ask the children to count together from zero to 20. Check to see who can say all of the number names, and who is still not sure. Record children's progress with knowing the number names in order on 'Counting record'. Ask, for example: *What number comes after 10… 11…12…14…19…?*

Puppet count

Learning objectives
Green Stepping Stones:
● Show confidence with numbers by initiating or requesting number activities.
ELGs/NNS:
● Recite the number names in order, continuing the count forwards from a given number.

Activity
Explain to the children that the puppet will count. Ask them to listen carefully to what the puppet says, and to put up their hand if they think that the puppet has made an error. Begin with numbers to ten, such as:
● *One, two, three, four, six…*
● *Four, five, six, nine, eight…*
Then, for those working towards the ELGs/NNS, extend the count into the teen numbers:
● *Eleven, twelve, thirteen, fourteen, fiveteen…*
● *Eight, nine, ten, oneteen…*
Ask the children to say what the number should be.

Plenary & assessment
Ask the children to count together, from zero to about 20. Then ask them to listen to the puppet count. Make errors as above. Ask:
● *What did the puppet do wrong?*
● *What should the number be?*
● *Who would like to say the count for me?*

Counting forwards and backwards

Learning objectives
ELGs/NNS:
● Recite the number names in order, continuing the count forwards or backwards from a given number.

Activity
Ask the children to count with you from zero to 15, and back again. Repeat the counting back several times until the children are confident with this. Now invite the children to begin the count, counting forward from three… six… nine… ten… When they are confident with this, ask them to count back from 15… 13… 11…

Plenary & assessment
Make a note of the children's counting forwards and backwards ability on 'Counting record'. Ask questions such as: *What number comes before/after 5… 7… 8… 10… 13… 14… 18… 19…?*

2 Sessions

Preparation

Photocopy 'Duck counting cards' onto card. If preferred, colour in the cards, then laminate them to make a long-lasting set. Photocopy 'Duck counting cards 2' onto card and cut out, making enough for one set between two children. Onto each tray, put five containers. Put one item into the first container, two in the next, and so on. Each tray should be themed, so that one tray contains marbles, another counting tiles and so on.

Learning objectives

Main teaching activity
ELGs/NNS
- Order a given set of numbers, for example, the set of numbers 1 to 6, given in random order.

Vocabulary

compare, order, first, second, third… tenth, last, last but one, before, after, next, between, zero, one, two, three… to ten

You will need:
Photocopiable pages
'Duck order' for the teacher's/LSA's reference, see page 88.

CD pages
'Duck counting cards', photocopied onto card and coloured if desired and 'Duck counting cards 2', photocopied onto card, one set per pair of children (see General resources).

Equipment
Four trays; 20 containers; counting tiles, conkers, marbles and so on.

WHOLE CLASS TEACHING

Main teaching activity

Begin with CD pages 'Duck counting cards' for quantities one to five, in counting order. Explain to the children that you have a set of cards with some ducks on. Invite five children, one at a time, to come to the front of the group and take a card. Say: *How many ducks are there on this card?* Ask the five children to stand at the front of the class, so that everyone can see the cards. Now invite the other children to take turns to stand at the front. Say:

- *Gemma, stand in the two-card place instead of Peter.*
- *Marcus, take the card that has one more than three ducks.*
- *Naima, take the card that has one fewer than two ducks.*

Repeat this until everyone has had a turn at standing at the front.

    Collect the cards and shuffle them so that they are out of number order, but make sure that one, then five, are the first two cards. These will mark the beginning and end of a picture number line for the children. Hold up a card and say: *How many ducks?* Invite the child who answers to stand at the front with the card. Hold up the next card and ask: *How many?* Invite another child to stand at the front. Discuss where the two children should stand, and what numbers will come between one and five.

    Repeat this procedure for the other cards, each time asking the children to decide where the person with the card should stand. Then repeat the whole exercise, this time with the cards not in order. Over time, extend to quantities up to ten.

GROUP ACTIVITIES

Duck order

Learning objective
ELGs/NNS:
- Order a given set of numbers, for example, the set of numbers 1 to 6, given in random order.

Activity
The detail of this activity is given on CD page 'Duck order'. Ask a group of six to eight children, in

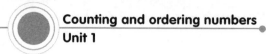

pairs, to work with the LSA. Provide each pair with a set of one to five cards from CD page 'Duck counting cards 2'. The LSA can ask the children to put their cards in a pile, then to take turns to take the top card, and to place the card in front of them. The object of the game is to put the cards in order, from left to right, one to five. As the children work, ask:

● *How many ducks are there on this card?*
● *Where will this card go?*
● *Why do you think that?*

Plenary & assessment

Shuffle the teaching set of one to five 'Duck counting cards', and ask a child to turn over the top card. Ask:

● *Where do you think this card will go?*
● *What goes one before/after this?*

Repeat this until all five cards are ordered. For older or more confident children, repeat the exercise and include cards six to ten.

Order these

STRUCTURED PLAY

Learning objectives

ELGs/NNS:
● Order a given set of numbers, for example, the set of numbers 1 to 6, given in random order.

Activity

Work with a group of six to eight children, working in pairs. Ask each pair to choose one of the trays of things to order. Invite the children to order these, from one to five. When they have done this, check that they are correct and ask them to muddle up the containers so that these are now out of order. They can swap their tray with another pair. Repeat this several times.

Plenary & assessment

Choose one tray and ask the children to help you to order the things on it. Ask:

● *Which comes first? Why is that?*
● *Which comes last? Why is that?*
● *What comes after one… three…?*
● *What comes before two… four…?*

Name	Date

One, two, buckle my shoe

Say the rhyme together and do the actions.

One, two, buckle my shoe

One, two, buckle my shoe.
Do up shoe.
Three, four, knock at the door.
Knock with knuckles on the floor.
Five, six, pick up sticks.
Pretend to pick up sticks from the floor.
Seven, eight, lay them straight.
Putting sticks into a straight line.
Nine, ten, a big fat hen.
Making a large circle shape.
Eleven, twelve, dig and delve.
Child digging.
Thirteen, fourteen, maids a-courting.
Hold hands with next-door child
Fifteen, sixteen, maids in the kitchen.
Pretend to cook.
Seventeen, eighteen, maids in waiting.
Stand with hands behind your back.
Nineteen, twenty, my plate's empty.
Rub tummy.

Duck order

You will need a set of 'Duck counting cards 2' for each pair of children.

Work with a group of six to eight children, in pairs.

Provide each pair with a set of one to five 'Duck counting cards 2'.

Ask the children to put their cards in a pile, then to take turns to take the top card, and to place the card in front of them.

The object of the game is to put the cards in order, from left to right, one to five.

As the children work, ask:

- *How many ducks are there on this card?*
- *Where will this card go?*
- *Why do you think that?*

For more confident children, extend the activity to include cards six to ten.

Record the children's achievements. It would be helpful to record which children can confidently order quantities one to five, or one to ten.

Child's name	What happened	What to do next time

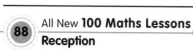

Counting, adding and partitioning

Children count out a given quantity of objects from a larger group. They count out a set, then a second set, combine these, and say the total. They partition a set into two groups, count each group, then count all to say the total.

LEARNING OBJECTIVES

Topics	Stepping Stones	Early Learning Goals & NNS Learning Objectives
	Green	
Counting	● Count out up to six objects from a larger group.	● **Count reliably up to 10 everyday objects** (first to 5, then 10, then beyond), giving just one number name to each object.
Adding and subtracting	● Find the total number of items in two groups by counting all of them.	● Begin to use the vocabulary involved in adding and subtracting. ● **Begin to relate addition to combining two groups of objects**, counting all the objects. ● Separate (partition) a given number of objects into two groups.

1 Session

Learning objectives

Starter
ELGs/NNS
● Recite the number names in order, continuing the count forwards or backwards from a given number.
● Order a given set of numbers, for example, the set of numbers 1 to 6 given in random order.

Main teaching activity
Green Stepping Stones
● Count out up to six objects from a larger group.
ELGs/NNS
● **Count reliably up to 10 everyday objects** (first to 5, then 10, then beyond), giving just one number name to each object.

Vocabulary

zero, one, two, three… to ten, how many …?

You will need
Photocopiable pages
'Count some out', for the teacher's/LSA's reference, see page 94.

CD pages
'Duck counting cards', photocopied onto card, for the teacher's/LSA's reference, and 'Partitioned work mat', for each child (see General resources).

Equipment
A tray with ten counting toys on it; ten counting tiles for each child in a group of eight.

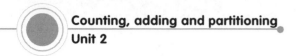
WHOLE CLASS TEACHING

Starter bank

These Starter bank ideas can be used throughout the unit.

Counting forwards and backwards

Ask the children to count with you, from zero or one, to ten and back. Repeat this several times. Now ask them to count with you to 15. Count back again. At first you may need to say some of the number names for the children, but over time they will become familiar with the order. Extend this to 20 when the children are confident with counting to 15.

Counting from a given number

Ask the children to count with you from a given number, such as 1, 2, 3… to 10… 15… 20 and back to the given number. Count with them, saying the number names loudly at first, until they are confident with this. Repeat the activity, this time counting around the group from the given number. Repeat this several times so that every child has the opportunity to say a number, in order, at least three times.

Order these

Use the CD pages 'Duck counting cards'. Hand out a card each to three children and ask them to stand at the front of the group. Make sure that the children are not in number order. Ask the other children:

● *How many ducks are there on the card that Marisa is holding? What about Andrej's card?*
● *How many on Sam's card? Are the cards in number order? Who do we need to move?*

Invite the children to explain how to rearrange the cards so that they are in number order. Repeat this for other sets of three, random, cards. If the children find this difficult with three cards at first, use just two. When they are confident with ordering three numbers, use four cards.

Main teaching activity

Show the children the tray with ten counting toys on it. Invite a child to come out and to count out five of the toys. Ask the child to put the five toys separately from the others so that everyone can see. Ask: *How many did you count?* Repeat this for other quantities from one to ten. Over time this can be repeated with different objects, so that the children begin to understand that it is possible to count out some of a group of objects.

GROUP ACTIVITIES

Count some out

Learning objectives
Green Stepping Stones:
● Count out up to six objects from a larger group.
ELGs/NNS:
● **Count reliably up to 10 everyday objects** (first to 5, then 10, then beyond), giving just one number name to each object.

Activity

This activity is provided in detail on CD page 'Count some out' for the adult's reference and so they can record the children's achievements and difficulties for use during feedback. Work with a group of six to eight children. Each child will need a copy of CD page 'Partitioned work mat' and ten counting tiles. Ask the children to put their tiles onto one section of the work mat and to count how many they have. Say: *What was the last number you said? How many tiles have you?* Now ask the children to count out three/four/five/nine of the tiles, which they can put onto the second section

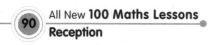

of their mat. Repeat this several times for different quantities.

For children working towards the Green Stepping Stones, begin with quantities to five, then extend to six, seven… For children working towards the ELGs/NNS, extend the quantity to 15, then 20.

Plenary & assessment

Invite a child to count out, say, seven tiles onto the second section of their work mat. Ask:

- *What was the last number you said? How many tiles did you count?*
- *Count how many are left. How many tiles are there altogether?*

Repeat this for other quantities so that several children have the opportunity to count out. Talk about how you can count out how many you need from a larger number.

2 Sessions

Learning objectives

Main teaching activity

ELGs/NNS

- **Begin to use the vocabulary involved in adding and subtracting.**
- **Begin to relate addition to combining two groups of objects**, counting all the objects.

Vocabulary

add, more, and, make, sum, total, altogether, one more, two more, is the same as

You will need:

Photocopiable pages
'Finger totals', for the teacher's/LSA's reference, see page 95.

CD pages
'Partitioned work mat' for each child (see General resources).

Equipment
A tray with ten counting toys; two hoops; pot with ten counting tiles per child.

WHOLE CLASS TEACHING

Main teaching activity

Put the tray with ten counting toys on it onto a table with two hoops. Invite a child to count out three toys into one hoop. Ask: *What was the last number you said? How many did you count?* Invite another child to count out two toys into the other hoop and say: *What was the last number you said? How many did you count?* Ask a third child to count the toys in the two hoops and say again: *What was the last number you said? How many did you count?* Say together as a group, as you point to the toys in one, then the other hoop: *One, two, three. one, two. Altogether, there are one, two, three, four, five. Three add two is five.* Emphasise 'add' and 'and' when pointing from one hoop to the other. Say, for example: *How many have you in this hoop? And how many here? Altogether, that is one, two, three, four, five. So three add two is five.*

Repeat this for other amounts, at first keeping the total to about seven, then extending to totals up to ten over time.

GROUP ACTIVITIES

Two set totals

Learning objectives

ELGs/NNS:

- Begin to use the vocabulary involved in adding and subtracting.
- **Begin to relate addition to combining two groups of objects**, counting all the objects.

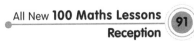

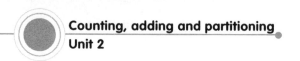

Activity

Give a group of six to eight children CD page 'Partitioned work mat' and a pot of counting tiles. Ask them to count some tiles onto each part of the mat, and then to count how many there are altogether. Start with small combinations, but extend to totals up to ten over time. Say, for example for four and three: *How many have you on this part? And how many here? Altogether, that is one, two, three, four, five, six, seven. So four add three is seven.*

Plenary & assessment

Invite a child to count out five toys into one hoop, and three into the other. Ask the children to count each set of toys as you point: *One, two, three, four, five. One, two, three.* Ask:

- *How many is that altogether? Let's count together: One, two, three, four, five, six, seven, eight.*
- *So what is 5 add 3?*

Say together: *Five add three is eight.* Repeat this for other totals between about five and ten.

Finger totals

Learning objectives
ELGs/NNS:

- Begin to use the vocabulary involved in adding and subtracting.
- **Begin to relate addition to combining two groups of objects**, counting all the objects.

Activity

This activity is provided in detail on CD page 'Finger totals' for the adult's reference and so they can record the children's achievements and difficulties for use during feedback. Ask four to six children to work with the LSA in a finger-counting game.

Plenary & assessment

Repeat the activity from the CD page 'Finger totals', keeping the pace sharp. Encourage the children to count their fingers quickly and accurately. Say for each total:

- *Show me three fingers on one hand. Show me four fingers on your other hand.*
- *How many fingers is that altogether? Let's count: One, two, three, four, five, six, seven. So three add four is seven.*

2 Sessions

Preparation

Cut the A4 paper in half to make fields for the animals.

Learning objectives

Main teaching activity
ELGs/NNS

- **Begin to use the vocabulary involved in adding and subtracting.**
- Separate (partition) a given number of objects into two groups.

Vocabulary

take (away), leave, how many are left/left over? how many have gone?

You will need:

CD pages
'Partitioned work mat' for each child (see General resources).

Equipment
Ten counting toys; two hoops; farm animals; sheets of green A4 paper; animal tiles; plates and biscuits; beads; pegboards and pegs.

WHOLE CLASS TEACHING

Main teaching activity

Put five counting toys in one hoop, with an empty hoop alongside. Ask one child to come and count the toys while the others count by pointing. Tell the children to shut their eyes, then move

one toy into the empty hoop. Say: *Open your eyes. What can you see?* Encourage the children to say that there are four toys in one hoop and one in the other. Invite two children to come and count the toys, taking one hoop each. Ask: *How many toys in this/that hoop? How many toys altogether?*

Repeat this, so that children consider partitions of one and four; two and three; three and two; four and one. Over time, this can be repeated for other partitions of amounts from two up to ten.

GROUP ACTIVITIES

Farm animals

Learning objectives
ELGs/NNS:
- Begin to use the vocabulary involved in adding and subtracting.
- Separate (partition) a given number of objects into two groups.

Activity
Provide pairs of children with some toy farm animals and sheets of green paper. Ask the children to put out five animals between the two fields. Encourage them to find different ways of doing this. (For example, two and three, four and one, and so on.) Over time, repeat this with other quantities of animals.

This activity can be repeated using different equipment, such as plates and biscuits; threading beads in two colours; pegs and pegboards.

Plenary & assessment
Invite a pair of children to show a pair of fields with five animals in total. Ask:
- *How many animals are there in this/that field? So how many animals altogether?*
Put out six animals in one field and say:
- *How many are there? Watch.* (Put four animals into the other field.) *How many here? And here?*
- *So if I take away four animals, there are two left.*
Repeat this for other amounts.

Animal splits

Learning objectives
ELGs/NNS:
- Begin to use the vocabulary involved in adding and subtracting.
- Separate (partition) a given number of objects into two groups.

Activity
Work with a group of six to eight children. Each will need CD page 'Partitioned work mat' and ten animal tiles. Ask the children to count out the animals that you say. For example: *Count out four animals. Put three of those animals on the other part of your mat. How many on this/that side? So three add one is four.*

Repeat this for other quantities from three to ten.

Plenary & assessment
Ask a child to take a handful of animal tiles and to put these onto one part of their mat. Ask another child to count them by touching and counting. Say, for example for six tiles:
- *How many animals are there?*
- *Now move two of these into the other part of the mat.*
- *How many are left? So six take away two is four.*
Repeat this several times, asking different children to take handfuls of tiles as a starting point.

Count some out

You will need:

- ten counting tiles for each child
- copy of 'Partitioned work mat' for each child.

Work with a group of six to eight children.

Ask the children to put their tiles onto one section of
the work mat and to count how many they have. Say:

- *What was the last number you said?*
- *How many tiles have you?*

Now ask the children to count out three/four/five/nine of the tiles, which they can put onto the
second section of their mat. Repeat this several times for different quantities.

For children working towards the Green Stepping Stone, begin with quantities to five, then gradually
extend this to six... seven...

For children working towards the ELGs/NNS extend the quantity to 15 then 20 over time.

Record the children's achievements. It would be helpful to record which children can count out
quantities to six... eight... ten with confidence.

Child's name	What happened	What to do next time

Finger totals

Work with four to six children.

Say:

- *Show me three fingers on one hand.*

- *Show me two fingers on your other hand.*

- *How many fingers is that altogether?*
  Let's count: One, two, three. One, two. One, two, three, four, five.

- *So three add two is five.*

Repeat this for other amounts, up to five add five, such as three and one, four and two...

Record the children's achievements. It would be helpful to record which children can count accurately to find totals.

Child's name	What happened	What to do next time

Children name common 3-D and 2-D shapes and describe some of their properties. They choose sorting criteria for a group of objects. They sort the objects and explain how they have sorted.

LEARNING OBJECTIVES

| Topics | Stepping Stones | Early Learning Goals & |
	Green	NNS Learning Objectives
Exploring pattern, shape and space	● Begin to use mathematical names for 'solid' 3-D shapes and 'flat' 2-D shapes and mathematical terms to describe shapes. ●Choose suitable components to make a particular model.	● Begin to name solids such as a cube, cone, sphere, and flat shapes such as circle, triangle, square, rectangle. Use a variety of shapes to make models, pictures and patterns, and describe them.
Reasoning about numbers or shapes		● Solve simple problems or puzzles in a practical context, and respond to 'What could we try next?' ● Sort and match objects, pictures or children themselves, justifying the decisions made.

4 Sessions

Learning objectives

Starter
ELGs/NNS
● **Begin to use the vocabulary involved in adding and subtracting.**
● **Begin to relate addition to combining two groups of objects,** counting all the objects.
● Separate (partition) a given number of objects into two groups.

Main teaching activity
Green Stepping Stones
● Begin to use mathematical names for 'solid' 3-D shapes and 'flat' 2-D shapes and mathematical terms to describe shapes.
● Choose suitable components to make a particular model.
ELGs/NNS
● Begin to name solids such as a cube, cone, sphere, and flat shapes such as circle, triangle, square, rectangle. Use a variety of shapes to make models, pictures, patterns, and describe them.
● Solve simple problems or puzzles in a practical context, and respond to 'What could we try next?'

Vocabulary

shape, pattern, flat, curved, straight, round, hollow, solid, corner, face, side, edge, end, sort, make, build, draw, cube, pyramid, sphere, cone, circle, triangle, square, rectangle, star

You will need:
Photocopiable pages
'Make a model' and 'Sand shapes' for the teacher's/LSA's reference, see pages 101–102.

Equipment
Red hoop, blue hoop; sorting hoops; sets of 2-D shape tiles; sets of 3-D shapes; 'junk' 3-D shapes; building bricks; construction kits; sand trays.

WHOLE CLASS TEACHING

Starter bank
These Starter bank ideas can be used throughout the unit.

Finger add
Ask the children to hold up two fingers on one hand and one finger on the other. Say:
- *How many fingers is that altogether? One, two. One. One, two, three.*
- *So, two add one is three.*

Repeat this for other quantities of fingers, each time counting each hand separately, then together, then saying the addition sentence. Addition sentences can be from one add one to five add five.

Show me fingers
Explain to the children that you will say a number. You would like them to show you that number of fingers, using both hands. For example, if you say four, they might show you one add three, two add two… Each time, invite several children to come to the front and show their fingers. Count each hand separately, then together, then say the addition sentence together. For example, for five this could be: *One, two . One, two, three. Altogether that is one, two, three, four, five. So two add three is five.*
Repeat this for other quantities, from four to ten.

Six children
You will need a red and a blue hoop. Invite six children to stand at the front. Ask the others to decide who will stand in which hoop. When the children have been moved, ask:
- *How many children are standing in the red hoop?*
- *How many are standing in the blue hoop?*
- *How many are there altogether?*
- *So two add four is six.*

Repeat this several times for different partitions of six. Over time, repeat the activity for seven, eight, nine and ten.

Main teaching activity
Show the children the models of a cube, cone, pyramid and sphere, then choose one of them such as the cube and say: *What is this called?* Invite the children to describe the shape, for example, that the faces are flat or that it has 'points'. Repeat this for the other 3-D shapes. When all of the shapes have been described, talk about which shapes are good for building, and why that is. For example: *A cube is good at the bottom of a tower because all its faces are flat. A cone is better at the top of a tower, because it can balance on its circle face.* Invite the children to demonstrate what they say with the shapes. Also demonstrate how a sphere, for example, would be hopeless at the bottom of a tower because nothing will balance on it.
Repeat this on another occasion, this time with the 2-D shapes of circle, triangle, square, rectangle and star. Discuss which shapes have straight sides, which curved, and whether the 'points' are out, or out and in, as in a star.

GROUP ACTIVITIES

3-D shape sort

Learning objectives
Green Stepping Stones:
- Begin to use mathematical names for 'solid' 3-D shapes and mathematical terms to describe shapes.

ELGs/NNS:
- Begin to name solids such as a cube, cone, sphere.

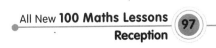

● Solve simple problems or puzzles in a practical context, and respond to 'What could we try next?'

Activity

Provide a group of four children with a selection of 3-D shapes (these could be building bricks, cardboard 'junk' shapes and so on) and some sorting hoops. Ask the children to decide how to sort the shapes. They might sort them by those with flat faces, curves and so on.

Plenary & assessment

Ask the children to explain how they decided to sort their shapes. Encourage them to use the mathematical names of the shapes, where appropriate, and if they are not sure of these, remind them of the names. Ask questions such as:
● *How did you sort the shapes?*
● *What is the same about this set? And this set?*
● *What is different between these two sets of shapes?*

2-D shape sort

STRUCTURED PLAY

Learning objectives

Green Stepping Stones:
● Begin to use mathematical names for 'flat' 2-D shapes and mathematical terms to describe shapes.

ELGs/NNS:
● Begin to name flat shapes such as circle, triangle, square, rectangle.
● Solve simple problems or puzzles in a practical context, and respond to 'What could we try next?'

Activity

Provide a group of four children with a set of 2-D shape tiles for sorting and some sorting hoops. Ask the children to decide how to sort the shapes. For example, they might put all the shapes with three sides together, all those with curves together and so on.

Plenary & assessment

Ask the children to explain how they decided to sort their shapes. Encourage them to use the mathematical names of the shapes, where appropriate and, if they are not sure of these, remind them of the names. Ask questions such as:
● *How did you sort the shapes?*
● *What is the same about this set? And this set?*
● *What is different between these two sets of shapes?*

Make a model

STRUCTURED PLAY

Learning objectives

Green Stepping Stones:
● Begin to use mathematical names for 'solid' 3-D shapes and 'flat' 2-D shapes and mathematical terms to describe shapes.
● Choose suitable components to make a particular model.

ELGs/NNS:
● Begin to name solids such as a cube, cone, sphere, and flat shapes such as circle, triangle, square, rectangle.
● Use a variety of shapes to make models, pictures, patterns, and describe them.
● Solve simple problems or puzzles in a practical context, and respond to 'What could we try next?'

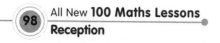

Activity

This activity is provided in detail on CD page 'Make a model' for the adult's reference and so they can record the children's achievements and difficulties to feedback. Provide a set of building blocks, 'junk' shapes, or a construction kit for a group of four children. Ask them to work in pairs and to begin by deciding what model they will build. Encourage the children to plan their model. If they are working towards the ELGs/NNS, encourage them to make a simple sketch of what they would like to build. Give them time to make the model and, as they work, ask them to evaluate what they are doing, asking, for example: *What else could you try? How could you make your model even better?*

Plenary & assessment

Ask each pair to explain what they have made. Encourage them to explain why they chose particular shapes, and why these were good for building. Check that they are using the appropriate vocabulary, such as 'flat', 'curved' and so on. Ask questions such as:

- *How could you make your model even better?*
- *Which shapes were good for the bottom of this model?*
- *Why do you think that is?*
- *Does your model look as you planned? How have you changed it? Why did you do that?*

Sand shapes

ADULT SUPPORTED

Learning objectives

Green Stepping Stones:

- Begin to use mathematical names for 'solid' 3-D shapes and 'flat' 2-D shapes and mathematical terms to describe shapes.
- Choose suitable components to make a particular model.

ELGs/NNS:

- Begin to name solids such as a cube, cone, sphere and flat shapes such as circle, triangle, square, rectangle.
- Use a variety of shapes to make pictures, patterns, and describe them.
- Solve simple problems or puzzles in a practical context, and respond to 'What could we try next?'

Activity

This activity is provided in detail on CD page 'Sand shapes' for the adult's reference and so they can record the children's achievements and difficulties for use during feedback. Ask three or four children to work with sand. Provide some items that they can use to make impressions in the sand. Invite the children to make impressions in the sand with the items. Talk about what they have done, and encourage the children to describe the shapes that they have made. Ask the children to use one of the shapes, and, with a finger, to draw around the shape. Again, encourage them to describe the shape, whether it is straight or curved, or a combination of both.

Plenary & assessment

Ask the children to talk about some of the shapes that they have made in the sand, and to describe them. Listen to the vocabulary that they use, and provide the mathematical words if they are not sure. Ask questions such as:

- *Which things made curved…straight… straight and curved lines?*
- *Which things could you use to make a hollow in the sand?*
- *Of an impression you have made in the sand) What do you think made this outline? Why do you think that?*
- *What else could we use to make a straight/curved line in the sand?*

1 Session

Learning objectives

Main teaching activity
ELGs/NNS
- Sort and match objects, pictures or children themselves, justifying the decisions made.

Vocabulary

compare, count, sort, group, set, match

You will need:
Equipment
Tray with a collection of classroom equipment, such as some marbles, bricks, rods, shells, counters; four red and five blue bricks; sets of objects for the children to sort such as coins and a cash register, toy cars, play people, shells of various types, leaves and so on.

WHOLE CLASS TEACHING

Main teaching activity

Explain to the children that today they will be sorting, matching and counting things. Show the children the tray of objects and ask: *How could we sort these? What do you suggest?* Invite the children to explain their suggestions. For example, they might suggest:
- *Put the round things together.*
- *Put the shells in one pile, and the bricks in another…*

Now show the children the bricks and ask: *How can we sort these?* The children will probably sort the bricks by colour. Ask: *How many red/blue bricks are there? Which has more, red or blue?* This can be repeated for other sets of items, such as rods in two colours, matching cups to their saucers and so on.

GROUP ACTIVITIES

Sorting

STRUCTURED PLAY

Learning objective
ELGs/NNS:
- Sort and match objects, pictures or children themselves, justifying the decisions made.

Activity
Provide groups of four children with a set of objects to sort and a sorting tray or hoops. Ask the children to decide how they will sort the objects. When they have done this ask: *Is there another way that you could sort these?* Over time, the groups of children can each try sorting the different sets that are available.

Plenary & assessment
Invite the groups to show how they have sorted their objects. Encourage the children to explain what they have done, sorting by colour, shape, type of thing, use. Ask questions such as:
- *How did you sort these?*
- *Are there more shells or more bricks?*
- *How can you tell?*
- *What other ways could we sort these?*

Where children suggest alternative ways of sorting, ask them to demonstrate this with the object.

Make a model

You will need some building blocks, 'junk' shapes, or a construction kit.

Work with a group of four children.

Ask the children to work in pairs and to begin by deciding what model they will build. Encourage the children to plan their model.

If they are working towards the ELG/NNS, encourage children to make a simple sketch of what they would like to build.

Give the children time to make the model and, as they work, ask them to evaluate what they are doing, asking, for example:

- *What else could you try?*
- *How could you make your model even better?*

Record the children's achievements. It would be helpful to record whether the children can name and describe the shapes that they used.

Child's name	What happened	What to do next time

Sand shapes

You will need:

- damp sand in a tray
- sand play items.

Work with three or four children.

Ask the children to make impressions in the sand with the items.

Talk about what they have done, and encourage the children to describe the shapes that they have made.

Ask the children to use one of the shapes and, with a finger, to draw around the shape. Again, encourage them to describe the shape, whether it is straight or curved or a combination of both.

Ask questions such as:

- *What shape do you think this will make in the sand?*
- (Of an impression you have made in the sand) *What do you think made this? Why do you think that?*

Record the children's achievements. It would be helpful to record which children can use appropriate vocabulary to describe shapes and their outlines.

Child's name	What happened	What to do next time

Spring term Unit 4
Counting and filling containers

Children count from zero to 20 and back again. Then they count on and back from a small number. They say the number one before and after a given number. Children estimate then make a direct comparison of the capacity of two containers by filling and pouring.

LEARNING OBJECTIVES

Topics	Stepping Stones	Early Learning Goals & NNS Learning Objectives
	Green	
Counting	● Begin to count beyond 10.	● Recite the number names in order, continuing the count forwards or backwards from a given number.
Comparing and ordering measures	● Order two items by capacity.	● **Use language such as more or less, to compare two capacities**, then more than two, by filling and emptying comtainers.

2 Sessions

Learning objectives

Starter
ELGs/NNS
● Recite the number names in order, continuing the count forwards or backwards from a given number.
● **Begin to relate addition to combining two groups of objects**, counting all the objects.

Main teaching activity
Green Stepping Stones
● Begin to count beyond 10.
ELGs/NNS
● Recite the number names in order, continuing the count forwards or backwards from a given number.

Vocabulary

zero, one, two, three… to twenty, count, count (up) to, count on (from, to), count back (from, to)

You will need:
Phtocopiable pages
'Count on and back', for the teacher's/LSA's reference, see page 108.

Equipment
Puppet.

WHOLE CLASS TEACHING

Starter bank

These Starter bank ideas can be used throughout the unit.

Count on

Ask the children to count from and to the numbers that you say. For example:

- *Start from two. Hold it in your head. Count on to seven… three, four, five, six, seven.*
- *Start from three. Hold it in your head. Count on to nine… four, five, six, seven, eight, nine.*

  Repeat this for different starting and finishing numbers, keeping the range within one to ten. Over time, and for the more confident children, this can be extended to 15, then to 20.

Count back

Ask the children to count back from and to the numbers that you say. For example:

- *Start from five. Hold it in your head. Count back to one… four, three, two, one.*
- *Start from nine. Hold it in your head. Count back to three… eight, seven, six, five, four, three.*

  Repeat this for different starting and finishing numbers, keeping the range within one to ten. Over time, and for the more confident children, this can be extended to 15, then to 20.

How many?

Ask the children to use their fingers. Explain that you would like them to show you one of the numbers you say on one hand, and the other number on the other hand. Then you would like them to count all. Say, for example:

- *Show me three on one hand. Now show me three on the other hand. Let's count: One, two, three. One, two, three. Now let's count all: one, two, three, four, five, six. So three add three is six.*
- *Show me four on one hand. Now show me three on the other hand. Let's count: One, two, three, four. One, two, three. Now let's count all: one, two, three, four, five, six, seven. So four add three is seven.*

  Repeat this for other amounts, up to five add five.

Main teaching activity

Begin by asking the children to count with you from zero, to ten, then back to zero. Repeat this several times, keeping the pace sharp. Extend this to counting to and from 15, then to 20. Now ask them to count from the number that you say, up to 10… 15… 20 then back to zero, such as: *Count from two… five… ten…*

Ask the children to say the number that comes before and after the number that you say. Say, for example:

- *What comes before three / after three?*
- *What comes before nine / after nine?*

  Repeat this, at first keeping the numbers in the range one to ten, then over time extend the range to 15, then to 20.

Now ask the children to count from and to the numbers that you say. For example: *Start at three. Hold it in your head. Count to nine: three, four, five, six, seven, eight, nine.* Repeat this for counting back, from nine… to three… Over time extend this to 15, then to 20.

Ask the children to use their fingers. Ask them to count several numbers from a given number: *Count on three numbers from five… six, seven, eight. Count back four numbers from nine… eight, seven, six, five.* Repeat this, extending the range to 15, then to 20.

This main teaching activity should be repeated two or three times, extending the number range.

GROUP ACTIVITIES

Count on and back

Learning objectives
Green Stepping Stones:
● Begin to count beyond 10.
ELGs/NNS:
● Recite the number names in order, continuing the count forwards or backwards from a given number.

Activity
This activity is provided in detail on CD page 'Count on and back' for the adult's reference and so they can record the children's achievements and difficulties for use during feedback. Ask a group of six to eight children to work with the LSA and to count together to ten, from zero, and back again. The LSA should keep the pace snappy. The children may find it helpful to slap their knees in time with the counting. The LSA can repeat this several times and then ask the children to count around the group, again keeping the pace sharp. If a child falters, the LSA can provide the number name for them to keep the pace. Then the LSA can ask the children to count on/back from a number that you say, such as: *Count on from four to eight… five, six, seven, eight. Count back from nine to six… eight, seven, six.* The LSA can invite the children to repeat this several times. When the children are confident with counting to ten, this can be extended to 15, then to 20.

Plenary & assessment
Briefly repeat the activity and check that the children can count on/back to given numbers. Begin with the range zero to ten, then extend this to 15, then to 20. Say, for example:
● *Count from 3… 6… 9… 14… to 7… 10… 13… 18…*
● *Count back from 7… 10… 16… to 4… 6… 11…*

Count up, count down

Learning objectives
Green Stepping Stones:
● Begin to count beyond 10.
ELGs/NNS:
● Recite the number names in order, continuing the count forwards or backwards from a given number.

Activity
Work with a group of six to eight children. Explain that you will ask them to count on from a number. The children may find it helpful to use their fingers to keep count. Say, for example:
● *Count on three numbers from five: six, seven, eight.*
● *Count on four, starting from eight: nine, ten, eleven, twelve.*
  Now ask them to count back, in the same way, such as *Count back three numbers from five: four, three, two. Count back four numbers from nine: eight, seven, six, five.*
  Extend the range for counting to 15, then to 20, as the children become more confident.

Plenary & assessment
Ask the children to listen to the puppet counting. The puppet will make mistakes, and encourage the children to correct these. Say, for example:
● *I will count on three numbers from seven: eight, nine, eleven.*
● *I will count back four numbers from nine: eight, seven, six.*
Encourage the children to say what the count should be.

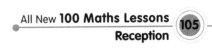

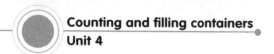
3 Sessions

Learning objectives

Main teaching activity
Green Stepping Stones
- Order two items by capacity.

ELGs/NNS
- **Use language such as more or less, to compare two capacities**, then more than two, by filling and emptying containers.

Vocabulary

full, half full, empty, holds, container, guess, estimate, enough, not enough, too much, too little, nearly, close to, about the same as, just over, just under, measure, size, compare, more, most, less, least

You will need:
Photocopiable pages
'Ordering', for the teacher's/LSA's reference, see page 109.

Equipment
Transparent containers which hold various amounts, including some that hold the same but are of different shapes; scoops; spoons; sand; water; home area with crockery; cutlery; teapot and kettle.

WHOLE CLASS TEACHING

Main teaching activity

Show the children two transparent containers. Ask: *Which do you think will hold more?* Encourage the children to explain why they think that one container will hold more. Fill the larger container with sand, then ask a child to pour the sand into the smaller one. Ask: *Will all the sand fit in this container? So which holds more?* Repeat this for another pair of containers.

Now ask of two differently-sized containers: *Which do you think will hold less? How could we find out?* Again, encourage the children to explain their thinking. Ask a child to pour sand into the smaller container, then to pour this into the larger container. Agree which holds less and which holds more. Say together: *This tub holds less than that box. This box holds more than that tub.*

GROUP ACTIVITIES

Fill it up

Learning objectives
Green Stepping Stones:
- Order two items by capacity.

ELGs/NNS:
- **Use language such as more or less, to compare two quantities**, then more than two, by filling and emptying containers.

Activity

You will need some containers of different sizes and sand or water. Work with a group of four to six children, with the children in pairs. Ask each pair to choose a container and fill it. When they have done this, ask them to empty it, then to fill it so that it is half full. Now say: *Pour some more in until it is nearly full. Pour out water until it is nearly empty.*

Ask the children to repeat this using different containers.

Plenary & assessment

Pour some water into a transparent container and ask: *How much water is in here?* Encourage the children to explain using language such as 'about full', 'empty', 'nearly full', 'nearly empty', 'half full' and so on. Now fill another container to about half way and ask: *How much is in here?* Repeat this for different containers, checking that the children can use the vocabulary of estimating capacity.

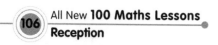

Ordering

Learning objectives
Green Stepping Stones:
- Order two items by capacity.

ELGs/NNS:
- **Use language such as more or less, to compare two quantities**, then more than two, by filling and emptying containers.

Activity
This activity is provided in detail on CD page 'Ordering' for the adult's reference and so they can record the children's achievements and difficulties for use during feedback. Work with four children in the sand area. Invite them to choose two containers and to estimate, or guess, which holds more. Ask them to check by filling and pouring. Discuss with them their decisions and ask them to explain why they think one holds more, and one holds less than the other. Repeat this with other containers. Now provide two containers that hold about the same and repeat the activity. Talk about how containers may not be the same height but that they can still hold about the same.

Extend ordering to three containers, when children are confident with two. Talk about which holds more, most, and which holds less and least.

Plenary & assessment
Choose two containers and say: *Which do you think holds more/less?* Invite two children to compare their capacities by filling and pouring. Ask: *Did you make a good guess? So which holds more/less?*

When the children are confident comparing two containers, ask them to compare three.

Tea party

Learning objectives
Green Stepping Stones:
- Order two items by capacity.

ELGs/NNS:
- **Use language such as more or less, to compare two quantities**, then more than two, by filling and emptying containers.

Activity
Ask the children to have a tea party. They can pour water from the teapot into cups. As they work ask them to, for example:
- *Fill the cup.*
- *Pour in enough so that the cup is half full.*
- *Empty the cup.*

Plenary & assessment
Talk about the tea party. Ask, for example:
- *Why are cups not filled to the very top?* (Because it would be difficult to lift the cup without spilling.)
- *Which of these cups do you think will hold more/less? Why do you think that? How could you check?*

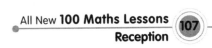

Count on and back

Work with a group of six to eight children.

Ask them to count together to ten, from zero, and back again. Keep the pace sharp. The children may find it helpful to slap their knees in time with the counting. Repeat this several times.

Now ask the children to count around the group, again keeping the pace snappy. If a child falters, provide the number name for them to keep the pace.

Now ask the children to count on/back from a number that you say, such as: *Count on from four to eight... five, six, seven, eight. Count back from nine to six... eight, seven, six.* Repeat this several times.

When the children are confident with counting to 10, extend this to 15, then to 20.

Record the children's achievements. It would be helpful to record how far children can count confidently, and whether they can count on/back from given numbers.

Child's name	What happened	What to do next time

■SCHOLASTIC
photocopiable

Ordering

You will need:

- sand tray
- various differently-sized containers that can be filled (include two that hold about the same but are different shapes, such as shampoo bottles).

Work with four children in the sand area.

Ask them to choose two containers and to estimate, or guess, which holds more. Ask them to check by filling and pouring.

Discuss with them their decisions and ask them to explain why they think one holds more, and one holds less than the other.

Repeat this with other containers.

Now provide two containers that hold about the same, and repeat the activity. Talk about how containers may not be the same height but they can still hold about the same.

When children are confident with ordering two containers, extend to ordering three containers. Talk about which container holds 'more', 'most', and which holds 'less' and 'least'.

Record the children's achievements. It would be helpful to record how well the children can use the vocabulary of estimation and capacity.

Child's name	What happened	What to do next time

Spring term
Unit 5

Counting, subtracting and using coins

Children count items in a picture by coordinating the point and count. In practical activities they take away a small quantity from a set and count what is left. They say the subtraction sentence. They use coins in practical activities. They count out from ten 1p coins and say how much is left.

LEARNING OBJECTIVES

Topics	Stepping Stones	Early Learning Goals & NNS Learning Objectives
	Green	
Counting	● Count out up to six objects from a larger group.	● **Count reliably up to 10 everyday objects** (first to 5, then 10, then beyond), giving just one number name to each object. ● Count reliably in other contexts such as clapping or hopping movements.
Adding and subtracting	● Count actions or objects that cannot be moved.	● **Begin to use the vocabulary involved in adding and subtracting.** ● **Begin to relate subtraction to 'taking away'** and counting how many are left.
Problems involving 'real life' or money	● Sometimes show confidence and offer solutions to problems.	● Begin to understand and use vocabulary related to money. Sort coins, including the £1 and £2 coins, and use them in role play to pay and give change.

1 Sessions

Preparation

Enlarge 'Teddy bears' picnic' to A3. This can be coloured in, if desired.

Learning objectives

Starter
ELGs/NNS
● Begin to use the vocabulary involved in adding and subtracting.
● **Begin to relate addition to combining two groups of objects,** counting all the objects.
● Separate (partition) a given number of objects into two groups.

Main teaching activity
Green Stepping Stones
● Count out up to six objects from a larger group.
● Count actions or objects that cannot be moved.
ELGs/NNS
● **Count reliably up to 10 everyday objects** (first to 5, then 10, then beyond), giving just one number *name to each object.*
● Count reliably in other contexts such as clapping or hopping movements.

Vocabulary

zero, one, two, three… to twenty, how many…?

You will need:
CD pages
'Teddy bears' picnic', photocopied to A3, for the teacher's/LSA's reference (see General resources).

Equipment
Ten teddies or sorting bears; a red and a blue sorting hoop; ten toy cars and a garage; ten sorting toys, all different, such as a set of vehicles.

WHOLE CLASS TEACHING

Starter bank

These Starter bank ideas can be used throughout the unit.

Finger add

Ask the children to use their fingers. Say: *Show me three on one hand. Show me four on the other hand. Let's count how many. One, two, three. One, two, three, four. Altogether that is one, two, three, four, five, six, seven. So three add four is seven.* Repeat this for other quantities of fingers, up to five add five. Invite children to say the addition sentence individually.

Teddy partition

Use ten teddies, or sorting bears. Put out five of the bears into the red sorting hoop so that all the children can see them. Invite a child to come to the front and count out three of these and put them into the blue sorting hoop. Ask: *How many teddies are there in the red hoop?* (Point to each one.) *One, two. And how many in the blue hoop?* (Point to each one.) *One, two, three. So how many teddies are there altogether? One, two, three, four, five.* Repeat this for different partitions of five. Then repeat this over time for partitions of from six to ten.

Car add

Put the ten toy cars by the garage. Ask a child to put two cars into the garage and count these together: *One, two.* Now say: *Three more cars arrive. Let's count these. One, two, three. How many cars are there in the garage now? Let's count these together: One, two, three, four, five. So two add three is five.* Repeat this for other additions, counting all of the cars each time. Invite individual children to say the addition sentence once all of the cars have been counted.

Main teaching activity

Pin up the poster 'Teddy bears' picnic' and ask the children to look carefully at the pictures. Ask them to count by pointing. Say, for example:

- *Where are the birds? How many birds can you see?*
- *How many teddies are there?*
- *How many apples are there? Are there enough apples for the teddies to have one each?*

After each answer, invite a child to come out and to touch the items whilst all of the children count them together. Ask, for example: *Did we count all of the teddies?* Continue asking questions in this way. The count can be extended to 15, then to 20, by combining things to count.

GROUP ACTIVITIES

Vehicle count

Learning objectives

Green Stepping Stones:

- Count out up to six objects from a larger group.
- Count actions or objects that cannot be moved.

ELGs/NNS:

- **Count reliably up to 10 everyday objects** (first to 5, then 10, then beyond), giving just one number name to each object.

Activity

Work with a group of four to six children. Put out the set of vehicle sorting toys and invite a child to choose four of the toys. Ask them to put them in a straight line. Make one of them, say the motorbike, the second toy in the line. Now say: *Count the toys for me, starting with the motorbike.* Check to see how the child counts, for example, by touching, and that they count all the toys. Ask of the others: *Do you agree? Are there four?* Invite another child to count the toys, this time starting

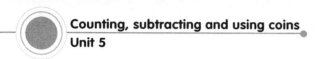

with a different toy. Repeat this, until everyone has had a turn. Now increase the number of toys to five, six and so on. (For those working towards the Green Stepping Stones, begin with three toys.)

Plenary & assessment

Put out five of the toys in a line, with the motorbike third in line. Ask one of the children to count the toys, starting with the motorbike. Ask the others:
- *How many toys are there? Did Jose count all of the toys?*
- *If I asked you to count them again, starting with the lorry, how many toys would there be?*
   Repeat this with a different arrangement of toys, then with more than five.

2 Sessions

Learning objectives

Main teaching activity
ELGs/NNS
- **Begin to use the vocabulary involved in adding and subtracting.**
- **Begin to relate subtraction to 'taking away'** and counting how many are left.

Vocabulary

take (away), leave, how many are left/left over? how many have gone?

You will need:
Photocopiable pages
'Biscuit subtract' for the teacher's/LSA's reference, see page 115.

Equipment
Ten sorting toys; ten play biscuits, two plates, dolls, dolls' furniture and dolls' house.

WHOLE CLASS TEACHING

Main teaching activity

Put out the sorting toys, and ask a child to count out four of the toys. Say: *I am going to take one toy away. How many are left? How can we find out?* The children will probably suggest counting what is left. Do this together, with a child touching each one as everyone counts. Say together: *One, two, three, four. Take away one. One, two, three left. So four take away one leaves three.*
   Repeat this for other subtractions, at first for starting quantities up to five, then extend this over time to six, seven… ten.

GROUP ACTIVITIES

Biscuit subtract

ADULT SUPPORTED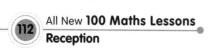

Learning objectives
ELGs/NNS:
- **Begin to use the vocabulary involved in adding and subtracting.**
- Begin to relate subtraction to taking away and counting how many are left.

Activity

This activity is provided in detail on CD page 'Biscuit subtract' for the adult's reference and so they can record the children's achievements and difficulties for feedback. Ask four to six children to work with the LSA in the home area. You will need ten play biscuits and two plates. The LSA asks one of the children to count out five biscuits onto one of the plates and invites the other children to check by pointing and counting. They ask another child to take away two of the biscuits and place these onto the other plate. They say: *How many biscuits are left?* Count together: *There were one, two, three, four, five biscuits. Take away two: One, two. This leaves one, two, three. So five take away two leaves three.* Repeat this for other amounts up to, eventually, a starting number of ten.

Plenary & assessment

Ask the children to watch as you model a subtraction with the biscuits. Say: *Here are six biscuits. I take away two. How many are left?* Invite a child to count each plate and all of them to say the sentence: *six take away two leaves four.* Repeat this for other quantities, up to, over time, ten.

Counting chairs

Learning objectives

ELGs/NNS:
- **Begin to use the vocabulary involved in adding and subtracting.**
- Begin to relate subtraction to taking away and counting how many are left.

Activity

Ask two children to work with the dolls, furniture and dolls' house. Ask them to arrange the furniture and the dolls. Say, for example: *How many chairs are in the dining room?* Ask the children to count them: *One, two, three, four, five, six. Now put two of those chairs into the lounge. How many chairs are left in the dining room?* Again, ask the children to count the chairs: *One, two, three, four.* Say together the subtraction sentence: *Six take away two leaves four.* Repeat this for other amounts up to ten, furniture and dolls.

This activity can also be carried out with other mini worlds, such as garage and cars.

Plenary & assessment

Ask one of the children to put seven chairs into the dolls' dining room and say: *Are there seven chairs? Who will count them for us?* Encourage the other children to point and count as one of the children touches and counts. Now say: *Put three of those chairs into the bedroom. How many chairs are left in the dining room?* Ask the children to count together, as one of them touches and counts: *One, two, three, four. So seven take away three leaves four.*

Repeat this for other quantities, checking that the children can accurately count, by touching and by pointing, and that they can say the subtraction sentence.

2 Sessions

Preparation

Set up a class shop.

Learning objectives

Main teaching activity

ELGs/NNS
- Begin to understand and use vocabulary related to money. Sort coins, including the £1 and £2 coins, and use them in role play to pay and give change.

Vocabulary

money, coin, penny, pence, price, cost, buy, sell, spend, spent, pay, change, how much…? how many…? total

You will need:

Photocopiable pages
'10p game' for the teacher's/LSA's reference, see page 116.

Equipment
1p, 2p, 5p, 10p coins; feely box or bag; items from the class shop; 1–6 spot dice; forty 1p coins.

WHOLE CLASS TEACHING

Main teaching activity

Put the coins into the feely box and explain that you will pass the box around the group. Ask each child to feel in the box for a coin, bring it out, look at it carefully and name it. When each child has had two turns at this, explain that coins are not all worth the same. Show the children a 2p coin and say: *This coin is worth the same as two 1p coins.* Show the children two 1p coins. Repeat this for a 5p coin, comparing it with five 1p coins, then one 10p coin with ten 1p coins.

Now show the children something from the class shop and say: *This costs 4p. How could I pay for this?* Ask a child to count out the penny coins: *1p, 2p, 3p, 4p.*

Repeat this, this time for something that you say costs 3p. Again, encourage one of the children to count out the coins.

Explain that you have ten 1p coins in your hand. Count the coins together: *1p, 2p, 3p, 4p, 5p…10p.* Say: *This costs 7p. How many pennies will I have left?* Invite a child to count out the seven 1p coins, and another child to count the coins left. Say: *There is 3p left.* Repeat this for other amounts.

GROUP ACTIVITIES

Shopping

Learning objectives
ELGs/NNS:
- Begin to understand and use vocabulary related to money.
- Sort coins, including the £1 and £2 coins, and use them in role play to pay and give change.

Activity
Work with a group of six to eight children in the class shop. Provide each pair with ten 1p coins and ask each pair to choose something to buy. Say: *This costs… Count out the money for me. How much do you have left?* Encourage the children to count out the coins and to count up their 'change'.

If children find 10p too large an amount to begin with, limit this to 5p and extend to higher amounts over time.

Plenary & assessment
Show the children something from the class shop and say: *This costs 6p. Here is 10p. Count out the coins for me. How many pennies do you have left?* Repeat this for different amounts.

10p game

Learning objectives
ELGs/NNS:
- Begin to understand and use vocabulary related to money.
- Sort coins, including £1 and £2 coins, and use them in role play to pay and give change.

Activity
This activity is provided in detail on CD page '10p game' for the adult's reference and so they can record the children's achievements and difficulties for use during feedback. The LSA will need about forty 1p coins and a spot 1–6 dice. Ask four children to work with the LSA. Ask them to take turns to roll the dice. They count the spots and take that quantity of pennies. The first child to collect 10p wins the game. This can be played several times by the children.

For those children who can count confidently to 20, extend the game, using more 1p coins, and ask the children to collect 20p.

Plenary & assessment
Ask questions about money. Show the children 1p, 2p, 5p and 10p coins and say for each coin: *How much is this worth?* Now ask questions such as: *How many pennies do I need to make 5p…10p?* Invite individual children to count out the appropriate number of pennies for the amount that you say, from 1p to 10p, then extend this to 20p.

Biscuit subtract

You will need:

- two plates
- ten play biscuits.

Work in the home area with four to six children.

Ask one of the children to count out five biscuits onto one of the plates. Invite the other children to check by pointing and counting.

Now ask another child to take away two of the biscuits and place these onto the other plate.

Say:

- *How many biscuits are left?* (Count together.)
- *There were one, two, three, four, five biscuits. Take away two: one, two. This leaves one, two, three.*
- *So five take away two leaves three.*

Repeat this for other amounts up to, eventually, a starting number of ten.

Record the children's achievements. It would be helpful to record how well the children can use the vocabulary of subtraction.

Child's name	What happened	What to do next time

10p game

You will need:

- forty 1p coins
- a 1–6 spot dice.

Work with four children.

Ask them to take turns to roll the dice and count the spots. They take that quantity of pennies.

Ask questions such as:

- *How much money have you?*
- *How many pennies have you?*
- *How many pennies do I need to make 5p... 10p...?*

The first child to collect 10p wins the game.

This can be played several times by the children.

For those children who can count confidently to 20, extend the game using more 1p coins, and ask the children to collect 20p.

Record the children's achievements. It would be helpful to record how well the children count the penny coins and can say how much money they have collected.

Child's name	What happened	What to do next time

Counting, reading numerals, and comparing and ordering numbers

Children count from zero to 20. They begin to recognise the numerals for one to five, then up to ten, in practical activities. They say the number that is one more or one less than a given number.

LEARNING OBJECTIVES

Topics	Stepping Stones	Early Learning Goals & NNS Learning Objectives
	Green	
Counting	● Begin to count beyond 10.	● **Say and use the number names in order in familiar contexts** such as number rhymes, songs, stories, counting games and activities (first to five, then ten, then twenty and beyond).
Reading and writing numbers	● Recognise numerals 1 to 5, then 1 to 9.	● **Recognise numerals 1 to 9,** then 0 to 10, and beyond 10.
Comparing and ordering numbers	● **Say with confidence the number that is one more than a given number.**	● **Use language such as more or less, greater or smaller, to compare two numbers** and say which is more or less, and say a number that lies between two given numbers.

1 Session

Learning objectives

Starter
ELGs/NNS
● **Say and use the number names in order in familiar contexts** such as number rhymes, songs, stories, counting games and activities (first to five, then ten, then twenty and beyond).
● Begin to understand and use vocabulary related to money. Sort coins, including the £1 and £2 coins, and use them in role play to pay and give change.

Main teaching activity
Green Stepping Stones
● Begin to count beyond 10.
ELGs/NNS
● **Say and use the number names in order in familiar contexts,** such as number rhymes, songs, stories, counting games and activities (first to 5, then 10, then 20 and beyond).

Vocabulary

zero, one, two, three… to twenty

You will need:
Photocopiable pages
'Count to 20', for the teacher's/LSA's reference, see page 122.

CD pages
'Rhymes for 10' and 'Counting record' for the teacher's/LSA's reference (see General resources).

Equipment
Items to buy and sell from the class shop; a tub of penny coins; a tub of mixed coins including 1p, 2p, 5p, 10p, 20p, 50p, £1 and £2; hand puppet.

WHOLE CLASS TEACHING

Starter bank
These Starter bank ideas can be used throughout the unit.

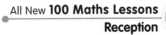

Rhymes for ten

You will need sheet 'Rhymes for 10', which contains three number rhymes. Choose one of the rhymes and begin by saying the words. Encourage the children to join in as you repeat the rhyme several times. Each time a number word is said, hold up that quantity of fingers and encourage the children to do the same. Ask questions such as: *What numbers did we say? How many fingers is that?* Repeat this for the other rhymes, over time.

Coin recognition

Explain to the children that you will pass the tub of mixed coins around the group. Ask each child in turn to find the coin that you say. Say, for example: *Hold up a 1p coin; a coin that is worth the same as two 1p coins. What is this coin called? Hold up a 5p coin. How many 1p coins is worth the same as that?*

Shopping

Explain to the children that you have some things to sell. Show them the items from the class shop and the tub of pennies. Invite a child to come out and to take five pennies. Say: *This… costs 4p. Please give me 4p for it. How much money do you have left?* Invite the other children to use their fingers to work out how much is left. They can put up five fingers, count them, then put down four fingers, counting as they do this. Say a subtraction sentence together: *five take away four leaves one. So 5p take away 4p leaves 1p.* Repeat this for other amounts, over time extending to up to 10p.

Main teaching activity

Ask the children to join with you in counting from zero to 20. Keep the pace sharp, and if the count falters when saying the teen numbers, keep it going yourself, using a strong voice. Repeat this several times. Now ask the children to count around the class, one by one. Again, if a child falters, supply the missing number in order to keep the pace. Repeat this, and when the children can count confidently, ask them to put their arms in the air when it is their turn to count. This will produce a wave effect, and the children will enjoy watching this.

Using the puppet, explain that the puppet will count. Ask the children to listen to the counting and to tell you by putting up their hands if the puppet makes a mistake. Say, for example:
- *Thirteen, fourteen, fiveteen…*
- *Eighteen, nineteen, tenteen…*

Ask the children to say the count correctly for the puppet to hear.

GROUP ACTIVITIES

Count to 20

ADULT SUPPORTED

Learning objectives

Green Stepping Stones:
- Begin to count beyond 10.

ELG/NNS:
- **Say and use the number names in order in familiar contexts** such as number rhymes, songs, stories, counting games and activities (first to five, then ten, then twenty and beyond).

Activity

This activity is provided in detail on CD page 'Count to 20' for the adult's reference and so they can record the children's achievements and difficulties for use during feedback. Work with a group of about ten children. Explain that you would like them to count with you, from zero to 20. Keep the pace sharp, and, if the children falter in the count, supply the number name and continue with the count. Invite children to count. Explain that you will point to one of them to start the count, and when you point to the next child, that child takes over. When they reach 20, explain that the next child should begin again at zero.

Record children's progress on CD page 'Counting record'.

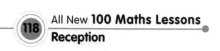

Plenary & assessment

Ask the children to count around the group, from zero to 20. Now ask:

- *What comes after ten?*
- *What is the next number after 14?*

2 Sessions

Preparation

Photocopy 'Number and picture cards 1 to 10' onto card and cut out the numerals. Photocopy '0 to 20 number cards' and 'Number picture cards' onto card, and make sufficient sets for each child to have one. Sort out the numeral cards for one to five from both '0 to 20 number cards' and 'Number and picture cards 1 to 10' and the picture cards from 'Number picture cards'. Put up the washing line.

Learning objectives

Main teaching activity
Green Stepping Stones

- Recognise numerals 1 to 5, then 1 to 9.

ELGs/NNS

- **Recognise numerals 1 to 9,** then 0 to 10, and beyond 10.

Vocabulary

number, one, two, three, four, five

You will need:

Photocopiable pages
'Card hold up', for the teacher's/ LSA's reference, see page 122.

CD pages
'Number and picture cards 1 to 10', photocopied onto card, and 'Reading numbers record', for the teacher's/LSA's reference; and '0 to 20 number cards' and 'Number picture cards', photocopied onto card for each child (see General resources).

Equipment
Washing line, pegs.

WHOLE CLASS TEACHING

Main teaching activity

Show the children the teaching set of numerals 1 to 5 from 'Number and picture cards'. Look at each one in turn and, with a child touching each picture, count together how many pictures are on each card. Say the number for each card, point to the digit and say: *This is how we write the number....* Ask the children to read each number with you and invite a child to peg the cards onto the washing line so that the cards are in number order. Point to each card in turn and say: *What does this say?* The pictures on the card can be counted by the children if they are unsure. Now point to each number, but out of order, and say: *What does this card say?* Remove the cards from the line and hand them, one each, to five children. Ask the children to stand at the front of the class, with the cards in order. Say to the other children: *Sarah, go and hold number one; Rajan, go and hold number two,* and so on until all of the children holding the cards originally have been replaced. Repeat this, this time, saying the numbers out of number order.

When the children are confident with the numerals 1 to 5, extend this to include 6 to 10.

GROUP ACTIVITIES

Card hold up

Learning objectives
Green Stepping Stones:
- Recognise numerals 1 to 5, then 1 to 9.
ELGs/NNS:
- **Recognise numerals 1 to 9,** then 0 to 10, and beyond 10.

Activity

This activity is provided in detail on CD page 'Card hold up' for the LSA's reference and so they can record the children's achievements and difficulties for use during feedback. Ask a group of five

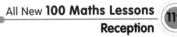

children to work with the LSA. Provide each child with a digit card from CD page '0 to 20 number cards', of numerals one to five. The LSA explains that they will say a number and whoever has that number on their card holds it up. The LSA should keep the pace of this snappy. When everyone has had a turn at holding up their cards, the LSA can take the cards in, shuffle them and repeat this, with each child having a different card this time.

When the children are confident with this, the LSA can extend the activity by providing each child with a set of 1 to 5 digit cards so that each child can hold up the appropriate card each time.

Over time extend to include the numerals to 10.

Plenary & assessment

Hold up a digit card and say: *What number is this?* Repeat this, checking which numbers children are confident with reading. Record confidence on 'Reading number record'.

Number snap

STRUCTURED PLAY

Learning objectives
Green Stepping Stones:
● Recognise numerals 1 to 5, then 1 to 9.
ELGs/NNS:
● **Recognise numerals 1 to 9,** then 0 to 10, and beyond 10.

The children can play this game in pairs. Provide each pair with a set of 1 to 5 numeral cards and a set of 1 to 5 picture cards from CD pages '0 to 20 number cards' and 'Number picture cards'. Ask the children to shuffle their set of cards and to place them face down, in a stack. The children take turns to take a card, placing it in front of them, face up. When two cards match (that is the numeral and the quantity match for number), the first child to say *Snap!* takes their cards and their partners' cards. The game continues until all the cards have been taken. The child with the most cards wins.

When the children are confident with this, extend it by including the numerals to ten.

Plenary & assessment

Use a set of 1 to 5 picture and numeral cards. Shuffle the cards together, and ask the children to look at each card you hold up and to say either how many or the numeral name. When the children have done this for all the cards, spread them out, face up, and say: *Who can find me a pair of cards worth the same? How many are on that card? What is the number on this card?* Repeat this until all the cards have been paired. Note which children can read the numerals one to five with ease, and who will need more practice.

1 Session

Preparation

Put up the washing line. Enlarge CD page 'Ten tracks' to A3. Write in some numbers, as shown below, and pin to the flip chart.

1	2	3	–	5	–	7	8	–	10
1	–	–	4	–	6	7	–	–	–
–	–	3	4	–	–	7	–	9	–
–	2	–	–	–	6	–	8	–	10

Learning objectives

Main teaching activity
ELGs/NNS
● **Use language such as more or less, greater or smaller, to compare two numbers and say which is more or less,** and say a number that lies between two given numbers.

Vocabulary

More, fewer, smaller, less, most, fewest, least, one more, one less, compare

You will need:
Photocopiable pages
'Number track' photocopied onto A3, for the teacher's/LSA's reference, see page 123.

CD pages
'Duck counting cards' and 'Ten tracks', for the teacher's/LSA's reference and 'Number cards' for each child (see General resources).

Equipment
Washing line and pegs.

WHOLE CLASS TEACHING

Main teaching activity

Explain that you would like the children to say the number that is one more/one less than the number that you say, for example: *Say the number that is one more than three…, one less than seven…* Repeat this for numbers to ten. Then, when the children are confident with this, extend it to numbers to 15, then to 20.

Now explain that you will peg some picture cards from CD page 'Duck counting cards' onto the washing line. Ask the children to watch carefully and encourage them to count the pictures by co-ordinating, pointing and counting. Put up the cards with one, two, three, five pictures on. By this time the children should notice that the card with four pictures on has been missed. Invite a child to pick out the card with four ducks from the rest of the cards. Continue like this, sometimes pinning up the correct card, and sometimes making a mistake. Encourage the children to put up their hands when they see an error and to say which card should be placed next.

Show the children the CD page 'Ten tracks'. Explain that you have written some numbers in, but that some are missing. Together, read the numbers that are there, pause at the missing number and ask the children to say what is missing. Write the number into the track, and repeat until all the numbers have been written in.

If the children are not yet confident with numbers to ten, fold the track halfway and begin with writing in just numbers for up to five. Extend to up to ten over time.

GROUP ACTIVITIES

Number track

Learning objectives

Green Stepping Stones:

● Say with confidence the number that is one more than a given number.

ELGs/NNS:

● **Use language such as more or less, greater or smaller, to compare two numbers** and say which is more or less, and say a number that lies between two given numbers.

Activity

This activity is provided in detail on CD page 'Number track' for the adult's reference and so they can record the children's achievements and difficulties for use during feedback. Ask a group of six to eight children, in pairs, to work with the LSA. Each pair will need a set of 1 to 10 numeral cards from CD page 'Number cards'. The LSA asks the children to remove the 1 and the 10 cards, and then shuffle the rest. Then the LSA asks them to place the cards face down in a stack in front of them. The children place the 1 card at the beginning of an imaginary number track, and the 10 at the end of it. They take turns to turn over the top card and decide where it will go in the number track. As the children work, the LSA can ask questions such as:

● *Which card will go next to …?*

● *Where does this card go?*

● *What is one more/one fewer than this card?*

When the children are confident at placing the cards, the LSA can suggest that they include the 1 and 10 cards in the shuffled pack.

Plenary & assessment

Shuffle one set of 1 to 10 cards and turn over the top card. Invite the children to say what is one more and one less than the number and where it should go in an imaginary number track. Repeat this until all the cards have been placed. Ask questions such as:

● *What is one more/less than three?*

● *Where does this card go? Why is that?*

● (when most of the cards have been placed) *Which numbers are still missing?*

Count to 20

You need a copy of 'Counting record'.

Work with a group of about ten children.

Explain that you would like them to count with you, from zero to 20.

Keep the pace sharp, and if the children falter in the count, supply the number name and continue with the count.

Invite the children to count. Explain that you will point to one of them to start the count, and when you point to the next child, that child takes over.

When they reach 20, explain that the next child should begin again at zero.

Children's counting ability can be recorded on 'Counting record'. It would be helpful to note who can say all the number names, confidently, and in order.

Card hold up

You need a set of 1 to 5 digit cards from '0 to 20 number cards' for each child.

Work with a group of five children. Provide each child with just one digit card, from '0 to 20 number cards'.

Explain that you will say a number and whoever has that number on their card holds it up. Keep the pace of this snappy. When everyone has had a turn at holding up their cards, take the cards in, shuffle them and repeat this, with each child having a different card this time.

When the children are confident with this, extend it by providing each child with a set of 1 to 5 digit cards so that each child can hold up the appropriate card each time.

Children's confidence with reading numbers 1 to 5 can be recorded on 'Reading numbers record'.

Over time, extend to include the numerals covered to 10.

Number track

You will need three or four sets of 1 to 10 numeral cards from CD page 'Number cards'.

Work with a group of six to eight children in pairs.

Each pair will need a set of 1 to 10 numeral cards.

Ask the children to remove the 1 and the 10 cards, and then shuffle the rest. Ask them to place the 1 card at the beginning of an imaginary number track, and the 10 card at the end of it. They take turns to turn over the top card and decide where it will go on the number track.

As the children work, as questions such as:

- *What card will go next to five?*
- *Where does this card go?*
- *What is one more/one fewer than the number on this card?*

When the children are confident at placing the cards, suggest that they include the 1 and 10 cards in the shuffled card.

Child's name	What happened	What to do next time

Counting objects, recognising numerals and adding strategies

Children count out a given quantity of objects and match the written numeral to how many objects there are. They count out two given quantities of objects and count on from one quantity to find the total. They say the addition sentence.

LEARNING OBJECTIVES

Topics	Stepping Stones Green	Early Learning Goals & NNS Learning Objectives
Counting	● Count out up to six objects from a larger group.	● **Count reliably up to 10 everyday objects** (first to 5, then 10, then beyond) giving just one number name to each object.
Reading and writing numbers	● Recognise numerals 1 to 5, then 1 to 9.	● **Recognise numerals 1 to 9,** then 0 to 10, and beyond 10.
Adding and subtracting	● Find the total number of items in two groups by counting all of them.	● **Begin to relate addition to combining two groups of objects,** counting all the objects. ● Begin to relate addition to counting on.

2 Sessions

Preparation

Separate out from several sets of number cards, the numbers one to five, and six to ten. Put up the washing line.

Learning objectives

Starter
ELGs/NNS
● **Recognise numerals 1 to 9,** then 0 to 10, and beyond 10.
● Separate (partition) a given number of objects into two groups.

Main teaching activity
Green Stepping Stones
● Count out up to six objects from a larger group.
● Recognise numerals 1 to 5, then 1 to 9.
ELGs/NNS
● **Count reliably up to 10 everyday objects** (first to 5, then 10, then beyond) giving just one number name to each object.
● **Recognise numerals 1 to 9,** then 0 to 10, and beyond 10.

Vocabulary

number, zero, one, two, three… to twenty; how many…? count, more than, less than, add

You will need
CD pages
'0 to 20 number cards', 'Number and picture cards 1 to 10', three or four sets of 'Duck counting cards 2', 'Counting objects record' and 'Reading numbers record', for the teacher's/ LSA's reference (see General resources).

Equipment
Washing line and pegs; ten toys for counting on a tray; hoop; for each pair a 1–6 spot dice, a 1–6 numeral dice and 20 counters.

WHOLE CLASS TEACHING

Starter bank

These Starter bank ideas can be used throughout this unit.

Which number?

Give each child a numeral card, from 1 to 5 from CD page '0 to 20 number cards', so that there are several children with the same number. Explain to the children that you will say a number. If they are holding that card, ask them to hold it up. Say the numbers, out of order: *three, one, five, two, four*. Repeat this, asking the children to swap their card with a friend so that they have a different number. Do this several times. Extend the range to up to 10 over time, as the children's confidence with reading numbers increases.

I am thinking of…

Decide whether to use the number and picture cards (CD page 'Number and picture cards 1 to 10') or the number cards (CD page '0 to 20 number cards'), depending upon the children's confidence with reading numerals. Pin up the cards chosen in number order and, as you do, encourage the children to read the numerals. Now explain that you will ask a question. Whoever answers correctly can come and collect that card. Say, for example: *This number is one more than two/one less than five/ is between six and eight…* Continue like this until all the cards have been taken. Invite the children holding the cards to come out and to peg their cards back onto the line in order and repeat the activity. For the less confident children, this activity can be limited to one to five initially.

Finger partition

Explain to the children that you would like them to use both hands to show you a number. Say, for example: *Four*. They could show one and three; two and two; three and one. Invite a child to come to the front to show their partition and say the addition sentence: *One add three is four*…. Repeat this until all three number sentences are shown at the front by children. Then repeat the activity for another addition, up to five add five.

Main teaching activity

You will need the ten toys on a tray, and the large 1 to 10 numeral cards from CD page '0 to 20 number cards'. Begin by inviting children to peg the large numeral cards onto the washing line, in order. Ask: *What comes at the beginning? Yes, one. What is next… and next?* until all of the cards are ordered on the line. Now explain that there are some toys on the tray. Invite a child to remove the number of toys that you say, such as five. These can be counted by being removed from the tray and placed into a hoop. Ask: *How many toys are there? So which number card is five?* Invite a child to remove the card from the line and to hold it by the toys. Say: *There are five toys. This is number five.* Repeat this for different quantities of toys, from one to ten. However, if the children are not confident with reading numbers from six on, begin by limiting this to the numbers one to five, and extend over time to up to ten.

GROUP ACTIVITIES

Duck count

Learning objectives
Green Stepping Stones:
- Count out up to six objects from a larger group.
- Recognise numerals 1 to 5, then 1 to 9.

ELGs/NNS:
- **Count reliably up to 10 everyday objects** (first to 5, then 10, then beyond) giving just one number name to each object.
- **Recognise numerals 1 to 9,** then 0 to 10, and beyond 10.

Activity

The LSA will need a set of CD page 'Duck counting cards 2' and a set of 1 to 10 numeral cards from CD page '0 to 20 number cards' for pairs of children in a group of six to eight. Begin with the cards for 1 to 5. The LSA should ask the children to spread out the numeral cards in front of them, in number order, then to shuffle the duck counting cards and to place these in a stack. They take turns to take a duck card, count how many and place it underneath the appropriate numeral card. When they have sorted the cards for 1 to 5, the activity can be repeated for 1 to 10.

Plenary & assessment

Spread out the number cards, and ask the children to help you to order them, from 1 to 5, or from 1 to 10. Choose one of the duck cards and say: *How many ducks are there? So, which number card has that number?* Repeat this for other quantities, checking that the children count accurately and can read the appropriate number.

Dice match

STRUCTURED PLAY

Learning objectives

Green Stepping Stones:
- Count out up to six objects from a larger group.
- Recognise numerals 1 to 5, then 1 to 9.

ELGs/NNS:
- **Count reliably up to 10 everyday objects** (first to 5, then 10, then beyond) giving just one number name to each object.
- **Recognise numerals 1 to 9,** then 0 to 10, and beyond 10.

Activity

This is an activity for pairs of children. Each pair will need a 1–6 spot dice, a 1–6 numeral dice and some counters. The children take it in turns to roll both dice and to say the score on both dice. If the scores match, they take a counter. The child who is first to collect five, six… ten counters wins the game.

Plenary & assessment

Explain that you will roll both dice. Ask the children to look carefully and to read the scores. Repeat this several times. Say, for example:
- *How many are there on this dice?*
- *What number is on this dice?*
- *Do these match?*
- *Jasmine, can you turn the number dice until it matches the spot dice?*

3 Sessions

Learning objectives

Main teaching activity
Green Stepping Stones
- Find the total number of items in two groups by counting all of them.

ELGs/NNS
- **Begin to relate addition to combining two groups of objects,** counting all the objects.
- Begin to relate addition to counting on.

Vocabulary

add, more, and, make, sum, total, altogether, score

You will need:
Photocopiable pages
'Show me fingers', for the teacher's/LSA's reference, see page 129 and 'Race track', one per pair, see page 130.

Equipment
A tray of ten counting toys; two hoops; opaque bag and ten counting tiles; for each pair a red and blue counter, and a dice marked 1, 1, 2, 2, 3, 3.

WHOLE CLASS TEACHING

Main teaching activity
Ask a child to count out four of the toys from the tray and to put these into a hoop. Now ask another child to count out another two toys and put these into another hoop. Say: *There are four toys here and two toys here. How many toys are there in total? How can we find out?* Count all, by counting: *One, two, three, four, we're at four, so we hold that in our heads and count on the toys in the other hoop, five, six. One, two, three, four, five, six. So four add two makes six.* Repeat this for several more additions. Now say to the children: *Sacha, count out three toys. Mark count out two toys. Now let's count how many altogether. There are three here, and* (pointing to the second hoop of two toys) *four and five. So three add two makes five.* Repeat this for, for example, four and three, encouraging the children to count on with you, this time, from four. Repeat for further examples, keeping the total to up to ten.

GROUP ACTIVITIES

Into the bag

TEACHER DIRECTED

Learning objectives
Green Stepping Stones:
- Find the total number of items in two groups by counting all of them.

ELGs/NNS:
- **Begin to relate addition to combining two groups of objects**, counting all the objects.
- Begin to relate addition to counting on.

Activity
Work with a group of six to eight children. Show them the opaque bag and the counting tiles. Explain that you will put some tiles into the bag and that you want the children to say how many tiles there are in total. Begin by saying: *Count how many I put into the bag.* Drop four tiles into the bag, one at a time. Say: *How many are there?* Now say: *I will put some more in.* Put in a further tile and encourage the children to count on from the previous count. Say: *I put in four tiles and one more so how many are there altogether? Yes, four add one makes five.* Tip the tiles out onto the table top and ask a child to count them all, to check. If the children are not sure about this, separate the tiles into four and one and count them all, so that they can see how this works. Repeat this several times, using different amounts and each time encouraging the children to count on from the first batch of tiles to find the total.

Plenary & assessment

Repeat the activity again, this time for, say, four and three. Say:

- *Count how many go into the bag.*
- *Now count on as I put three more into the bag. How many are there altogether?*
  Repeat this several times.

Show me fingers

Learning objectives

Green Stepping Stones:

- Find the total number of items in two groups by counting all of them.

ELGs/NNS:

- **Begin to relate addition to combining two groups of objects**, counting all the objects.
- Begin to relate addition to counting on.

Activity

This activity is provided in detail on CD page 'Show me fingers' for the adult's reference and so they can record the children's achievements and difficulties for use during feedback. Work with a group of four to six children. Explain that you will say a number which they will show on one hand, then another number for the other hand. Say, for example: *Show me four on one hand. Now show me two on the other hand. Now let's count how many that is altogether.* Say:

- *You have four on this hand and we carry on counting onto this hand: five, six.*
- *So four add two makes six.*
  Repeat this for other amounts, up to five add five.

Plenary & assessment

Ask the children to show you three on one hand and two on the other. Say: *How many is that altogether?* Check which children count on from one hand to the other. Remind any children who do not count on yet of how to do this. Repeat this for other amounts up to five add five.

Race track

Learning objectives

Green Stepping Stones:

- Find the total number of items in two groups by counting all of them.

ELGs/NNS:

- **Begin to relate addition to combining two groups of objects**, counting all the objects.
- Begin to relate addition to counting on.

Activity

This is a game for two children. They will need a copy of CD page 'Race track', a red and a blue counter and a dice marked 1, 1, 2, 2, 3, 3. Ask the children to take turns to roll the dice. They move their counter that number. From their second turn on they say how many they have moved, and what number they have landed on. The winner is the one who reaches the end first. The children can play this game several times.

Plenary & assessment

Play the game with a group of children, using just one counter. Ask questions such as:

- *What number is the counter on?*
- *What number does the dice say?*
- *So, where do you think the counter will land?*

Show me fingers

Work with a group of four to six children.

Explain that you will say a number which they will show on one hand, then another number for the other hand.

Say, for example: *Show me four on one hand. Now show me two on the other hand. Now let's count how many that is altogether. You have four and five, six. So four add two makes six.*

Repeat this for other amounts, up to five add five.

Record the children's achievements. It would be helpful to record how well the children can count on to find a total.

4 and 5, 6. So 4 add 2 makes 6.

Child's name	What happened	What to do next time

Name	Date

Race track

Work with a partner.
You need a red counter, blue counter and
a dice marked 1, 1, 2, 2, 3, 3.

Take turns to roll the dice.
Say your start number.
Move your counter the number on the dice.
Say your stop number.
The winner is the one who gets to 'Finish' first.

◼ S C H O L A S T I C
photocopiable

Making patterns and reasoning

Children copy and continue patterns. They make symmetrical shapes by folding and cutting. They follow position and direction instructions in order to find things in the room.

LEARNING OBJECTIVES

Topics	Stepping Stones	Early Learning Goals & NNS Learning Objectives
	Blue	
Reasoning about numbers or shapes	● Show awareness of symmetry.	● **Talk about, recognise and recreate patterns**: for example, simple repeating or symmetrical patterns in the environment.
Exploring pattern, shape and space	● Find items from positional/directional clues. ● Describe a simple journey. ● Instruct a programmable toy.	● **Use everyday words to describe position**: for example, follow and give instructions about positions, directions and movements in PE and other activities.

3 Sessions

Learning objectives

Starter

ELGs/NNS

● **Count reliably up to 10 everyday objects** (first to 5, then 10, then beyond) giving just one number name to each object.

● **Recognise numerals 1 to 9,** then 0 to 10, and beyond 10.

Main teaching activity

Green Stepping Stones

● Show awareness of symmetry.

ELGs/NNS

● **Talk about, recognise and recreate patterns**: for example, simple repeating or symmetrical patterns in the environment.

Vocabulary

shape, pattern, make, build, draw, sort

You will need:

Photocopiable pages

'Butterflies', for the teacher's/LSA's reference, see page 135.

CD pages

'Number cards' for the teacher's/LSA's reference (see General resources).

Equipment

Ten toys and a tray; coloured beads and laces; computer and a drawing package; mosaic tiles; safety mirrors; paints, large sheets of paper, safety scissors.

WHOLE CLASS TEACHING

Starter bank

These Starter bank ideas can be used throughout the unit.

Toy count

Explain to the children that you will show them some toys on a tray. Ask them to count them by pointing as quickly as they can. Now say: *What was the last number you counted? So how many toys are there? Who would like to find the number card for that number?* Repeat this several times for quantities of toys from three to ten.

Show me

Provide each child with a numeral card from one to ten from CD page 'Number cards'. Explain that you will describe a number. If the children think that it is their number, when you say *Show me* they hold up their card. Say, for example: *I am thinking of a number that is between one and three; I am thinking of a number between two and six; My number is one more… less than eight….* Where there are several possible answers, discuss why this is so.

Human number track

Use the large 1 to 10 number cards from CD page 'Number cards'. Invite a child to hold the 'one' card and to stand at the front. Now, ask a child to hold the 10 card and to decide where to stand. The others can help with where they think this should be. Now give the 3 card to a child and ask the child to stand in the line. Discuss why there is a space between one and three. Continue until all the cards are held in line. Now invite other children to swap places in order to hold a particular card. Say, for example: *Sophie, go and hold 5… Leanne, hold the card that is between 6 and 8.* Continue until every child has had a turn, pitching the questions at their current level of confidence in reading numbers.

Main teaching activity

Explain to the children that you will make a pattern with some beads. Begin by threading alternatively red and blue beads. When there are six beads on the lace say: *What comes next? Why is that? And what will come after that?* Continue the pattern, encouraging the children to say the next bead colour before you thread it. Repeat this, making a different repeating pattern.

Now show the children a paper shape, such as a rectangle. Say: *What shape do you think I will make if I fold it in half?* Show the children the shape by folding. Now show them how to make the image of the whole shape by holding the paper by a mirror.

GROUP ACTIVITIES

Computer patterns

Learning objectives
Green Stepping Stones:
- Show awareness of symmetry.

ELGs/NNS:
- **Talk about, recognise and recreate patterns**: for example, simple repeating or symmetrical patterns in the environment.

Activity

Ask two children to work with the LSA at the computer. The LSA can ask the children to make a pattern on screen. As they work the LSA can discuss the shapes that they have used and the colours they have chosen. At first, the patterns may not be patterns at all, but pictures or randomly-placed shapes. The LSA can talk about how the shapes could be moved in order to make a pattern which repeats.

Plenary & assessment

Choose two shapes and draw these on the computer screen. Ask the children to suggest where the two shapes should go, then what should come next, and so on, in order to make a simple ABAB repeating pattern. Ask questions such as:
- *Which shape shall we put first? What comes next? What would be next… and next…?*

Mosaic patterns

Learning objectives
Green Stepping Stones:
● Show awareness of symmetry.
ELGs/NNS:
● **Talk about, recognise and recreate patterns**: for example, simple repeating or symmetrical patterns in the environment.

Activity
Work with a group of four to six children in pairs. Each pair will need some mosaic tiles and a safety mirror. Invite the children to make designs with their tiles and then to look at the finished result in the mirror. Encourage them to talk about what they have done, and where particular shapes have been placed. Now encourage the children to make another design that has a pattern, such as using alternating colours or shapes. Encourage the children to 'say' their pattern or design to you.

Plenary & assessment
Look together at the different patterns and designs that have been made. Use a mirror and show the reflection of the design in the mirror. Encourage the children to say what they can see. They may notice, for example, that the design is 'back to front' when seen in the mirror, or symmetrical. Ask:
● *Which shapes can you see?*
● *What pattern can you see?*
● *What do you see in the mirror?*

Butterflies

Learning objectives
Green Stepping Stones:
● Show awareness of symmetry.
ELGs/NNS:
● **Talk about, recognise and recreate patterns**: for example, simple repeating or symmetrical patterns in the environment.

Activity
This activity is provided in detail on CD page 'Butterflies' for the adult's reference and so they can record the children's achievements and difficulties for use during feedback. Ask four children to work with the LSA. They will each need a large sheet of paper and access to paint.

Plenary & assessment
Talk about the designs that the children have made and how these are symmetrical. Examine some of the butterflies with a mirror, looking at the reflection of one wing, then the other. Encourage the children to talk about what they can see. Say:
● *Tell me about your butterfly wings. Are they the same as each other?*
● *What do you notice when you look at a wing in the mirror?*

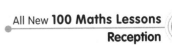

1 Session

Preparation

Enlarge 'Where is it?' to A3. This can be coloured in to make an attractive poster, then laminated so that it can be used many times.

Learning objectives

Main teaching activity
Green Stepping Stones
● Find items from positional/directional clues.
ELGs/NNS
● **Use everyday words to describe position**, for example, follow and give instructions about positions, directions and movements in PE and other activities.

Vocabulary

position, over, under, above, below, top, bottom, side, on, in, outside, inside, around, in front, behind, front, back, before, after, beside, next to, opposite, apart, between

You will need:
CD pages
'Where is it?', photocopied onto A3, for the teacher's/ LSA's reference (see General resources).

WHOLE CLASS TEACHING

Main teaching activity

Pin up the poster from CD page 'Where is it?' so that the children can see it clearly. Talk about the picture and what is happening. Ask questions such as:
● *What do you think the kitten is doing?*
● *What will grandma say when she wakes up?*

When the children have shown that they understand the story being shown, of Grandma asleep, and the kitten tangling the knitting, ask position questions, such as:
● *Where is the dog/kitten/knitting?*
● *What is on/under the table?*
● *What is next to / on top of / beside…?*

Encourage the children to respond to these questions by saying a sentence, rather than just naming an object in the picture.

GROUP ACTIVITIES

I spy

TEACHER DIRECTED

Learning objectives
Green Stepping Stones:
● Find items from positional/directional clues.
ELGs/NNS:
● **Use everyday words to describe position**, for example, follow and give instructions about positions, directions and movements in PE and other activities.

Activity
Play 'I spy' with a group of children. This can be a group of six to eight children, or the whole class:
● *I spy with my little eye something on top of the cupboard.*
● *I spy something under the table / on the chair / beside…*

The children will enjoy looking for what you can see and, when they are confident with this, the game can be played with one of them being in charge, saying: *I spy…*

Plenary & assessment
Ask the children to look around the room. Tell them that you can see a ball/bookcase… Ask the children to describe its position. Repeat this for several other items.

Butterflies

Work with four children.

The children will each need a large sheet of paper and access to paint.

Ask the children to begin by folding their piece of paper in half like this:

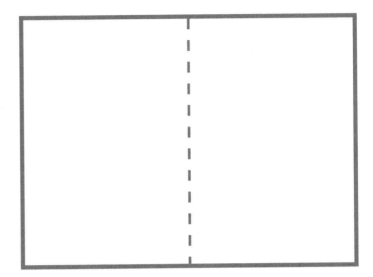

Ask the children to open out their paper and place it down, with the inside created by the fold uppermost.

Now they can decorate one half of their paper with paint 'blobs' to make a decoration. When they are satisfied, they can fold their paper again and carefully rub their hands over the outside in order to press the paint into both halves of the paper.

Ask the children to open out their paper and let the paint dry. When the paint is dry either ask the child to draw half a butterfly on the outside, or draw this for them, and ask them to cut it out, being careful not to cut away the fold.

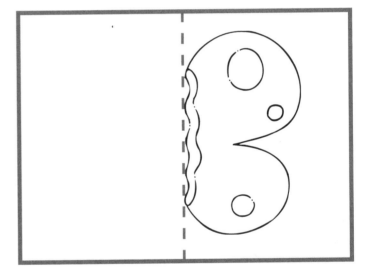

The children can then open out their paper to see the symmetrical butterfly that they have made. Talk about the symmetry. They may like to look at one wing in a mirror to see how it matches the other wing.

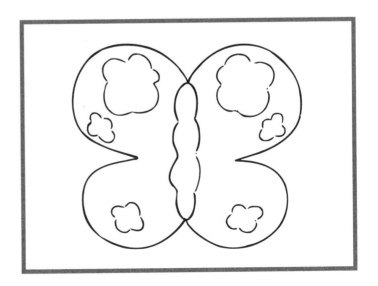

Counting, reading numerals, comparing and adding numbers, and days of the week

Children count from zero to 20 and back. They count starting and finishing on given numbers. They repeat this, reading the start number within the range 1 to 9. Using a programmable toy they use language such as 'more' or 'less'/'longer' or 'shorter' to describe how close the toy is to the desired position. They recite the days of the week and answer questions about today/tomorrow.

LEARNING OBJECTIVES

Topics	Stepping Stones	Early Learning Goals &
	Green	**NNS Learning Objectives**
Counting	● Begin to count beyond 10.	● **Recite the number names in order in familiar contexts**, continuing the count forwards and backwards from a given number.
Reading and writing numbers	● Recognise numerals 1 to 5, then 1 to 9.	● **Recognise numerals 1 to 9,** then 0 to 10, and beyond 10.
Comparing and ordering numbers	● **Say with confidence the number that is 1 more than a given number.**	● **Use language such as more or less, greater or smaller, to compare two numbers** and say which is more or less, and say a number that lies between two given numbers.
Days of the week		● Begin to know the days of the week in order.

2 Sessions

Learning objectives

Starter
Green Stepping Stones
● Find the total number of items in two groups by counting all of them.
ELGs/NNS
● **Begin to relate addition to combining two groups of objects,** counting all the objects.
● Begin to relate addition to counting on.

Main teaching activity
Green Stepping Stones
● Begin to count beyond 10.
● Recognise numerals 1 to 5, then 1 to 9.
ELGs/NNS
● **Recite the number names in order,** continuing the count forwards or backwards from a given number.
● **Recognise numerals 1 to 9,** then 0 to 10, then beyond 10.

Vocabulary

zero, one, two, three… twenty, count, count (up) to, count back (from, to)

You will need:

Photocopiable pages
'Count on, count back', for the teacher's/LSA's reference, see page 142.

CD pages
'0 to 20 number cards', one set for each pair, and one set for the teacher's/LSA's reference (see General resources).

WHOLE CLASS TEACHING

Starter bank

These Starter bank ideas can be used throughout the unit.

Finger add

Ask the children hold up the number of fingers that you say on one hand, then another quantity on the other hand. Ask them to count all of their fingers to say how many are held up. Say, for example: *Hold up four fingers on one hand, and now hold up two fingers on the other hand. How many is four add two. Let's count together. One, two. One, two, three, four. So altogether that is one, two, three, four, five, six. So four add two makes six.* Repeat this for other quantities, up to five add five.

Finger add on

This is similar to the 'Finger add' activity above. This time, invite the children to count on from the quantity on one hand. So, for four add two they would say *four and five, six. So four add two makes six.* Repeat this for quantities up to five add five.

Explain that you will tell the children an addition number story. Ask them to count on, using their fingers to help them, from one of the numbers, to find the total. Say, for example: *Tom has three apples. His mum gives him two more apples. How many has he now?* Encourage the children to respond: *Three add two is three, four, five. So Tom has five apples.* Repeat this for other addition number stories, keeping within the limits of up to five add five.

Main teaching activity

Ask the children to count with you, from zero, to 20, and back. Keep the pace sharp. The children can slap their knees in time with the count. Repeat this several times. Now ask the children to count from a given number, such as: *Start on three. Hold it in your head. Count on to nine: four, five, six, seven, eight, nine.* Repeat this several times for different starting and finishing numbers within the range of zero to 20. Now say: *Count on three numbers from six... seven, eight, nine.* Again, repeat this for several different starting numbers and within the range of zero to 20.

Explain to the children that you will hold up a numeral card (from CD page 'Number cards) to show their starting number. Ask them to count on or back from that number until you say *Stop!* Hold up six... nine... three...

Now explain to the children that you would like them to count around the circle. Explain that you will hold up a numeral card to show the start number. Begin by asking the children to count forwards. Then repeat this, with counting back. Here keep the range within one to nine.

GROUP ACTIVITIES

Count on, count back

Learning objectives
Green Stepping Stones:
- Begin to count beyond 10.
- Recognise numerals 1 to 5, then 1 to 9.

ELGs/NNS:
- Recite the number names in order, continuing the count forwards or backwards from a given number.
- **Recognise numerals 1 to 9,** then 0 to 10, then beyond 10.

Activity

This activity is provided in detail on CD page 'Count on, count back' for the adult's reference and so they can record the children's achievements and difficulties for use during feedback. Ask a group of six to eight children to sit in a circle with the LSA. The LSA explains that they have some shuffled numeral cards for 1 to 9 in front of them and that they will show the children a numeral card from CD page 'Number cards'. The LSA asks a child to begin the count from that number, and for the count to continue around the circle. When a child reaches 20, the next child begins the count back, and the count stops at the start number on the card. Repeat this several times for different start numbers from 1 to 9 and encourage the children to keep the pace sharp. If the count falters, say the next number in order to keep the count going.

For children working towards the Green Stepping Stones, begin by limiting the count to 12, 13… and the numerals to be recognised to 1 to 5. Extend this, over time, to numerals 1 to 9, and the count to 20 and back.

Plenary & assessment

Invite the children to count around the circle from a number which you show them with a numeral card and explain that you will say *Stop!* during the count. After saying *Stop!* ask:
- *What was the last number you said?*
- *What would the next number be?*
- *What was the number before seven?*
  Repeat this for different start and stop numbers.

One more and one less

STRUCTURED PLAY

Learning objectives
Green Stepping Stones:
- Begin to count beyond 10.
- Recognise numerals 1 to 5, then 1 to 9.

ELGs/NNS:
- **Recite the number names in order**, continuing the count forwards or backwards from a given number.
- **Recognise numerals 1 to 9,** then 0 to 10, then beyond 10.

Activity

Provide each pair of children with a set of cards from CD page '0 to 20 number cards', or for those working towards the Green Stepping Stones, a set for 1 to 5. This can be increased to 1 to 10 over time. Ask the children to shuffle their cards, then to place them in a stack, face down. They take turns to turn over the top card and to say the number that is one more than and one less than the number on the card. Partners take it in turns to check each other's work.

This can be extended by asking the children to turn over the top card and to count together on to 20, and back to the start number.

Plenary & assessment

Explain that you will show the children a number card. Ask questions such as:
- *What number is this?*
- *What is one more than this number?*
- *What is one less than this number?*
  Repeat this for other numbers.

2 Sessions

Preparation

Roamer can be decorated to become a postman. Set up a space in the classroom for Postman Roamer, with cardboard houses, and a road marked in as shown on the CD page 'Postman Roamer'.

Learning objectives

Main teaching activity
Green Stepping Stones
● Order two or three items by length.
ELGs/NNS
● **Use language such as more or less, longer or shorter, heavier or lighter to compare two quantities,** then more than two, by making direct comparisons of lengths.

Vocabulary

length, width, height, depth, long, short, high, low, wide, narrow, deep, shallow, thick, thin, longer, shorter, taller, higher… and so on, longest, shortest, tallest, highest… and so on, far, near, close.

You will need:
Photocopiable pages
'Beanbag throw', for the teacher's/LSA's reference, see page 143.

CD pages
'Postman Roamer' for the teacher's/LSA's reference (see General resources).

Equipment
Roamer or other programmable toy; four cardboard houses; beanbags; hoop.

WHOLE CLASS TEACHING

Main teaching activity

Introduce the children to Roamer. Explain that it is possible to make Roamer move by putting in numbers and pressing 'Go'. Demonstrate this by asking Roamer to move forward one. Invite a child to programme Roamer. Ask: *Where shall we send Roamer this time? What number do you think you should press?* Encourage the children to suggest where Roamer should go, and estimate the number required to get Roamer there. Use language such as 'far', 'near', 'close', to describe how close Roamer is to the goal. Repeat this several times for sending Roamer to different places in the room.

The children will find it useful to understand that there is a forward and a back input for Roamer. Decide whether to introduce the turn function. If you do, then re-programming this function to work with smaller numbers may help the children to use it successfully. (See the instruction manual for Roamer, or the other programmable toy for how to do this.)

GROUP ACTIVITIES

Postman Roamer

Learning objectives
ELGs/NNS:
● **Use language such as more or less, longer or shorter, heavier or lighter to compare two quantities,** then more than two, by making direct comparisons of lengths.

Activity

Work with a group of four to six children. Read them the story on CD page 'Postman Roamer' about Roamer the postman. Explain that Roamer needs to visit each house in turn to deliver the letters. Encourage the children to estimate how far Roamer needs to travel to reach the first house. Ask one of the children to input the chosen number, and to press 'Go'. Encourage the children to evaluate how well they estimated. If Roamer did not reach the destination, then ask: *How much further has Roamer to go? What number do you think we should use?* If Roamer overshot the destination, remind children of the back button and ask them to estimate how far back Roamer needs to go. Continue in this way until Roamer has visited all the houses.

This activity can be simplified to include two or three houses to be visited in a straight line. It can be extended by altering the story so that Roamer visits three of the four houses, and by putting in a road which runs diagonally from the second to the fourth house. This will challenge the more able.

Plenary & assessment

Alter the distance between the two houses. Invite the children to estimate how far Roamer will need to travel from one house to the next. Then invite one of the children to input the number and press go. Ask:

- *Did you make a good guess?*
- *How did you work out your guess?*
- (Where Roamer over- or under-shot a house) *How shall we move Roamer now?*

Bean bag throw

ADULT SUPPORTED

Learning objectives

Green Stepping Stones:
- Order two or three items by length.

ELGs/NNS:
- **Use language such as more or less, longer or shorter, heavier or lighter to compare two quantities**, then more than two, by making direct comparisons of lengths.

Activity

This activity is provided in detail on CD page 'Beanbag throw' for the adult's reference and so they can record the children's achievements and difficulties for use during feedback. This activity will need some room, so it may be better to work outside or in a larger space. Put out the hoop. Ask four to six children to work with the LSA, and give each child a beanbag. The LSA asks the children to stand in a line and to take turns throwing their beanbag, aiming for the inside of the hoop. As the children work, the LSA can ask them to say how well they threw the beanbag, using words such as 'far', 'near', 'close'…

Plenary & assessment

Invite each child to have another turn at throwing their beanbag. Ask:

- *Whose beanbag landed near to the hoop?*
- *Whose was far away?*

Encourage the children to compare their beanbag landings, and to use the vocabulary of distance as they describe where the beanbags are.

1 Session

Preparation

If no commercial days of the week chart is available, make one from card.

Learning objectives

Main teaching activity
ELGs/NNS
- Begin to know the days of the week in order.

Vocabulary

Sunday, Monday, Tuesday, Wednesday, Thursday, Friday, Saturday, Sunday, day, week, today, yesterday, tomorrow, before, after, next, last

You will need:
Photocopiable pages:
'Days of the week' for the teacher's/LSA's reference, see page 144.

Equipment
Days of the week chart. (This can be a commercial chart or one that is home made, with removable days cards to slot into spaces for today, tomorrow, yesterday.)

WHOLE CLASS TEACHING

Main teaching activity

Begin by saying the days of the week in order. If the children do not yet know the days of the week, say these several times and the children will begin to join in with you. Now, as you say each day, hold up the card with the word for that day on it. Repeat this several times. Show the children the days of the week chart. Ask them to help you to decide what day it is today. Invite a child to put the appropriate card into the 'Today' slot. Repeat this for 'yesterday' and for 'tomorrow'.

This activity will need to be repeated several times. As the children become more confident about the days of the week, invite them to answer questions, such as:

- *What day is it today?*
- *What day was it yesterday?*
- *What day will it be tomorrow?*
- *What do you do that is special on Sunday, Monday...?*

GROUP ACTIVITIES

Days of the week

Learning objectives
ELGs/NNS:
- Begin to know the days of the week in order.

Activity

Use the poem on 'Days of the week' with a group of six to eight children. Say the poem to the children and repeat it several times. Encourage the children to join in with you, so that they begin to know it too. Ask the children questions about the poem such as:

- *Who makes beds on Saturdays?*
- *Who rests or plays on Sundays?*

To finish the activity, encourage the children to say the poem again, then to say the days of the week, in order.

Plenary & assessment

Invite the children to say the poem through with you. Ask them questions such as:

- *What day is it today?*
- *What day was it yesterday?*
- *What day will it be tomorrow?*
- *Which is your favourite day of the week? Why is that?*

Count on, count back

You will need a set of '1 to 20 number cards'.

Work with a group of six to eight children.

Explain that you have some shuffled numeral cards for 1 to 9 in front of you. Ask the children to sit in a circle, and that you will show them a numeral card. Ask a child to begin the count from that number, and for the count to continue around the circle.

When a child reaches 20, the next child begins the count back, and the count stops at the start number on the card. Repeat this several times for different start numbers from 1 to 9 and encourage the children to keep the pace sharp. If the count falters, say the next number in order to keep the count going.

For children working towards the Green Stepping Stones, begin by limiting the count to 12, 13... and the numerals to be recognised to 1 to 5. Extend this, over time, to numerals 1 to 9, and the count to 20 and back.

Record the children's achievements. It would be helpful to record how confident they are with counting on and back and the number range with which they are currently comfortable.

Child's name	What happened	What to do next time

Beanbag throw

This activity will need some room, so it may be better to work outside or in a larger space.

You will need a hoop and some beanbags.

Put out the hoop. Work with four to six children, and give each child a beanbag.

Ask the children to stand in a line, and to take turns throwing their beanbag, aiming for the inside of the hoop.

As the children work, ask them to say how well they threw the beanbag, using words such as 'far', 'near', 'close'... Say:

- *Whose beanbag was close to the hoop?*
- *Whose was far / further away?*

Record the children's achievements. It would be helpful to record how confident they are with understanding and using the vocabulary of distance.

Child's name	What happened	What to do next time

Name	Date

Days of the week

Work with a group of six to eight children.

Working week

Monday raining,
Stay indoors.
Tuesday foggy,
Do the chores.
Wednesday sunny,
Hang the washing.
Thursday cloudy,
There's the ironing.
Friday thunder,
Bake a cake.
Saturday lightning,
Beds to make.
Sunday, thank goodness!
This is best:
Now I can have –
A day of rest!

Neela Mann

Say the poem 'Working week' to the children and repeat it several times. Encourage the children to join in with you so that they begin to know it too. Ask the children questions about the poem such as:

- *Who makes beds on Saturdays?*
- *Who rests or plays on Sundays?*

To finish the activity, encourage the children to say the poem again, then to say the days of the week, in order.

Counting, reading numbers, adding, solving problems and reasoning

Children count objects and find the numeral for how many there are. Children use coins to help them to solve problems, using the counting on strategy for addition.

LEARNING OBJECTIVES

Topics	Stepping Stones Green	Early Learning Goals & NNS Learning Objectives
Counting	● Count an irregular arrangement of up to 10 objects.	● **Count reliably up to 10 everyday objects** ● **Recognise numerals 1 to 9,** then 0 to 10, then beyond 10.
Reading and writing numbers	● Recognise numerals 1 to 5, the 1 to 9.	● Begin to relate addition to counting on.
Adding and subtracting	● Sometimes show confidence and offer solutions to problems.	● Begin to understand and use the vocabulary related to money. Sort coins, including the £1 and £2 coins, and use them in role play to pay and give change.
Problems involving real-life and money		●Sort and match objects, pictures or children themselves, justifying the decisions made.
Reasoning about numbers or shapes	● Match some shapes by recognising similarities and orientation.	

2 Sessions

Preparation

Basket of toys, such as teddies, dolls, toy cars in a treasure box. Have between one and ten of each type of toy and sufficient for each child to have one. Photocopy CD page 'Labels' onto thin card and cut out.

Learning objectives

Starter
ELGs/NNS
- ● **Recite the number names in order**
- ● **Recognise numerals 1 to 9,** then 0 to 10, then beyond 10.
- ● Begin to know the days of the week in order.

Main teaching activity
Green Stepping Stones
- ● Count an irregular arrangement of up to 10 objects.
- ● Recognise numerals 1 to 5, then 1 to 9.
- ● Match some shapes by recognising similarities and orientation.

ELGs/NNS
- ● **Count reliably up to 10 everyday objects**
- ● **Recognise numerals 1 to 9,** then 0 to 10, then beyond 10.
- ● Sort and match objects, pictures or children themselves, justifying the decisions made.

Vocabulary

count, sort, group, set, match, list

You will need:

Photocopiable pages:
'Days of the week' for the teacher's/LSA's reference, see page 144, and 'Animal sort', one for each pair, see page 151.

CD pages
'Number cards' and 'Labels', photocopied onto A3 for the teacher's/LSA's reference (see General resources).

Equipment
Days of the week chart, as made for Unit 10; basket of toys, treasure box; 'treasures' that can be categorised into shiny, dull, hard, soft, smooth, rough… such as beads, pieces of fabric, shiny and dull papers…; hoops; scissors; glue; paper.

WHOLE CLASS TEACHING

Starter bank
These Starter bank ideas can be used throughout this unit.

Count up, count back
Ask the children to count from zero to 20 and back again. Repeat this several times, keeping the pace sharp. Now ask the children to count from a number that you say to another number, such as: *Count from three to nine; count from two to twelve… count back from eight to two; count back from fifteen to seven…* Repeat this several times.

Show me fingers
Explain that you will hold up a number card and when you say *Show me*, you would like the children to hold up that number of fingers. Begin with numbers from one to five, then extend to nine. Over time, include zero and ten.

Days of the week
Begin by saying together the rhyme 'Days of the week' on CD page 'Days of the week'. Say this several times, encouraging the children to join in. Now, with the days of the week chart beside you, say: *What day is it today?* and invite a child to find the appropriate card and place it on the chart. Repeat this for: *What day will it be tomorrow?* and *What day was it yesterday?* Repeat this each day this week.

Main teaching activity
You will need numeral cards for 1 to 10 for this activity and the basket of toys. Show the children the basket of toys and invite them to each take a toy so that everyone has one. Now explain to the children that you would like their help in sorting the toys. Say: *Who has a teddy? Come and stand by the… Who will count all the children with teddies? How many teddies are there? Which number card has that number on it?* Ask one of the children with a teddy to hold the number card. *Who has a doll? Stand by the…* and so on until all of the toys have been grouped, counted and there is an appropriate number card with the group.

Ask each group to place their toys on a table so that everyone can see them, with the numeral card alongside. Say:

- *How many teddies are there?*
- *How many dolls?*
- *How many…?*
- *Are there more teddies or more dolls? How do you know that?*
- *Are there fewer teddies than dolls? How do you know that?*

Agree with the children that the toys have been sorted into sets that are of the same thing.

GROUP ACTIVITIES

Shiny and dull

TEACHER DIRECTED

Learning objectives

Green Stepping Stones:

- Count an irregular arrangement of up to 10 objects.
- Recognise numerals 1 to 5, then 1 to 9.
- Match shapes by recognising similarities and orientation.

ELGs/NNS:

- **Count reliably up to 10 everyday objects**
- **Recognise numerals 1 to 9,** then 0 to 10, then beyond 10.
- Sort and match objects, pictures or children themselves, justifying the decisions made.

Activity

Work with four to six children. You will need the treasures box, some hoops, the labels and a set of 1 to 10 numeral cards from CD page 'Number cards'. Explain to the children that you would like them to sort the items in the treasures box. Ask the children to each take something from the box and to feel it and look at it. Ask: *Is it shiny? Is it dull? Is it hard… smooth… rough… soft…?* Encourage the children to describe what they have. Read the labels on the hoop then ask each child to place their item into the appropriate labelled hoop. Repeat this for the other items in the treasures box.

When all the objects have been sorted, ask the children to count how many there are in each hoop. Then they can choose the appropriate numeral card to place by the hoop.

For children working towards the Green Stepping Stones, limit the quantity for each category to about five at first. Over time extend this to ten and beyond.

Plenary & assessment

Ask individual children to explain what each hoop contains. Ask questions about how the items have been categorised, such as:

- *What is special about these?*
- *Are these the same as the dull… ones? What is different about them?*
- *How many… are there?*
- *Are there more/fewer… than …?*

Animal sort

ADULT SUPPORTED

Learning objectives
Green Stepping Stones:
- Count an irregular arrangement of up to 10 objects.
- Recognise numerals 1 to 5, then 1 to 9.
- Match some shapes by recognising similarities and orientation.

ELGs/NNS:
- **Count reliably up to 10 everyday objects**
- **Recognise numerals 1 to 9,** then 0 to 10, then beyond 10.
- Sort and match objects, pictures or children themselves, justifying the decisions made.

Activity
Ask four to six children to work with the LSA. Provide each pair with the CD page 'Animal sort'. The LSA asks the children to cut out the cards, and then to sort out the cut-out animals into sets and encourages them to talk about which animals go into which set and why. When they have sorted them, the children can glue the tiles onto a sheet of paper, putting all the animals in one set together. The LSA asks the children to count how many in each set and to place an appropriate numeral card beside that set.

Plenary & assessment
Talk about which animals are in which set and why the children have sorted them in this way. Ask:
- *What is the same about this set of animals?*
- *How many animals are there in this set?*
- *How many animals in that set?*
- *Which set has more/fewer than…?*

3 Sessions

Preparation
Use copies of 'Price labels' photocopied onto thin card to price the items in the class shop between 1p and 5p so that no total of two items can be greater than 10p.

Learning objectives

Main teaching activity
Green Stepping Stones
- Sometimes show confidence and offer solutions to problems.

ELGs/NNS
- Begin to relate addition to counting on.
- Begin to understand and use the vocabulary related to money. Sort coins, including the £1 and £2 coins, and use them in role play to pay and give change.

Vocabulary
zero, one, two, three… to ten and beyond, money, coin, penny, pence, pound, price, cost, buy, sell, spend, spent, pay, change, how much…? how many…? total

You will need:
CD pages
Copies of 'Price labels' photocopied onto card, for the teacher's/LSA's reference (see General resources).

Equipment
Tub of penny coins for each table group; tub of mixed coins and a sorting tray for each pair of children; items from the class shop.

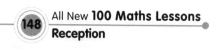

WHOLE CLASS TEACHING

Main teaching activity

Ask the children to sit at tables. Explain that you will ask them some money questions. Tell them that they can use the penny coins in the tub in front of them to help them. Ask questions such as: *Tom buys an orange for 4p and an apple for 3p. How much does he spend altogether?* Say to the children: Tom's orange is 4p. Hold that in your heads. He spends another 3p. Use the coins to help you. Put out 3p. *Now 4p and 5p, 6p, 7p. So Tom spends 7p altogether because 4 add 3 is 7.* Repeat this for other amounts where the total is no more than 10p. Encourage the children to hold one price in their heads each time and count on, using coins to help them, for the second price.

GROUP ACTIVITIES

Shopping

Learning objectives

Green Stepping Stones:

- Sometimes show confidence and offer solutions to problems.

ELGs/NNS:

- Begin to relate addition to counting on.
- Begin to understand and use the vocabulary related to money.
- Sort coins, including the £1 and £2 coins, and use them in role play to pay and give change.

Activity

Ask a group of four children to work with the LSA in the class shop. The LSA begins by acting as shopkeeper, and the children as customers. The LSA invites the children to choose two things to buy, and to work out how much they cost in total. The LSA encourages the children to put one of the prices 'in their heads' and to count on, using pennies for the second price. For example, for 3p and 2p: 3p and 4p, 5p. The LSA asks the children to count out the appropriate number of coins to pay for the items. The children can then take turns to be shopkeeper, whilst the LSA checks that they calculate the price of two items correctly each time.

Plenary & assessment

Choose two items from the class shop and say: *How much are these in total?* Ask: *How did you work that out?* Check that the children count on from one price to the next, either using coins or their fingers to help them. Repeat this for other pairs of items.

Shopping problems

Learning objectives

ELGs/NNS:

- Begin to relate addition to counting on.
- Begin to understand and use the vocabulary related to money.
- Sort coins, including the £1 and £2 coins, and use them in role play to pay and give change.

Activity

Explain to the children that you will ask them some money problems. Provide tubs of mixed coins so that they can use the coins to help them to solve the problem. For example:

- *Tom spent 2p and 5p. How much did he spend altogether?*
- *Shala spent £4 and £2. How much did she spend altogether?*
- *Nancy had a 10p coin. She spent 1p. How much change did she have.*

For each problem, ask the children to explain how they worked it out. In particular, praise those children who used a counting on method to find the answer. Give more problems similar to the ones above, where the total is no more than ten each time.

Plenary & assessment

Ask another problem such as: *Claire buys a chew for 3p and a sherbet for 5p. How much does she spend altogether?* Ask:

- *How did you work it out?*
- *If she had 10p, how much change would she have? How did you work that out?*

Repeat this for other, similar problems, checking that the children are beginning to use counting on methods for addition.

Coin sort

Learning objectives

Green Stepping Stones:

- Sometimes show confidence and offer solutions to problems.

Activity

This is an activity for pairs of children. Provide each pair with some mixed coins and a sorting tray. Ask the children to sort the coins into the sorting tray by how much each is worth.

Plenary & assessment

Ask the children to name each coin and to describe its colour. Ask questions such as:

- *What is this coin called?*
- *What colour is it?*
- *Can you find me some more coins like this?*

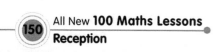

Name   Date

Animal sort

Cut out the cards.
Sort the animals.

LEARNING OBJECTIVES

	Topics	Stepping Stones Green	Early Learning Goals & NNS Learning Objectives
1	Counting	● Show confidence with numbers by initiating or requesting number activities.	● **Say and use the number names in order and in familiar contexts** such as number rhymes, songs, counting games and activities (first to five, then ten, then twenty and beyond).
	Comparing and ordering numbers		● Order a given set of selected numbers: for example, the set 2, 5, 1, 8, 4.
2	Counting	● Count out up to six objects from a larger group.	● Count reliably up to 10 everyday objects (first to 5, then 10, then beyond), giving just one number name to each object.
	Reading and writing numbers	● Recognise some numerals of personal significance. ● Recognise numerals 1 to 5, then 1 to 9.	● **Recognise numerals 1 to 9**, then 0 to 10, then beyond 10. ● Begin to record numbers, initially by making marks, progressing to simple tallying and writing numerals.
	Adding and subtracting		● Begin to relate the addition of doubles to counting on. ● Find a total by counting on when one group of objects is hidden.
3	Exploring pattern, shape and space	● Show awareness of symmetry.	● Talk about, recognise and recreate simple patterns: for example, simple repeating or symmetrical patterns in the environment.
	Reasoning about numbers or shapes	● Order two items by length or height.	● Make simple estimates and predictions: for example, of the number of cubes that will fit in a box or strides across the room.
4	Reading and writing numbers	● Begin to represent numbers using fingers, marks on paper or pictures.	● Begin to record numbers, initially by making marks, progressing to simple tallying and writing numerals.
	Comparing and ordering measures	● Order two items by weight. ● Instruct a programmable toy.	● **Use language such as heavier or lighter to compare two quantities,** then more than two, by making direct comparisons of masses.
5	Counting	● Recognise numerals 1 to 5, then 1 to 9.	● Count in tens. ● **Recognise numerals 1 to 9**, then 0 to 10, then beyond 10.
	Adding and subtracting		● Remove a smaller number from a larger and find how many are left by counting back from the larger number.
	Problems involving 'real life' or money	● Sometimes show confidence and offer solutions to problems.	● Sort coins, including the £1 and £2 coins, and use them in role play to pay and to give change. ● **Use developing mathematical ideas and methods to solve practical problems** involving counting and comparing in a real or role play context.
6	Assess and review		

	Topics	Stepping Stones	Early Learning Goals & NNS Learning Objectives
		Green	
7	Counting	● Show increased confidence with numbers by spotting errors. ● Count an irregular arrangement of up to ten objects.	● Estimate a number in the range that can be counted reliably, then check by counting.
	Reading and writing numbers	● Begin to represent numbers, using fingers, marks on paper or pictures.	● Begin to record numbers, initially by making marks, progressing to simple tallying and writing numerals.
	Comparing and ordering numbers		● Begin to understand and use ordinal numbers in different contexts.
8	Counting	● Show increased confidence with numbers by spotting errors. ● Count an irregular arrangement of up to ten objects.	● Count in twos.
	Adding and subtracting	● Begin to represent numbers, using fingers marks on paper or pictures.	● Select two groups of objects to make a given total. ● Begin to find out how many have been removed from a larger group of objects by counting up from a number.
9	Exploring pattern, shape and space	● Find items from positional/directional clues. ● Describe a simple journey. ● Instruct a programmable toy.	● **Use everyday words to describe position,** direction and movement: for example, follow and give instructions about positions, directions and movements in PE and other activities.
	Reasoning about numbers or shapes.	● Choose suitable components to make a particular model. ● Select a particular named shape.	● Sort and match objects, pictures or children themselves, justifying the decisions made.
10	Reading and writing numbers	● Begin to represent numbers, using fingers, marks on paper or pictures. ● Select the correct numeral to represent 1 to 5, then 1 to 9, objects.	● Begin to record numbers, initially by making marks, progressing to simple tallying and writing numerals.
	Counting		● Estimate a number in the range that can be counted reliably, then check by counting.
	Comparing and ordering measures		● Begin to read o'clock time.
11	Counting		● Count in tens. ● Count in twos.
	Reading and writing numbers	● Begin to represent numbers, using finger, marks on paper or pictures. ● Select the correct numeral to represent 1 to 5, then 1 to 9, objects.	● Begin to record numbers, initially by making marks, progressing to simple tallying and writing numerals.
	Adding and subtracting		● Work out by counting how many more are needed to make a larger number.
	Problems involving real-life and money		● Sort coins, including £1 and £2 and use them in role-play to pay and give change. ● **Use developing mathematical ideas and methods to solve practical problems** involving counting and comparing in a real or role play context.
12	Assess and review		

Counting and ordering numbers

Children count from zero to 20 and back again, keeping the pace sharp. The count is extended to 30, then beyond 30. They order a set of numbers chosen at random from zero to ten.

LEARNING OBJECTIVES

| Topics | Stepping Stones | Early Learning Goals & |
	Green	NNS Learning Objectives
Counting	● Show confidence with numbers by initiating or requesting number activities.	● **Say and use the number names in order and in familiar contexts** such as number rhymes, songs, counting games and activities (first to five, then ten, then twenty and beyond).
Comparing and ordering numbers		● Order a given set of selected numbers, for example, the set 2, 5, 1, 8, 4.

3 Sessions

Learning objectives

Starter
ELGs/NNS
● **Recognise numerals 1 to 9,** then 0 to 10, and then beyond 10.

Main teaching activity
Green Stepping Stones
● Show confidence with numbers by initiating or requesting number activities.
ELGs/NNS
● **Say and use the number names in order and in familiar contexts** such as number rhymes, songs, counting games and activities (first to five, then ten, then twenty and beyond).

Vocabulary

number, zero, one, two, three to twenty and beyond, count

You will need:
Photocopiable pages
'Giant's breakfast' for the teacher's/LSA's reference, see page 159.

CD pages
'Number cards' and 'Number rhymes to 10' for the teacher's/LSA's reference (see General resources).

Equipment
Washing line and pegs; puppet; tape recorder and blank tape.

⌐ WHOLE CLASS TEACHING

Reading numbers
Use the numeral cards for 0 to 10 from CD page 'Number cards'. Explain to the children that you have some numeral cards. You will hold them up and you would like them to show you the number on the card with their fingers. Keep the pace of this sharp. Ask: *What number is this? So how many fingers are you showing me? Count your fingers.*

Find the number

Use the numeral cards for 0 to 10 from CD page 'Number cards'. Explain that you would like the children to help you to peg the number cards for 0 to 10 onto the washing line. Invite the children to come out, one at a time, to take a card. Ask: *Which card will come first? So which one is that?* (from the fan of cards in your hand). Repeat this until all the cards are pegged up. Now say: *Jane, take the card for three…* Repeat this until every card has been removed. Invite the children holding a card to hand their card to another child. Then ask these children, in number order, to peg their cards back onto the line.

Main teaching activity

Begin by counting to 20, from zero, then back again. Encourage the children to count briskly, keeping a good pace. They may like to stand up, in a space, and swing their arms in time with the count. Repeat this two or three times, and check that the children are confident with the count to 20. Say: *Listen to the puppet count.* Count, making errors, such as: *One, two, four, five* (missing three); *Six, seven, nine, eight, ten; Eight, nine, nine, ten.* Encourage the children to put up their hands when they hear a wrong count, and to explain what is wrong and to say the correct sequence. When they are confident with doing this to ten, extend the count by the puppet to 20: *eleven, twelve, thirteen, fourteen, fiveteen, eighteen, nineteen, tenteen.*

Count from zero again, to 30, keeping the pace sharp. With repetition the children will join in. When they are confident with counting to 30, count back to zero. The children will begin to learn the number names and to join in. Over time, use the puppet again, and make more errors: *twenty, twenty-one… twenty-nine, twenty-ten*; decide whether to extend the counting to 40.

GROUP ACTIVITIES

Giant's breakfast

ADULT SUPPORTED

Learning objectives
Green Stepping Stones:
● Show confidence with numbers by initiating or requesting number activities.
ELGs/NNS:
● **Say and use the number names in order and in familiar contexts** such as number rhymes, songs, counting games and activities (first to five, then ten, then twenty and beyond).

Activity

This activity is provided in detail on CD page 'Giant's breakfast' for the LSA's reference and so they can record the children's achievements and difficulties for use during feedback. The LSA needs CD page 'Number rhymes to 10'. CD page 'Giant's breakfast' counts from one to ten. CD page 'Counting' counts from ten back to zero. The LSA says one of the rhymes through, holding up their fingers for each number spoken. The LSA then encourages the children to join in with showing fingers, and to begin to join in with the words. The LSA can repeat the rhyme several times over time until the children become familiar with it and teach the other rhyme in the same way. The LSA can ask: *How many fingers are you holding up? What number comes before/after eight?*

Plenary & assessment

Invite the children to say the rhyme through with you, showing you the appropriate number of fingers for each number word. Ask questions such as: *How many fingers are you holding up? What if you hold up one more/fewer… How many then?*

Counting to 30

TEACHER DIRECTED

Learning objectives
Green Stepping Stones:
● Show confidence with numbers by initiating or requesting number activities.
ELGs/NNS:
● **Say and use the number names in order and in familiar contexts** such as number rhymes, songs, counting games and activities (first to five, then ten, then twenty and beyond).

Activity
Work with a group of eight to ten children. Invite them to count with you, from zero to 30. If they are unsure of counting beyond 20, say the count loudly so that they begin to join in. Now ask them to count around the group, keeping the pace brisk. If they falter, provide the missing number so that the count can continue. When the children are confident with this, count backwards from 30 to zero, again saying loudly the new counting number names.

Plenary & assessment
Explain that you will say some counting numbers. Ask the children to listen carefully. Invite them to correct your mistakes! Say:
● *Eighteen, nineteen, tenteen…*
● *Twenty-eight, twenty-nine, twenty-ten…*
● *Thirty-eight, thirty-nine, thirty-ten…*

Recorded counting

STRUCTURED PLAY

Learning objectives
Green Stepping Stones:
● Show confidence with numbers by initiating or requesting number activities.
ELGs/NNS:
● **Say and use the number names in order and in familiar contexts** such as number rhymes, songs, counting games and activities (first to five, then ten, then twenty and beyond).

Activity
Ask the children to work in groups of four. Show them how to record and play back using the tape recorder. They record their counting, from one to 20 or beyond, repeating this several times.

Plenary & assessment
Invite the children to listen to their counting. Ask: *Did you say all the numbers from one to 20?* Count again together from one to at least 20, keeping a good pace and rhythm to the count.

2 Sessions

Learning objectives

Main teaching activity
ELGs/NNS
- Order a given set of selected numbers: for example, the set 2, 5, 1, 8, 4.

Vocabulary

order, first, last, before, after, next, between

You will need:
Photocopiable pages
'Ordered numbers' for the teacher's/
LSA's reference, see page 160.

CD pages
'Number cards', for the teacher's/LSA's
reference and a set of 0 to 10 number
cards from '0 to 20 number cards' for
each pair (see General resources).

Equipment
Washing line and pegs; set of 1 to f
numeral cards for each pair.

WHOLE CLASS TEACHING

Main teaching activity

Choose three cards from the set of 0 to 10 numeral cards from '0 to 20 number cards'. Peg these,
out of order, to the washing line. Say: *Which numbers are these? Who will read them for me? Are they
in order? Which number comes first/next/between/last?* Repeat this for other sets of three, then four,
then five cards.

Choose six cards out of sequence and peg these to the washing line, such as: 6, 4, 10, 8, 3, 1. Ask
the children to put the numbers in order as before. 1, 3, 4, 6, 8, 10. Ask: *Which numbers are missing?
Where do they fit?* Encourage children to use the vocabulary of ordering numbers, such as: *The 2 fits
between the 1 and 3; the 5 is after 4....* Repeat this for other sets of random numbers.

GROUP ACTIVITIES

Ordered numbers

Learning objective
ELGs/NNS:
- Order a given set of selected numbers, for example, the set 2, 5, 1, 8, 4.

Activity

This activity is provided in detail on CD page 'Ordered numbers' for the LSA's reference and so they
can record the children's achievements and difficulties for use during feedback. Ask the LSA to work
with a group of four to ten children, in pairs. They shuffle a set of 1 to 10 numeral cards. One child
takes the top five cards and places them in a line as they come from the pack. The children take
turns to move one card at a time until the five cards are ordered. When the children are satisfied
that their cards are in order, they replace the five cards, shuffle the pack, and the other child takes
the top five cards.

If children find this activity difficult, the LSA can suggest that they begin with three cards.
The LSA can challenge the more able by asking them to take six cards at a time.

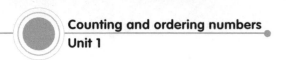
Plenary & assessment

Deal five cards, out of order, and invite the children to take turns to take a card and place it in the correct order. When the children are satisfied that the cards are in order, ask:

- *Which numbers are missing?*
- *Where does 3 fit?*
- *What comes between 5 and 7?*
- *What number is first/last?*

    This can be repeated for another five or six cards.

Card order

STRUCTURED PLAY

Learning objective

ELGs/NNS:

- Order a given set of selected numbers, for example, the set 2, 5, 1, 8, 4.

Activity

Ask the children to work in pairs. They shuffle the sets of 1 to 5 numeral cards and place these in a stack, face down. The children take turns to take a card and place it in front of both of them. The idea is to make a line of cards, in order, from 1 to 5.

Plenary & assessment

Repeat the activity. Ask for each card:

- *Where shall we put this card?*
- *What will come before/after it?*

Giant's breakfast

You will need:

- 'Number rhymes to 10' and 'Counting' CD pages.

Work with eight to ten children.

Explain to the children that you will teach them a new number rhyme, 'Giant's breakfast', about a giant who counts from one to ten. The children can show how many for each number that they say by holding up their fingers.

Say 'Giant's breakfast' and hold up your fingers for each number spoken. Encourage the children to join in with showing fingers and, with repetition of the words, to begin to join in with the words.

Repeat the rhyme several times over time until the children become familiar with the words. Ask:

- *How many fingers are you holding up?*
- *What number comes before... after...?*

The second rhyme, 'Counting', goes from ten back to zero. Teach this in the same way as 'Giant's breakfast'.

Record the children's achievements. It would be helpful to record whether or not children hold up the correct quantity of fingers for the number said.

Child's name	What happened	What to do next time

Ordered numbers

You will need:

- a set of 0 to 10 numeral cards for each pair from CD page 'Number cards'.

Work with a group of four to ten children.

Ask the pairs of children to shuffle a set of 1 to 10 numeral cards. One child takes the top five cards and places them in a line as they come from the pack.

The children take turns to move one card at a time until the five cards are ordered. When the children are satisfied that their cards are in order, they replace the five cards, shuffle the pack, and the other child takes the top five cards.

If children find this activity difficult, suggest that they begin with three cards. Challenge the more able by asking them to take six cards at a time.

Ask questions such as:

- *What number goes between 7 and 9?*
- *Which number comes first/last?*

Record the children's achievements. It would be helpful to record whether children can order the numerals 0 to 10, or any difficulties they have.

Child's name	What happened	What to do next time

Counting, reading and writing numbers, and adding

Children count out a given quantity of objects. This is checked by another child who counts that set, beginning with a different object. They begin to record numbers. They begin to add using doubles and to count on when a group is hidden. They say the addition sentence.

LEARNING OBJECTIVES

Topics	Stepping Stones	Early Learning Goals & NNS Learning Objectives
	Green	
Counting	● Count out up to six objects from a larger group.	● Count reliably up to 10 everyday objects (first to 5, then 10, then beyond), giving just one number name to each object.
Reading and writing numbers	● Recognise some numerals of personal significance. ● Recognise numerals 1 to 5, then 1 to 9.	**● Recognise numerals 1 to 9,** then 0 to 10, then beyond 10. ● Begin to record numbers, initially by making marks, progressing to simple tallying and writing numerals.
Adding and subtracting		● Begin to relate the addition of doubles to counting on. ● Find a total by counting on when one group of objects is hidden.

1 Session

Learning objectives

Starter
ELGs/NNS
● **Say and use the number names in order and in familiar contexts** such as number rhymes, songs, counting games and activities (first to five, then ten, then twenty and beyond).
● Order a given set of selected numbers: for example, the set 2, 5, 1, 8, 4.

Main teaching activity
Green Stepping Stones
● Count out up to six objects from a larger group.
ELGs/NNS
● Count reliably up to 10 everyday objects (first to 5, then 10, then beyond), giving just one number name to each object.

Vocabulary

number, zero, one, two, three… to ten and beyond, count

You will need:
CD pages
'Number rhymes to 10', 'Number cards' and 'Counting' for the teacher's/LSA's reference; and a set of 0 to 10 number cards from '0 to 20 number cards' for each pair, see General resources).

Equipment
Basket of about ten items from the room, suitable for counting out; for each pair a tub of small counting toys or tiles.

WHOLE CLASS TEACHING

Starter bank
These Starter bank ideas can be used throughout the unit.

Counting to and from ten
Use CD page 'Number rhymes to 10'. Invite the children to join in with you as you say the words of 'Giant's breakfast'. Ask them to show the appropriate number of fingers for each number as they say it in the rhyme. Then say the rhyme on CD page 'Counting'. Ask questions such as: *How many fingers are you showing? What number did we say?*

Count up, count down
Ask the children to count with you, from zero to 20 and back again. Keep the pace of this sharp. Then ask the children to count around the circle; the first child says 'zero', the second 'one', and so on, up to 20, then back again. Say the number if a child falters in order to keep the pace brisk. Repeat this several times, starting with a different child each time. When the children are confident count to 30, and beyond and, if appropriate, back again.

Order these
Use the 0 to 10 number cards from CD page 'Number cards'. Invite four children to stand at the front, each child holding a card chosen at random. Ask the other children to read the card numbers, starting with the one on their left. Say: *Are these in number order?* Invite individual children to reorder the children with the cards until the numbers are ordered. Say: *What comes first/last/ between?* Repeat until you can increase the quantity of cards to four, five, then six.

Main teaching activity
Show the children the basket of things from the room. Invite a child to count out a given number of things for the others to see. Say: *Josef, count out six things.* Invite another child to check by counting again, but starting with a different toy. Repeat this for other amounts, from about four to up to ten or more.

GROUP ACTIVITIES

Count them out

Learning objectives
Green Stepping Stones:
- Count out up to six objects from a larger group.

ELGs/NNS:
- Count reliably up to 10 everyday objects (first to 5, then 10, then beyond), giving just one number name to each object.

Activity
Ask the children to work in pairs, with a set of 0 to 10 numeral cards from '0 to 20 number cards'. They shuffle the cards and turn these face down in a stack. Then they take turns to turn over a card whilst their partner counts out that quantity of counting toys. The other child counts the toys again to check, starting with a different toy. For children working towards the Green Stepping Stones, limit the card range to up to 6. Challenge more able children by using cards from zero to 20.

Plenary & assessment
Invite a child to choose a number card from 4 to about 10. Invite another child to count out that quantity of toys. Ask: *How many are there? How can we check?* Encourage the children to count by starting with a different toy, still counting them all. Repeat this for other quantities to be sure that the children count accurately.

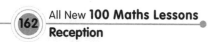

2 Sessions

Learning objectives

Main teaching activity

Green Stepping Stones
- Recognise some numerals of personal significance.
- Recognise numerals 1 to 5, then 1 to 9.

ELGs/NNS
- **Recognise numerals 1 to 9**, then 0 to 10, then beyond 10.
- Begin to record numbers, initially by making marks, progressing to simple tallying and writing numerals.

Vocabulary

number, zero, one, two, three… to ten and beyond, count

You will need:

Photocopiable pages
'Writing numbers', one for each child, see page 166.

CD pages
A set of 0 to 10 number cards from '0 to 20 number cards' for each pair (see General resources).

Equipment
A basket of up to ten toys for counting; dry sand tray and about ten small toys that can be buried in the sand; flip chart or board and pens.

WHOLE CLASS TEACHING

Main teaching activity

Explain that you would like the children to draw some numbers in the air. Turn so that your back is towards the children (or, if you can, draw the numeral in the air so that it is reversed for you but the correct way round for the children). Begin by drawing '1', then '2'. Describe the movement, always starting at the top of the number. Encourage the children to make large strokes with their whole arm in the air in order to 'feel' the shape of the number. Ask: *Is one a round number or a straight number? What about zero?* Repeat this for 3, 4 and 5.

Now say: *I shall draw a number in the air. Tell me what I have drawn.* Begin with 0 to 5, out of order, then, over time, extend this to up to 10. Each time, give the children the opportunity to draw it in the air for themselves.

Show the children the basket of toys. Invite a child to count out three of these. Invite all the children to draw '3' in the air. On the flip chart, record by using three tallies and ask a child to come out to count these. Alongside the tallies write '3'. Repeat this for other quantities of toys, from zero to five, then, over time, extended to up to ten.

GROUP ACTIVITIES

Buried treasure

Learning objectives

Green Stepping Stones:
- Recognise some numerals of personal significance.
- Recognise numerals 1 to 5, then 1 to 9.

ELGs/NNS:
- **Recognise numerals 1 to 9**, then 0 to 10, then beyond 10.
- Begin to record numbers, initially by making marks, progressing to simple tallying and writing numerals.

Activity

This is an activity for two children. Ask children to work in pairs. Each pair will need some paper, a pencil or crayon, a set of 0 to 5 numeral cards, and some small toys. Ask the children to take turns to bury some toys in the sand without their partner peeping. The child finds the numeral card for the number of toys buried, then either writes tally marks for that number or writes the numeral. The other children read the numeral card, count the tallies or read the written numeral, then find the buried treasure.

Plenary & assessment

Review the children's recording with them. Say: *How many did you bury? How many marks did you make on paper? Which number did you write?* Then encourage the children to draw the numbers that you say, from 0 to 5, in the air. Check that they draw these with reasonable accuracy.

Writing numbers

ADULT SUPPORTED

Learning objectives

ELGs/NNS:

- **Recognise numerals 1 to 9**, then 0 to 10, then beyond 10.
- Begin to record numbers, initially by making marks, progressing to simple tallying and writing numerals.

Activity

This is an activity for four to eight children. Provide each child with CD page 'Writing numbers'. Ask them to trace, with a finger at first, then with a pencil, the numerals at the top of the sheet. Then there is space for them to practise writing their own numerals, followed by counting how many, and writing the total as a numeral. Check that the children form the numerals correctly, starting at the top of the numeral.

Plenary & assessment

Review the children's written recording and check that this is reasonably accurate. Ask the children, this time without you drawing in the air, to draw in the air the numbers you say. Check that the children draw these the correct way round, and are forming them, starting at the top.

2 Sessions

Preparation

Enlarge 'Rabbit chase' to A3. This can be coloured in, then laminated so that it lasts, if required.
Photocopy 'Sheep' onto thin card. Cut out the sheep and fold along the dotted line so that the sheep will stand up.

Learning objectives

ELGs/NNS
- Begin to relate the addition of doubles to counting on.
- Find a total by counting on when one group of objects is hidden.

Vocabulary

add, more, and, make, sum, total, altogether, double

You will need:

Photocopiable pages
'Rabbit chase' for each pair or group of three and one copy enlarged to A3, see page 167.

CD pages
'Sheep' copied onto thin card, for the teacher's/LSA's reference (see General resources).

Equipment
Large 1–6 numeral teaching dice; box with a lid; ten small counting toys; 1, 1, 2, 2, 3, 3 numeral dice; counters in various colours.

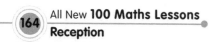

WHOLE CLASS TEACHING

Main teaching activity

Ask the children to play a dice game with you. Using a large teaching dice with numerals on it, begin by putting the dice down so that 2 is uppermost. Explain to the children that you would like them to work out what double two is, or 2 + 2' Say: *Put two in your heads. Now count on two: so two and three, four. So 2 + 2 is 4.* The children may find it helpful to count on, using their fingers to keep count. Repeat this for other doubles, at first using smaller ones, then up to five and six.

Now show the children some counting toys. Say: *I shall put three counting toys into this box. One, two, three* (dropping the toys into the box). *How many are in the box? There are three. Now here are some more* (showing the children two more). *Let's count them. There are three and four, five. So 3 + 2 is 5.* Repeat this for other small quantities, where one of them is known, but hidden from view.

GROUP ACTIVITIES

Rabbit chase

Learning objective
ELGs/NNS:
- Begin to relate the addition of doubles to counting on.

Activity

Ask a group of two or three children to work with the LSA. The children will need the enlarged version of CD page 'Rabbit chase', a 1, 1 2, 2, 3, 3 dice, and a counter each. The LSA explains to them that the idea of the game is to roll the dice, double their dice score and move their counter that number of moves. Whoever gets to the end first, wins the game. Whatever they roll on the dice they double by putting the number in their head then counting on. The LSA reminds them that they can use their fingers to help them to keep count if they like, and asks the children to say the addition sentence each time. For example: *3 + 3 = 6.*

Plenary & assessment

Play the game again. Ask the children to explain how they worked out their score each time. Ask them to say the addition sentence. When the game has been won, ask questions such as: *What is double two? How did you work that out?*

Sheep

Learning objective
ELGs/NNS:
- Find a total by counting on when one group of objects is hidden.

Activity

Work with a group of four to six children working in pairs. Each pair will need a copy of CD page 'Sheep' and ten small toys. Begin working as a group. Tell the children that you will hide five counting tiles under the sheep. Now say: *Here are three more tiles. How many are there altogether?* Encourage the children to count on from five: *Five, six, seven, eight. So 5 + 3 is 8.* When the children understand the activity and are confident with it, ask them to work in pairs, taking turns to hide and count out more counting tiles for the other one to total.

Plenary & assessment

Repeat the activity again with the whole group. Ask questions such as:
- *How many are hidden under the sheep? How many are there here? So how many is that altogether?*
- *How did you work that out?*

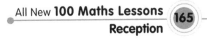

Name	Date

Writing numbers

Trace these numbers with your finger.
Now trace them with a pencil.

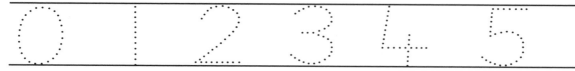

Write these numbers.
Write how many.

◼ S C H O L A S T I C

photocopiable

Name	Date

Rabbit chase

Work with a partner or in a three.
You will each need a counter.
You will need a 1, 1, 2, 2, 3, 3 dice.

Put your counters on 'Start'.

Take turns to roll the dice.

Double the score in your head.

Move your counter that number.

The winner is the one who gets to 'Finish' first.

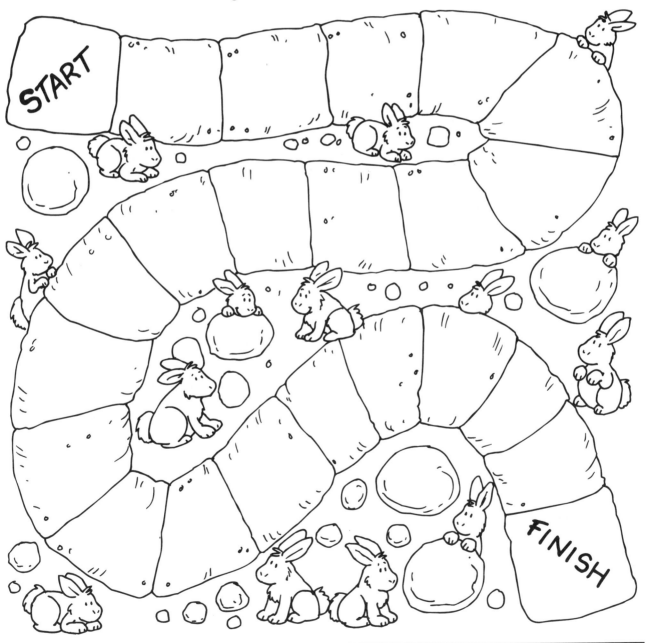

Patterns and reasoning

Children make simple symmetrical models and patterns. They make simple predictions in practical activities such as estimating how far away something is, or saying what they think is left in a bag when part of a set of numeral cards has been removed.

LEARNING OBJECTIVES

Topics	Stepping Stones	Early Learning Goals & NNS Learning Objectives
	Green	
Exploring pattern, shape and space	● Show awareness of symmetry.	● Talk about, recognise and recreate simple patterns: for example, simple repeating or symmetrical patterns in the environment.
Reasoning about numbers or shapes	● Order two items by length or height	● Make simple estimates and predictions: for example, of the number of cubes that will fit in a box or strides across the room.

2 Sessions

Learning objectives

Starter
ELGs/NNS
● **Recognise numerals 1 to 9,** then 0 to 10, then beyond 10.
● Begin to record numbers, initially by making marks, progressing to simple tallying and writing numerals.

Main teaching activity
Green Stepping Stones
● Show awareness of symmetry.
ELGs/NNS
● **Talk about, recognise and recreate simple patterns**: for example, simple repeating or symmetrical patterns in the environment.

Vocabulary

size, bigger, larger, smaller, symmetrical, pattern, repeating pattern, match

You will need:
Photocopiable pages
'Symmetrical patterns', one for each child, see page 173.

CD pages
'Number cards' for the teacher's/LSA's reference (see General resources).

Equipment
Flip chart and pen; individual white boards and pens; construction kits; building blocks including cube, cuboid, triangular prism, sphere, cone, pyramid; large safety mirror; small safety mirrors; red, blue, green and yellow crayons; 2-D shape tiles of squares, triangles, circles, rectangles in red, blue, green and yellow.

⌐ WHOLE CLASS TEACHING

Starter bank
These Starter bank ideas can be used throughout the unit.

Reading numbers
Use number cards for 0 to 10 from 'Number cards'. Explain to the children that you will hold up a card. Ask them to hold up fingers to show you how many for that number. Begin with smaller

amounts, from one to five, then extend to ten, including zero. Ask individual children to say the number on the card that you hold up.

Writing in the air

Explain to the children that you will hold up a number card. Ask them to look carefully at the number on the card, then write it with their whole arm in the air. This will make a large shape. Check that children are beginning at the top of the number and are making the shape in the 'writing direction'. If children are unsure, demonstrate by drawing a large numeral on the flip chart. Begin with numerals 0 to 5. Over time extend this to include numerals to 10.

Writing numerals

Provide each child with a white board and pen. Explain that you will say a number. Ask them to draw this on their board, and, when you say *Show me,* they hold up their board for you to see. Begin with numerals 0 to 5. Over time, extend this to include numerals to 10. If children have difficulty with writing, such as reversing the numeral or writing it beginning at the bottom of the numeral, use the flip chart to demonstrate this. It can help children who find this difficult to stand by you and help you to hold the pen. Then they can feel the direction of writing as you write on the flip chart.

Main teaching activity

Have beside you the building blocks. Ask the children to watch whilst you make a pattern with the blocks. Say: *What sort of pattern have I made?* Invite the children to explain the pattern. Say: *This pattern is symmetrical. That means that if we look at the first part of it in the mirror we will see the second part of it.* Invite children to come out and to look at the pattern in the mirror and then to look at the whole of the pattern.

Repeat this with other 3-D shapes so that the children have the opportunity to use the word 'symmetrical' in their descriptions.

GROUP ACTIVITIES

Making symmetrical structures

Learning objectives
Green Stepping Stones:
● Show awareness of symmetry.
ELGs/NNS:
● **Talk about, recognise and recreate simple patterns:** for example, simple repeating or symmetrical patterns in the environment.

Activity
The children can work in pairs, trios or fours, with building blocks or construction kits and a safety mirror. Ask them to make a symmetrical model. If they need further help, suggest that to begin with they make simple shapes, then use the mirror to help them to make the overall pattern symmetrical. Suggest that when the children have made a model which they think is symmetrical and of which they are proud, that they keep this one to one side for the Plenary.

Plenary & assessment
Look as a group at the models that the children have made. Use the large safety mirror and invite individual children to suggest where the mirror should be placed so that they can see the symmetrical model in the mirror as well as in 'real life'. Ask:
● *Why do you think this model is symmetrical? Where should we put the mirror?*
If any of the models are not symmetrical, the children will see this when the mirror is used. Invite the children to suggest how they could change the model in order to make it symmetrical. Help them to do this whilst the others watch, then check again using the mirror.

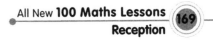

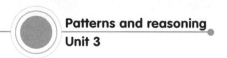

Symmetrical patterns

ADULT SUPPORTED

Learning objectives

Green Stepping Stones:
- Show awareness of symmetry.

ELGs/NNS:
- **Talk about, recognise and recreate simple patterns**: for example, simple repeating or symmetrical patterns in the environment.

Activity

Ask a group of four to six children to work with the LSA. Provide each child with a copy of CD page 'Symmetrical patterns'. The LSA asks the children to look at the first picture and to make it with the shape tiles. The children can decide which colours they will use. The LSA asks them then to make sure that their pattern is symmetrical by using a mirror to check. They will need to check for colour as well as shape. The LSA can ask questions such as: *How do you know that your pattern is symmetrical? Where will you put the mirror? Are the colours of this shape the same as there?* When they are satisfied that their pattern is symmetrical, the LSA can ask them to colour in what they have done on the sheet, and to check that they use the same colours as their shape tiles.

Plenary & assessment

Invite the children to show their coloured-in sheets. Use a mirror to demonstrate the symmetry of the pattern. Ask questions such as:
- *Where shall I put the mirror?*
- *Is this pattern symmetrical? How do you know?*

Main teaching activity

Show the children the covered tray. Explain that you have made a pattern, which is under the cloth.

4 Sessions

Preparation

On a tray place some counting toys in a pattern, such as car, car, aeroplane, car, car, aeroplane, car, aeroplane, car, car, aeroplane… making a deliberate error in the pattern repeats. Cover this with a cloth. Have some spare counting toys handy.

Learning objectives

Main teaching activity

Green Stepping Stones:
- Order two items by length or height.

ELGs/NNS
- Make simple estimates and predictions: for example, of the number of cubes that will fit in a box or strides across the room.

Vocabulary

pattern, puzzle, answer, right, wrong, what could we try next? how did you work it out? count, sort, group, set, match, list

You will need:

Photocopiable pages
'Strides', for the teacher's/LSA's reference, see page 174.

CD pages
A set of number cards from '0 to 20 number cards' for each pair (see General resources).

Equipment
Counting toys; one set of wooden or plastic numerals for 0 to 9, in an opaque bag; containers such as toy saucepans, cups, small boxes; interlocking cubes; flip chart and pens.

WHOLE CLASS TEACHING

Remove the cloth and ask the children to look at it. Say: *What is my pattern?* If the children do not spot that there is an error, ask: *Is the pattern right? What is wrong with it?* Invite a child to put the pattern right and to explain what is wrong. Repeat this for another pattern if the children need further experience of this.

Now show the children the opaque bag. Tell them that you have put one each of the numbers 0 to 9 into the bag. Invite ten children to come to the front. Ask the children to take turns to take out a number and to show it to the others until there are just three numbers left. Now say: *What do you think is left in the bag? Why do you think that?* If the children find it difficult to predict what is left, ask the children holding numbers to line up in number order, then ask the others to say what is missing. When the children are clear about what numbers are left, say to the three children who still have to take a number, just before they put their hand into the bag: *What number do you think you will take?* Talk about the choices they had and whether or not they could find by touch the number they said.

GROUP ACTIVITIES

Hidden numbers

TEACHER DIRECTED

Learning objective
ELGs/NNS:
● Make simple estimates and predictions: for example, of the number of cubes that will fit in a box or strides across the room.

Activity
Use the opaque bag and the 0 to 9 plastic or wooden numbers and work with a group of six to eight children. Spread the numbers out on the table and ask the children to check that all the numbers are there. They can put them in number order if they wish. Then say: *I am going to hide one of the numbers in this bag. Shut your eyes until I say open them.* Now mix up the numbers again, take one of them, place it in the bag and then ask the children to open their eyes. Ask: *Which number do you think is in the bag? Why do you think that?* The children can sort the numbers again, placing them in number order if they are not sure. Repeat the activity several times. The same activity can be repeated using transport tiles, farm animals and so on.

Plenary & assessment
Repeat the activity. Ask:
● *Which number do you think is in the bag?*
● *Why do you think that?*
● *How can we work it out without looking in the bag?*

Strides

ADULT SUPPORTED

Learning objectives
Green Stepping Stones:
● Order two items by length or height.
ELGs/NNS:
● Make simple estimates and predictions: for example, of the number of cubes that will fit in a box or strides across the room.

Activity

This activity is described in detail on CD page 'Strides' for the LSA's reference and so they can record the children's achievements and difficulties for use during feedback.

Ask a group of four to six children to work with the LSA and in a space where the children can take strides across the room. The LSA asks: *How many strides do you think you will need to take to get across the room? Why do you think it will be that many?* On the flip chart, the LSA records what each child said as an estimate. When the children have made their estimate, the LSA asks them to take turns, one at a time, whilst the others count, to take their strides across the room. The LSA records the number of strides they take on the flip chart and asks: *Did you make a good guess?* Repeat this for strides along the other length or width of the room.

Record the children's achievements. It would be helpful to record who made a reasonable estimate, and whether a child improves their estimate based on what they learned from the previous estimate/check.

Plenary & assessment

Take the children into another room or corridor, which has different dimensions from the classroom. Ask them to estimate how many strides they will take across the room, record this on the flip chart, then ask them to find out how many they take. Ask questions such as:

- *Why do you think you will take… strides?*
- *Did you make a good guess?*

Children will take different quantities of strides. For the more able children discuss why this is. Ask:

- *Why do you think that is? So, if you have longer/shorter legs than Jamie, will you take more or fewer strides?*

Packing cubes

STRUCTURED PLAY

Learning objective

ELGs/NNS:

- Make simple estimates and predictions: for example, of the number of cubes that will fit in a box, or the number of strides it takes to cross the room.

Activity

This is an activity for pairs of children. They will need containers and interlocking cubes. Ask them to decide how many cubes will fit into one of the containers, then to see how many they can pack in. Children can record their estimate and check using the number cards from CD page '0 to 20 number cards'. They repeat this for other containers.

Plenary & assessment

Invite the children to explain how they made their estimates and then compare these with their checks. Ask:

- *How many did you guess would fit?*
- *How many fitted?*
- *Did you make a good guess?*

Name	Date

Symmetrical patterns

Use shape tiles to copy these patterns.

Make the pattern symmetrical. Make sure the colours of the tiles are symmetrical too.

Colour in your pattern on the sheet.

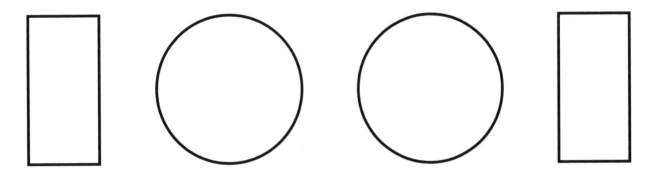

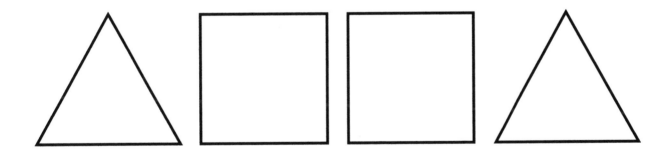

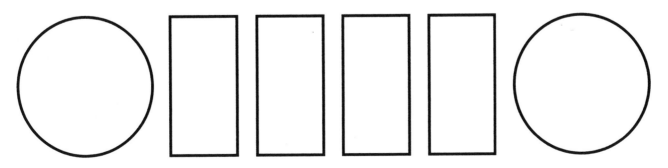

Strides

You will need:

- a flip chart and pen.

Work with a group of four to six children and in a space so that the children can take strides across the room.

Ask: *How many strides do you think you will need to take to get across the room? Why do you think it will be that many?* On the flip chart record what each child said as an estimate.

When the children have made their estimate ask them to take turns, one at a time, whilst the others count, to take their strides across the room.

Record the number of strides they take on the flip chart. Ask: *Did you make a good guess?* Repeat this for strides along the other length or width of the room.

Record the children's achievements. It would be helpful to record who makes a reasonable estimate, and whether a child improves their estimate based on what they learnt from their previous estimate and check.

Child's name	What happened	What to do next time

Writing numbers and comparing weights

Children practise writing the numbers 0 to 9 in practical situations. They estimate which is heavier and which is lighter of two parcels, then make a direct comparison using a bucket balance. This is extended to ordering by weight three parcels.

LEARNING OBJECTIVES

Topics	Stepping Stones	Early Learning Goals & NNS Learning Objectives
	Green	
Counting	● Begin to represent numbers, using fingers, marks on paper or pictures.	● Begin to record numbers, initially by making marks, progressing to simple tallying and writing numerals.
Measures, shape and space	● Order two items by weight.	● **Use language such as more or less, longer or shorter, heavier or lighter to compare two quantities,** then more than two, by making direct comparisons of masses.

3 Sessions

Learning objectives

Starter
ELGs/NNS
● **Say and use number names in order and in familiar contexts,** such as number rhymes, songs, counting games and activities (first to five, then ten, then twenty and beyond).
● Order a given set of selected numbers, for example, the set 2, 5, 1, 8, 4.

Main teaching activity
Green Stepping Stones
● Begin to represent numbers, using fingers, marks on paper or pictures.
ELGs/NNS
● Begin to record numbers, initially by making marks, progressing to simple tallying and writing numerals.

Vocabulary
zero, one, two, three… eight, nine.

You will need:
Photocopiable pages
A copy of 'Count and write' for each child and 'Counting numbers', see pages 179–181.

CD pages
'Number rhymes to 10' and 'Duck counting cards' for the teacher's/LSA's reference (see General resources).

Equipment
Flip chart or board and pen; Plasticine, modelling tools and boards.

WHOLE CLASS TEACHING

Starter bank
These starter ideas can be used throughout the unit.

Number rhymes to 10
Use the rhymes on CD page 'Number rhymes to 10'. Recite 'Giant's breakfast' together. Ask the children to hold up their fingers to show how many each time a number word is spoken. Ask: *How many did we say? How many fingers are you holding up?* Repeat this for the second rhyme, 'Counting'.

Round and round

Explain that you would like the children to sit in a circle. Ask a child to begin counting at zero, the next child one, and so on, to at least 30. Then ask the next child to begin counting back. If a child falters in the count, say the number name in order to keep the pace of the counting brisk. Repeat this several times, starting each time with a different child.

Who will say?

Ask the children to sit in a circle so that they can all see each other. Agree which way the counting will move around the circle. Ask questions such as:

- *If Jamie says four, who will say six?*
- *If Jasmine begins the count with zero, who will say eight?*
- *Let's count back. If Josh begins on 10, who will say seven?*

Main teaching activity

At all times during this activity check that children are making numbers starting from the top, and continuing in the writing direction. Gently correct any errors. This can be done by holding the child's hand and 'writing' in the air together. Use shuffled zero to nine cards from CD page 'Duck counting cards'. Explain to the children that you will hold up a card and would like them to count how many are on the card. Now ask the children to draw the number in the air, using large arm movements. Invite a child to write the number onto the flip chart. Repeat this until all the numbers from zero to nine have been written.

Now ask the children to take turns to come to the flip chart and to write the numbers, in order, starting with zero. Ask another child to find the appropriate duck counting card for each number. Finish by asking the children to sit in pairs. Ask them to take turns to 'write' a number that you say on their partner's back.

GROUP ACTIVITIES

Plasticine numbers

STRUCTURED PLAY

Learning objectives
Green Stepping Stones:
- Begin to represent numbers, using fingers, marks on paper or pictures.

ELGs/NNS:
- Begin to record numbers, initially by making marks, progressing to simple tallying and writing numerals.

Activity

This is an activity for a group of four to eight children, working independently. They will each need some Plasticine, a board, and some modelling tools. Ask the children to make Plasticine numbers. They can make all of them, from zero to nine, putting each finished one onto their board.

Plenary & assessment

Ask the children to point to each of their numbers and to say its name. Invite them to show you, by drawing in the air, how they made each number. Ask:

- *Which number is this… and this?*
- *How do you know that this is a three and not a five… two… eight…?*

Count and write

ADULT SUPPORTED

Learning objectives
Green Stepping Stones:
- Begin to represent numbers, using fingers, marks on paper or pictures.

ELGs/NNS:
- Begin to record numbers, initially by making marks, progressing to simple tallying and writing numerals.

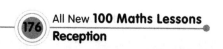

Activity

Ask a group of four to eight children to work with the LSA. Provide each child with a copy of CD page 'Count and write' and a pencil. The LSA asks: *How many are there?* for the first picture and asks the children to count and write the number. Repeat this for the other pictures on the sheet.

Plenary & assessment

Invite the children to read the numbers that they have written for you. Ask a child to come to the flip chart and to write the number that you say. Repeat, until everyone has had a turn. Check that the children write the numbers correctly, and gently correct any errors by holding the child's hand and writing it together. Ask questions such as: *Who can write the number for one more/less than six?*

Writing numbers

TEACHER DIRECTED

Learning objectives

Green Stepping Stones:
- Begin to represent numbers, using fingers, marks on paper or pictures.

ELGs/NNS:
- Begin to record numbers, initially by making marks, progressing to simple tallying and writing numerals.

Activity

This activity is intended for children who need further practice in writing numbers. Work with two to four children, giving them either CD page 'Counting numbers' (0 to 5) or (6 to 10). Ask the children to read the numbers, then to trace them with their finger. Check that they trace from the top and in the writing direction. If a child is unsure, hold their hand and trace together until they are sure. Then ask the children to trace over the numbers with their pencil, and then to write the numbers in the space provided.

Plenary & assessment

Work individually with children who have needed extra practice. Invite them to trace the numbers that you say with their fingers. Check that they read and trace correctly, beginning at the top.

2 Sessions

Preparation

Put 12 items for balancing and weighing onto the tray. Make sure that they are clearly different in weight, and that this can be felt by holding them in the hands.

Learning objectives

Main teaching activity

Green Stepping Stones
- Order two items by weight.

ELGs/NNS
- **Use language such as heavier or lighter to compare two quantities,** then more than two, by making direct comparisons of masses.

Vocabulary

weigh, weighs, balances, heavy/light, heavier/lighter, heaviest/lightest, weight, balance, scales

You will need:

CD pages
'Measures record' for the teacher's/LSA's reference (see General resources).

Equipment
Items for balancing and weighing from the classroom such as small toys; tray; bucket balances.

WHOLE CLASS TEACHING

Main teaching activity

Ask the children to sit in a circle. Choose two toys of different weights, such as a toy car and a play people doll, and pass these around the circle. Ask the children to hold one, then the other, and decide which is heavier and which is lighter. Ask them not to say anything to each other as they do this, but to keep their thoughts a secret until all have had a turn. Ask: *Which do you think is heavier? Which do you think is lighter?* Ask the children to suggest how you could check using a balance. Ask one of the children to place the toys, one in each balance pan. Say: *Did you make a good guess? So which is heavier/lighter?*

Repeat this, this time, passing around three things for the children to estimate the heaviest and lightest. Ask: *How can we check?* If necessary, explain that two items can be compared, then another two, until the heaviest and lightest become clear.

GROUP ACTIVITIES

Heavier and lighter

Learning objectives
Green Stepping Stones:
● Order two items by weight.
ELGs/NNS:
● **Use language such as heavier or lighter to compare two quantities,** then more than two, by making direct comparisons of masses.

Activity
Put 12 items for weighing on a tray and have ready some bucket balances. Ask four to six children, in pairs, to work with the LSA. The LSA asks each pair to choose two items from the tray. They then decide, by holding them in their hands, which item is heavier and which is lighter, then check by using the balance. The LSA asks: *Which do you think is lighter/heavier? Did you make a good guess?* The children can repeat this for several different comparisons.

Plenary & assessment
Choose two more items, and pass these around among the children. Ask: *Which do you think is heavier/lighter? Why?* Invite one of the children to check using the balance. Ask: *So which is heavier/ lighter? Did you make a good guess?* Record confidence on CD page 'Measures record' sheet.

Heaviest and lightest

Learning objectives
ELGs/NNS:
● **Use language such as heavier or lighter to compare two quantities,** then more than two, by making direct comparisons of masses.

Activity
Work with four to six children, in pairs. Ask each pair to choose three items from around the classroom. They then decide, by holding them in their hands, which item is heaviest and which is lightest, then check by using the balance. They will need to check pairs of items until they are sure that they have found the heaviest and the lightest. Ask: *Which is heaviest? Which is lightest? Which is heavier/lighter than the book?* The children can repeat this for several different comparisons, choosing three different items each time.

Plenary & assessment
Choose three more items, and pass these around among the children. Ask: *Which do you think is heaviest/lightest? Why do you think that?* Invite one of the children to check using the balance. Ask: *So which is heavier/lighter than the teddy? Which is heaviest/lightest? Did you make a good guess?*

Name	Date

Count and write

Count how many.
Write the number.

Name	Date

Counting numbers

Trace the numbers with your finger.

Trace the numbers with your pencil.
Write the number in the spaces.

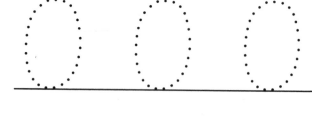

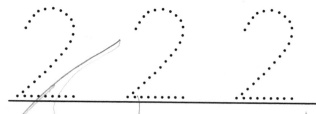

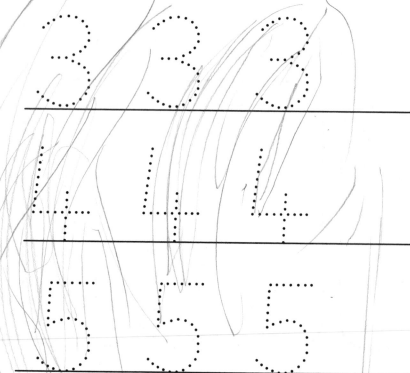

Name	Date

Counting numbers

Trace the numbers with your finger.

Trace the numbers with your pencil.
Write the number in the spaces.

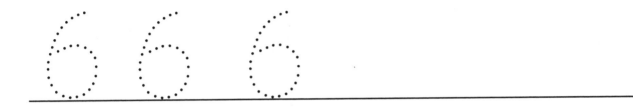

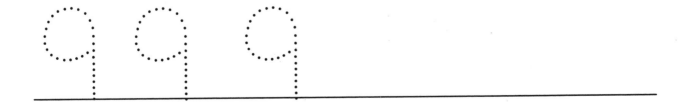

Counting, reading numbers, subtracting and solving problems

Children begin to count in tens, from zero to 100 and back again. They read numerals in practical situations. They count back from a larger number to a smaller number to find what is left after subtraction. They use the counting back method to work out how much change is left in shopping problems.

LEARNING OBJECTIVES

Topics	Stepping Stones	Early Learning Goals & NNS Learning Objectives
	Green	
Counting	● Recognise numerals 1 to 5, then 1 to 9.	● Count in tens. ● **Recognise numerals 1 to 9**, then 0 to 10, then beyond 10.
Adding and subtracting	● Sometimes show confidence and offer solutions to problems.	● Remove a smaller number from a larger and find how many are left by counting back from the larger number. ● Sort coins, including the £1 and £2 coins, and use them in role-play to pay and to give change. ● **Use developing mathematical ideas and methods to solve practical problems** involving counting and comparing in a real or role-play context.

1 Session

Learning objectives

Starter
ELGs/NNS
● Begin to know the days of the week in order.
● Count in tens.

Main teaching activity
ELGs/NNS
● Count in tens.

Vocabulary

zero, ten, twenty… one hundred, count in tens, count on (from, to), count back (from, to)

You will need:

Equipment
Commercial or school-made days of the week chart; floor number track, marked in tens from 10 to 100.

WHOLE CLASS TEACHING

Starter bank

These Starter bank ideas can be used throughout the unit.

Days of the week

Ask the children to recite the days of the week in order. Then, using the class days of the week chart, ask: *What day is it today?* Invite a child to change the day on the chart to the relevant day. Repeat this for 'yesterday' and 'tomorrow'. Finish by reciting the days of the week in order, again.

Use the following two Starters only after carrying out the first Main teaching activity in this unit.

Count in tens

Ask the children to count forward with you in tens. Keep the pace sharp. Repeat this for counting back in tens. When the children are confident with this, they can count around the group or class, from ten to 100, and back again, in tens.

What comes next?

Ask the children to count from ten to 100 and back again, in tens. Repeat this several times, keeping the pace sharp. Now ask questions such as:

- *What number comes just after 50?*
- *What number comes just before 80?*

Main teaching activity

Explain to the children that today's session will be about counting in tens. Begin by counting in tens: *0, 20, 30… 100.* Say this through several times until the children are joining in. When they are confident with counting forward in tens, introduce counting back in tens: *100, 90, 80… 0.* Again, repeat this several times.

Put down the large floor track and talk about how this is marked in tens. Ask the children to look carefully and point to each number on the track. Ask them to say them: *0, 10, 20… 100.* Discuss how the numbers are written – that is with a number then a zero. Invite a child to jump along the track, giving all of the children a turn, over time:

- *Count in tens along the track and stop at 60.*
- *Count on in tens from 20 to 80.*
- *Count back in tens from 90 and stop at 40.*

GROUP ACTIVITIES

Count in tens

Learning objective

ELGs/NNS:

- Count in tens.

Activity

Work with six to eight children, sitting in a circle. Ask them to count all together in tens, from zero to 100 and back again. Repeat this several times. Now ask them to count around the group, from ten to 100 and back again to zero. Again repeat this several times, until the children are confident with counting in tens. Ask questions such as: *What number comes just after/before 30, 60, 90?*

Plenary & assessment

Invite the children to count around the group in tens to and from 100. Ask questions such as:

- *If Tom says 30, who will say 70?*
- *If you start on 20 and count on two tens, what number will you say?*

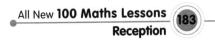

2 Sessions

Preparation

Use a blank dice and write on it 1, 1, 2, 2, 3, 3.

Learning objectives

Main teaching activity
Green Stepping Stones
● Recognise numerals 1 to 5, then 1 to 9.

ELGs/NNS
● **Recognise numerals 1 to 9,** then 0 to 10, then beyond 10.
● Remove a smaller number from a larger and find how many are left by counting back from the larger number.

Vocabulary

zero, one, two, three… to twenty and beyond, take away, count back (from, to) how many are left/left over? how many have gone?

You will need:
Photocopiable pages
'Dice roll', for the teacher's/LSA's reference, see page 187, and 'Count back', one copy for each pair, see page 188.

Equipment
Flip chart or board and pens; for each pair, two 1–6 numeral dice; a 1, 1, 2, 2, 3, 3 dice; counters.

⌐ WHOLE CLASS TEACHING

Main teaching activity
Explain to the children that they will be learning how to take away one number from another. Say: *I have five toffees. I eat two of them. How many are left?* Write '5' and '2' on the flip chart. Ask the children to put five in their heads and count back two. They may find it helpful to keep track using their fingers. *So five, four, three. Five take away two leaves three.* Repeat this for other examples, keeping the numbers to within six or seven to begin with. Over time, extend to include numbers to up to ten. Each time write the numbers from the subtraction sentence on the flip chart as a reminder to the children of the quantities involved.

⌐ GROUP ACTIVITIES

⌐ Dice roll

ADULT SUPPORTED

Learning objectives
ELGs/NNS:
● **Recognise numerals 1 to 9,** then 0 to 10, then beyond 10.
● Remove a smaller number from a larger and find how many are left by counting back from the larger number.

Activity
This activity is provided in detail on CD page 'Dice roll' for the LSA's reference and so they can record the children's achievements and difficulties for use during feedback. Ask four to eight children, in pairs, to work with the LSA. Each pair will need two 1–6 numeral dice. The LSA asks the children to take turns to roll both dice. The child who rolled the dice looks at the scores and decides which is the larger and which is the smaller number. They hold the larger number in their heads and count back for the smaller number. Then they say the subtraction sentence to their partner. Their partner checks by carrying out a similar calculation.

Plenary & assessment
Play the dice game as a group. Ask:
- *Which is the larger/smaller number?*
- *Which number do you put in your heads?*
- *How many do you count back?*

Check that the children understand how to subtract by counting back, and can do this with reasonable accuracy.

Count back

STRUCTURED PLAY

Learning objectives
Green Stepping Stones:
- Recognise numerals 1 to 5, then 1 to 9.

ELGs/NNS:
- **Recognise numerals 1 to 9**, then 0 to 10, then beyond 10.
- Remove a smaller number from a larger and find how many are left by counting back from the larger number.

Activity
This is an activity for pairs of children. They will need a copy of CD page 'Count back' a counter each and a 1, 1, 2, 2, 3, 3 numeral dice. Ask the children to start on the 10. They take turns to roll the dice and count back from ten for the dice number, placing their counter there. For their next turn they count back from the number where their counter is. The first one to reach 'Finish' wins the game. The children can play this game several times.

Plenary & assessment
Play the game together with you against the group. Invite the children to explain how they worked out where their counter should be. Ask:
- *Where is your counter? How many must you count back?*
- *So where will your counter be then?*

2 Sessions

Preparation
Enlarge 'Money cards' to A3 and cut out the cards, to make a teaching set. Make some sets of 'Money cards' for the children to use in pairs.

Learning objectives

Main teaching activity
Green Stepping Stones
- Sometimes show confidence and offer solutions to problems.

ELGs/NNS
- Sort coins, including the £1 and £2 coins, and use them in role play to pay and to give change.
- **Use developing mathematical ideas and methods to solve practical problems** involving counting and comparing in a real or role-play context.

Vocabulary
compare, count out, left, left over, money, coin, penny, pence, pound, price, cost, buy, sell, spend, spent, pay, change, dear, costs more, cheap, costs less, cheaper, costs the same as, how much…? how many…?

You will need:
CD pages
'Money cards' for the teacher's/LSA's reference, copied to A3, and a copy for each pair (see General resources).

Equipment
1p, 2p, 5p and 10p coins; tubs for the coins.

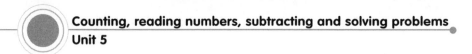
WHOLE CLASS TEACHING

Main teaching activity

Explain to the children that you have 10p to spend. Take one of the cards from the teaching set of CD page 'Money cards' and show the children the picture. Ask: *How much is the…?* Explain that to find out how much money will be left after buying this, the children can put ten in their heads and count back by the cost of it. So, for example, for the toy car at 5p, say: *Put ten in your heads. Now count back five. Ten, nine, eight, seven, six, five. So 10p take away 5p leaves 5p. I shall have 5p change.* Invite one of the children to model this for you, as you give a 10p piece and the child gives you either five 1p coins or a 5p piece. Repeat this for another price.

GROUP ACTIVITIES

Buying and selling

Learning objectives
Green Stepping Stones:
● Sometimes show confidence and offer solutions to problems.
ELGs/NNS:
● Sort coins, including the £1 and £2 coins, and use them in role play to pay and to give change.
● **Use developing mathematical ideas and methods to solve practical problems** involving counting and comparing in a real or role-play context.

Activity
Work with six to eight children. Put some coins in front of them. Use the teaching set of money cards from CD page 'Money cards', sorting out a set of 1p to 10p cards. Choose a card. Ask: *If I give the shopkeeper 10p, how much change will I have?* Encourage the children to work out the change using the counting back method. Invite a child to role-play this with you as the customer and the child as the shopkeeper. When the children have worked out how much change is due, the shopkeeper can count this out for you. Repeat this for other cards.

Plenary & assessment
Say: *I have 10p. I spend 4p in the shop. How much change will I have?* Check that the children understand that they should count back from 10p to 4p, and that the change will be 6p.

In the toy shop

Learning objectives
Green Stepping Stones:
● Sometimes show confidence and offer solutions to problems.
ELGs/NNS:
● Sort coins, including the £1 and £2 coins, and use them in role play to pay and to give change.
● **Use developing mathematical ideas and methods to solve practical problems**

Activity
Sort out sets of 1p to 10p cards from 'Money cards', and ask the children, in pairs, to play being the shopkeeper and the customer. The customer chooses a card, then gives 10p to the shopkeeper. They both work out the change and the shopkeeper gives the change.

Plenary & assessment
Choose two cards and say: *Which is cheaper / more expensive? How can you tell? So how much change will I have from 10p for this one… and that one…?* Repeat this for other pairs of cards.

Dice roll

You will need:

- two 1–6 numeral dice for each pair.

Work with four to eight children, in pairs.

Ask the children to take turns to roll both dice. The child who rolled the dice looks at the scores and decides which is the larger and which is the smaller number. They put the larger number in their heads, and count back for the smaller number. Then they say the subtraction sentence to their partner. Their partner checks by carrying out a similar calculation.

Ask questions such as:

- *Which is the larger... smaller number?*
- *Which number do you put in your heads?*
- *How many do you count back?*

This activity can be extended for the more able by using a 1–10 spinner.

Name   Date

Count back

**Work with a partner.
You will need a counter each and a 1, 1, 2, 2, 3, 3 dice.**

Put your counters on 'Start'.

Take turns to roll the dice.

Count back from 10 for your dice number.

Put your counter on this number.

The winner is the player who reaches 'Finish' first.

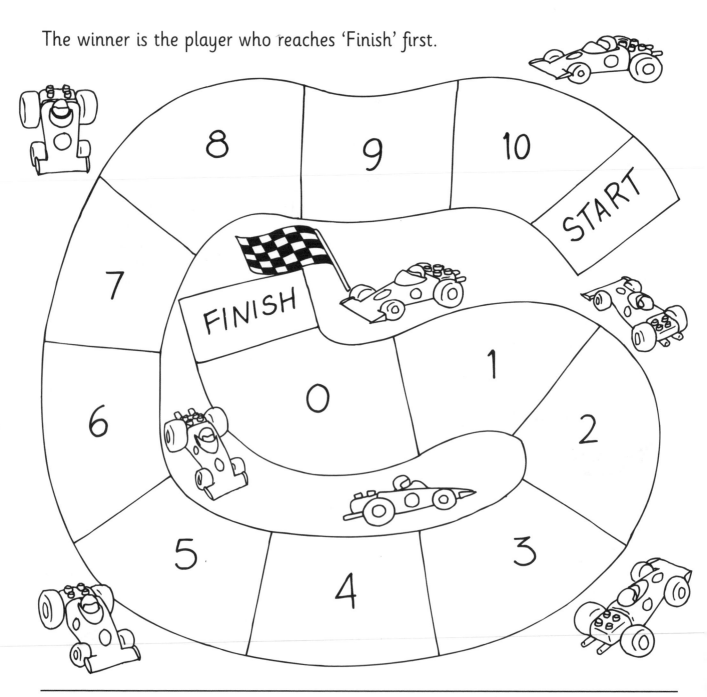

★SCHOLASTIC
photocopiable

Estimating, reading and writing numbers and ordinal numbers

Children order numerals from 0 to 10. They record numerals used in activities. They begin to use ordinal number in practical activities.

LEARNING OBJECTIVES

Topics	Stepping Stones	Early Learning Goals & NNS Learning Objectives
	Green	
Counting	● Show increased confidence with numbers by spotting errors.	● Estimate a number in the range that can be counted reliably, then check by counting.
Reading and writing numbers	● Count an irregular arrangement of up to ten objects.	● Begin to record numbers, initially by making marks, progressing to simply tallying and writing numerals.
Comparing and ordering number	● Begin to represent numbers, using fingers marks on paper or pictures.	● Begin to understand and use ordinal numbers in different contexts.

2 Sessions

Preparation

Enlarge two copies of 'Number worm' to A3 and pin to the flip chart. On one copy, mark the first number track '1' to '10', and the second number track with '1' and '10' only.

Learning objectives

Starter
ELGs/NNS
● Count in tens.
● Remove a smaller number from a larger and find how many are left by counting back from the larger number.

Main teaching activity
Green Stepping Stones
● Show increased confidence with numbers by spotting errors.
● Count an irregular arrangement of up to ten objects.
● Begin to represent numbers, using fingers marks on paper or pictures.
ELGs/NNS
● Estimate a number in the range that can be counted reliably, then check by counting.
● Begin to record numbers, initially by making marks, progressing to simply tallying and writing numerals.

Vocabulary

count, zero, one, two... nine, ten

You will need:

CD pages
'Number cards' and 'Number worm', two copies enlarged to A3, for the teacher's/LSA's reference (see General resources).

Equipment
Washing line and pegs; flip chart or board and pen; some books, with up to ten words on a page; Post-it Notes.

WHOLE CLASS TEACHING

Starter bank

These Starter bank ideas can be used throughout the unit.

Count in tens

Ask the children to count with you, in tens, from zero to 100. In order to keep a good pace, ask the children to gently swing their arms in time with the count. Repeat the count several times. Then, if they are confident with zero to 100, count back from 100 to zero. If this is repeated several times, children will begin to learn the number sequence for counting back.

Count around

Ask the children to sit in a group. Say who is to begin to count in tens. The children take turns to say the next ten around the group. When they get to 100, if they are confident, ask the children to count back in the same way. Repeat this several times, making sure that each time a different child has the chance to say zero.

Children's confidence with counting to 100 will increase with experience. Expect that, at first, you will have to say some of the numbers yourself whilst the children listen.

Count back

Explain to the children that you will say a number problem. Remind them that a way to solve this is to count back from the larger to the smaller number. Say, for example: *I have five sweets. Mark eats three of them. How many sweets do I have now?* Encourage the children to count back from five to three. They will find it helpful to use their fingers to keep track. Say together: *Five, four, three. So five take away three leaves two.* Repeat this for other amounts within five to begin with, and gradually extend to within ten.

Main teaching activity

Explain to the children that you would like them to peg the numbers 0 to 10 onto the washing line. Give out the cards in any order, one at a time, to different children. Ask the child with a card to decide where the card should go, and why. Invite the other children to say whether they agree, and why. As other cards are added there will probably need to be some replacing of cards so that they all fit. When the cards are all there, remove them all except for 0 and 10. Now say: *Where do you think 5 should be?* Invite a child to point to where they think 5 should go, and to explain why they think that. Repeat this for the other numbers, but do not place any cards, so that the children use just 0 and 10 to help them to estimate position.

Pin the enlarged blank version of CD page 'Number worm' to the flip chart. Invite a child to write '1' in the first box and another child to write '10' in the final box. Now ask different children to decide where 5, 2, 7… should go and to write these in. Each time, ask questions such as: *Do you agree? Why does the 3 go there?*

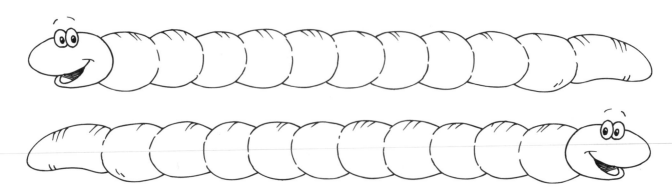

GROUP ACTIVITIES

Number track estimate

Learning objectives
ELGs/NNS:
- Estimate a number in the range that can be counted reliably, then check by counting.
- Begin to record numbers, initially by making marks, progressing to simply tallying and writing numerals.

Activity
Show the children the CD page 'Number worm', marked from 1 to 10 and invite them to say the numbers as you point to them. Do this in number order, then out of order. Now cover this up, and use the CD page 'Number track', marked only with '1' and '10'. Ask the children to say what they think will go into each space. Do this out of sequence, and ask the children to explain their thinking each time. Repeat this several times until the children are confident with this.

Plenary & assessment
Ask again: *What number goes here?* As you point to the number track where only 1 and 10 are marked, ask:
- *Why do you think that?*
- *So what goes here and here?* (pointing to the numbers on each side)
- *How can you check if you are right?*

How many words?

Learning objectives
Green Stepping Stones:
- Show increased confidence with numbers by spotting errors.
- Count an irregular arrangement of up to ten objects.
- Begin to represent numbers, using fingers, marks on paper or pictures.

ELGs/NNS:
- Estimate a number in the range that can be counted reliably, then check by counting.
- Begin to record numbers, initially by making marks, progressing to simply tallying and writing numerals.

Activity
Ask the children to work in pairs. They take it in turns to choose a page of a book, estimate how many words there are on the page and write this onto a Post-it Note. Then they count how many words there are and write this onto the Post-it Note. They stick this onto the page of the book. Their partner checks their work. They repeat this for each page.

Plenary & assessment
Ask the children to choose a page in their book and to say how many words they estimated. Now ask:
- *Did you make a good guess?*
- *Which page had five/seven/ten words on it?*
- *Did you have a page with no words? How did you write that?*
- *Which page do you think had the most words? How many were there?*

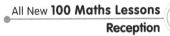

3 Sessions

Learning objectives

Main teaching activity
ELGs/NNS
● Begin to understand and use ordinal numbers in different contexts.

Vocabulary

first, second, third…, last

You will need:

Photocopiable pages
'Bead thread', for the teacher's LSA's reference, see page 194.

Equipment
Farm animals; toy cars in various colours; books and a shelf; laces and beads in different colours.

WHOLE CLASS TEACHING

Main teaching activity

Put out some farm animals in a line, for example, sheep, cow, pig, horse and donkey. Ask the children about the order of the animals. Say, for example: *Which animal is first/second/last?* Now ask a child to move one of the animals. For example: *How can we make the sheep the last animal? Who will make the cow the first?* When all of the animals have been reordered, ask questions such as: *Which animal is between the third and the fifth?* When the children are confident with ordinal numbers to five, add more animals until there are seven, and repeat.

GROUP ACTIVITIES

Bead thread

ADULT SUPPORTED

Learning objective
ELGs/NNS:
● Begin to understand and use ordinal numbers in different contexts.

Activity

This activity is provided in detail on CD page 'Bead thread' for the LSA's reference and so they can record the children's achievements and difficulties for use during feedback. Ask a group of six to eight children to work with the LSA. The LSA asks the children to thread beads, following the LSA's instructions. For example: *Thread a blue, then a blue, and then a red. Now thread a green bead. What colour is the first/second bead? You choose some beads and thread those. Tell the person next to you what to thread. Are your beads the same?* Repeat this for between six and ten beads on a lace.

Plenary & assessment

Ask the children to describe their bead threads. Invite them to say what colour is the first, second… and so on. Then take one of the threadings and say:
● *What colour is the third bead?*
● *What colour is the bead between the fourth and the sixth?*

Line up!

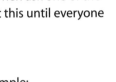

Learning objective
ELGs/NNS:
● Begin to understand and use ordinal numbers in different contexts.

Activity
Work with a group of up to ten children. Put ten toy cars in a line. Ask questions such as: *What colour is the third/sixth/ninth car? Which car is between the third and the fifth car?* Then ask one of the children to reorder the cars. Say, for example: *Make the yellow car the fifth.* Repeat this until everyone has had a turn.

Plenary & assessment
Reorder the cars again. Ask the children questions about their order. Say, for example:
● *Which car is first?*
● *Which car is between the fourth and the sixth?*

Book order

Learning objective
ELGs/NNS:
● Begin to understand and use ordinal numbers in different contexts.

Activity
Ask two or three children to tidy the bookshelf. When they have done this, invite them to question each other. Model the questions they might ask, for example: *Touch the first book. Which one is between the second and the fourth?*

Plenary & assessment
Talk about the order of the books. Remove some of them, and place them in a line. Ask questions such as:
● *Which book is third/sixth?*
● *Which book is between the seventh and the ninth?*
● *Who can make this book the last book?*
● *Now what is between the fifth and the seventh?*

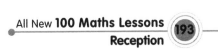

Bead thread

You will need:

- some laces and beads in different colours for each child.

Work with a group of six to eight children.

Ask the children to thread beads, following your instructions.
For example: *Thread a blue, then a blue, then a red. Now thread a green bead.*
What colour is the first/third bead?

Now say: *You choose some beads and thread those. Tell the person next to you what to thread. Are your beads the same?* Repeat this for between six and ten beads on a lace.

Record the children's achievements. It would be helpful to record who can use ordinal numbers up to tenth.

Child's name	What happened	What to do next time

Summer term
Unit 8

Counting in twos, and adding and subtracting

Children count in twos from 0 to 10, then up to 20. Given a total, children find different partitions to make that total. In practical situations they count up from a smaller to a larger number in order to find how many have been removed.

LEARNING OBJECTIVES

Topics	Stepping Stones Green	Early Learning Goals & NNS Learning Objectives
Counting	● Show increased confidence with numbers by spotting errors.	● Count in twos. ● Select two groups of objects to make a given total.
Adding and subtracting	● Count an irregular arrangement of up to ten objects. ● Begin to represent numbers, using fingers, marks on paper or pictures.	● Begin to find out how many have been removed from a larger group of objects by counting up from a number.

1 Session

Learning objectives

Starter
ELGs/NNS
● **Say and use the number names in order in familiar contexts.**
● Count reliably up to 10 everyday objects.
● Count in twos.

Main teaching activity
ELGs/NNS
● Count in twos.

Vocabulary

count in twos, two, four, six…, every other

You will need:

Photocopiable pages
'Count in twos', for the teacher's/LSA's reference, page 200.

CD pages
'2, 4, 6, 8: counting rhymes' for the teacher's/LSA's reference (see General resources).

Equipment
Number track and two colours of cubes.

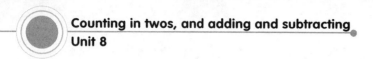

WHOLE CLASS TEACHING

Starter bank

These Starter bank ideas can be used throughout the unit.

Count around

Ask the children to sit in a circle. Begin by counting together from zero to 10… 15… 20…, as far as the children can count. Then count around the circle, from zero. Repeat this several times, beginning with a different child each time. This can be repeated to include counting back.

How many?

Ask the children to hold up the number of fingers that you say. Begin with numbers to five, then extend to ten. Keep the pace of this sharp.

Count in twos

This Starter can be used once the main teaching activity for counting in twos has been undertaken.

Ask the children to count with you, from zero. They say *zero* loudly, *one* quietly, *two* loudly, *three* quietly, and so on, up to ten. When the children are confident with this, they can say just the even numbers. Over time extend the count to 20.

Main teaching activity

Ask the children to sit in a circle and explain that they will begin today to count in twos. Say the rhyme 'Mary at the garden gate' from CD page '2, 4, 6, 8: counting rhymes'. Ask the children to hold up their fingers to show how many for each number that is said. Say the rhyme together several times so that the children become familiar with the words. Repeat this for the second rhyme, 'Ten crafty crocodiles'. Now ask the children to count with you, saying alternate numbers loudly and softly: *zero* (loudly), *one* (softly), *two* (loudly), *three* (softly)… Do this several times, then ask the children to count in twos with you: *two, four, six, eight, ten*. Explain that the children are saying every other number. Repeat this several times until they are confident with this. Extend the count beyond ten and up to 20, over time.

GROUP ACTIVITIES

Count in twos

ADULT SUPPORTED

Learning objective
ELGs/NNS:
- Count in twos.

Activity

This activity is provided in detail on CD page 'Count in twos' for the LSA's reference and so they can record the children's achievements and difficulties for use during feedback. The LSA will need a number track and two colours of cubes. Ask a group of four to six children to work with the LSA, who asks the children to place the cubes into the number track so that the cubes alternate in colour. The LSA asks the children to say aloud every other number as the LSA points at the track starting at two. Repeat this for starting at one. The LSA can ask: *Which numbers do we say when we start on one… two?* This activity can be repeated over time, extending the number range from ten to up to 20.

Plenary & assessment

Ask the children to count together in twos, from two to ten. Repeat this several times. Ask: *Which numbers do we say when we count in twos, starting from two?*

Repeat this for counting in twos, starting from one.

2 Sessions

Learning objectives

Main teaching activity
Green Stepping Stones
- Count an irregular arrangement of up to ten objects.

ELGs/NNS
- Select two groups of objects to make a given total.

Vocabulary

add, more, and, make, sum, total, altogether

You will need:
Equipment
Toy cars; two sheets of grey or black paper to represent car parks; paper, crayons; two 1–6 numeral dice; bricks in two colours.

WHOLE CLASS TEACHING

Main teaching activity
Show the children the toy cars, and explain that you would like one of them to count out six cars. Encourage the other children to count as the cars are put out. Now say: *Here are two car parks. How could we put these cars into the car parks?* Invite the children to take turns to come to the front and to put some of the cars in one car park, and some in the other. For each partition, say the number sentence. For example: *There are four cars here and two cars there. So four add two makes six.* This can be repeated, over time, for a different quantity, from five to ten, and in a different context, such as farm animals and fields.

GROUP ACTIVITIES

Six bricks

Learning objectives
Green Stepping Stones:
- Count an irregular arrangement of up to ten objects.
ELGs/NNS:
- Select two groups of objects to make a given total.

Activity
This is an activity for pairs of children. Provide some bricks in two colours. Ask the children to make towers of six bricks using the two colours. Challenge them to make each tower different. When they have made some towers, they can write on pieces of paper how many of each colour of brick are in the towers.

Plenary & assessment
Invite the children to show some of their towers and their pieces of paper. Ask questions such as:
- *How many red/blue bricks are there?*
- *Let's say the number sentence together: one add five makes six.*
- *Who can show a different number sentence from their bricks?*

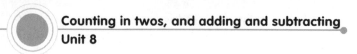

Dice scores

Learning objectives
Green Stepping Stones:
- Count an irregular arrangement of up to ten objects.

ELGs/NNS:
- Select two groups of objects to make a given total.

Activity
Work with a group of six to eight children. Show the children the two numeral dice, and ask two children to each roll a dice. Say: *How many have you scored?* for each of the dice and invite the children to add the scores. Ask: *How did you work that out?* Encourage the children to count on from one of the numbers. For five and two they say: *Five then six, seven. So five add two is seven.* Explain that you would like the children to work in pairs. They take turns to roll their two dice and find ways of scoring a total of six. If the children are confident with writing numbers, they can record on paper the numbers for each total of six.

Plenary & assessment
Invite the children to say which pairs of numbers total six. They should get '1, 5'; '2, 4'; '3, 3'; '4, 2'; '5, 1'. At this stage children will probably see, for example, '1, 5' as different from '5, 1'. Ask questions such as:
- *Which dice scores made six?*
- *Can you tell me some scores that did not make six?*

2 Sessions

Learning objectives

Main teaching activity
ELGs/NNS
- Begin to find out how many have been removed from a larger group of objects by counting up from a number.

Vocabulary

zero, one, two, three…, count, count (up) to, count on (from, to)

You will need:
Photocopiable pages
'How many pennies?'
for the teacher's/LSA's
reference, see page 201.

Equipment
Bricks or cubes; boxes; ten pennies.

Main teaching activity
Show the children the box and in front of them count five bricks into it. Say: *How many bricks are there in the box? Yes, there are five.* Now take out two bricks and put them onto the table. Ask: *How many bricks are left in the box?* Ask the children to count with you from two. They may find it helpful to keep a tally with their fingers. Say together: *on two, then three, four, five. There are three bricks in the box. Two add three is five. Five take away two is three.* Repeat this for other quantities of bricks, up to about seven, and for removing some in the same way.

GROUP ACTIVITIES

Hide some

STRUCTURED PLAY

Learning objective
ELGs/NNS:
● Begin to find out how many have been removed from a larger group of objects by counting up from a number.

Activity
Ask the children to work in pairs. They will need six bricks or cubes. They put the cubes into the box, then take turns to take some out and put these onto the table. Their partner works out how many are left by counting on from the number of the bricks on the table. This can be repeated for other quantities of bricks up to ten.

Plenary & assessment
Ask the children to count how many bricks you are putting into the box, such as seven. Now ask: *How many bricks are there in the box? How many have I put onto the table? So how many bricks are left in the box?* Invite the children to explain how they worked it out. Praise them for counting up. Encourage them to say an addition and a take away number sentence. Repeat this for another quantity removed from the box.

How many pennies?

ADULT SUPPORTED

Learning objective
ELGs/NNS:
● Begin to find out how many have been removed from a larger group of objects by counting up from a number.

Activity
This activity is provided in detail on CD page 'How many pennies?' for the LSA's reference and so they can record the children's achievements and difficulties for use during feedback. Ask a group of four to six children to work with the LSA. The LSA picks up six pennies, one at a time, and encourages the children to count them as the LSA does so. Say: *How many pennies are there in my hand?* Now put some of the pennies onto the table. Say: *How many pennies are there on the table? So how many are in my hand?* The LSA encourages the children to work out how many are in the LSA's hand by counting up from the number of pennies on the table. The LSA can ask the children to say an add and a take away sentence. For example, for four pennies on the table: *on four, then five, six. So there are two pennies in your hand. Four add two is six. Six take away four leaves two.* Repeat this for other amounts of money, up to about 10p.

Plenary & assessment
Count some pennies into your hand and ask: *How many pennies am I holding?* Now put some of the pennies onto the table and say: *How many of the pennies are on the table? So how many pennies are in my hand?* Encourage the children to say the counting up statement, and an addition and take away sentence.

Count in twos

You will need:

- a number track and cubes in two different colours.

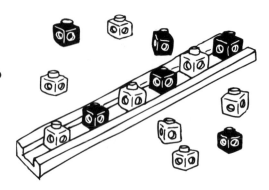

Work with a group of four to six children.

Ask the children to place the cubes into the number track so that the cubes alternate in colour.

Invite the children to say aloud every other number as you point at the track, starting at two. Repeat this for starting at one.

Ask:

- *Which numbers do we say when we start on 1... 2?*

This activity can be repeated over time, extending the number range from 10 to up to 20.

Record the children's achievements. It would be helpful to record who can count in twos, up to 10, starting from one or two.

Child's name	What happened	What to do next time

How many pennies?

You will need:

- ten pennies.

Work with a group of four to six children.

Explain that you will pick up some pennies. Pick up six pennies, one at a time, and encourage the children to count them as you do. Say: *How many pennies are there in my hand?*

Now put some of the pennies onto the table and hide the other pennies in your hand. Say: *How many pennies are there on the table? So how many are in my hand?* Encourage the children to work out how many are in your hand by counting up from the number of pennies on the table.

Ask the children to say an add and a take away sentence. For example, for four pennies on the table: 'Four, five, six. So there are two pennies in your hand. Four add two is six. Six take away four leaves two'.

Repeat this for other amounts of money, up to about 10p.

Record the children's achievements. It would be helpful to record who can count up to find how many have been taken away.

Child's name	What happened	What to do next time

Movement and reasoning

Through movement activities, children follow instructions which use position and movement vocabulary. They sort shapes for specific properties and explain their sorting.

LEARNING OBJECTIVES

Topics	Stepping Stones	Early Learning Goals &
	Green	**NNS Learning Objectives**
Exploring pattern, shape and space	● Find items from positional/directional clues. ● Describe a simple journey. ● Instruct a programmable toy.	● **Use everyday words to describe position,** direction and movement: for example, follow and give instructions about positions, directions and movements in PE and other activities.
Reasoning about numbers or shapes	● Choose suitable components to make a particular model. ● Select a particular named shape.	● Sort and match objects, pictures or children themselves, justifying the decisions made.

3 Sessions

Preparation

Prepare a floor space where Roamer can be moved. Some play people set out on the floor; with construction kit houses would be helpful. Roamer can be decorated to become an ice cream delivery van if wished.

Learning objectives

Starter
ELGs/NNS
● Count in twos.
● **Recognise numerals 1 to 9.**
● **Use language such as more or less, greater or smaller, to compare two quantities.**

Main teaching activity
Green Stepping Stones
● Find items from positional/directional clues.
● Describe a simple journey.
● Instruct a programmable toy.
ELGs/NNS
● **Use everyday words to describe position**, direction and movement: for example, follow and give instructions about positions, directions and movements in PE and other activities.

Vocabulary

position, over, under, above, below, on, in, outside, inside, behind, beside, before, after, next to, opposite, between, close, far, apart, middle, corner, top, bottom, front, back, side, direction, left, right, up, down, forwards, backwards, sideways, across, around, through, to, from, towards, away from, movement, roll, slide, turn, stretch, bend, along, in front, edge

You will need:

Photocopiable pages
'Where is it?' for the teacher's/LSA's reference, and 'Find the kittens' mothers', one for each child, see pages 207–208.

CD pages
'Number cards', for the teacher's/LSA's reference (see General resources).

Equipment
Crayons; Roamers or other programmable toys.

WHOLE CLASS TEACHING

Starter bank
These Starter bank ideas can be used throughout the unit.

Count in twos
Ask the children to count together in twos, starting on zero. They can gently swing their arms in time with the count to help to keep the momentum. Count to ten, then over time extend this to 20, when the children are confident. Repeat this, starting on one to count in twos for the odd numbers.

Recognising numerals
Hold up the shuffled number cards, one at a time, and say: *What number is this?* Invite the child who responds correctly to come to the front and to hold the card so that everyone can see it. When all nine cards are held at the front, invite a child who is still sitting to take the card for 1 and to stand at one end of the line. Ask: *What number will come next?* The child who responds correctly takes 2 and stands beside 1, and so on until all the cards are placed in order. Over time this can be repeated for recognising numerals beyond 9.

Comparing numbers
Ask the children to say the number that is one more or less than the numbers that you say. Ask, for example: *What is one more/less than three/nine/twelve?* Repeat this for several numbers. Then say: *Which is more/less, four or nine? How can you tell?* Repeat this for several numbers.

Main teaching activity
This activity can be carried out as part of a movement or PE session. Work in a large space. Ask the children to move around the space following your instructions. Begin with position words, such as: *Stand in front of / behind / opposite your partner. Work in a group of three. One of you stands between the other two.* As the children work, check that they are following the instructions quickly.

When the children are confident with position words, move on to movements and directions. For example, say: *Hop forwards, walk backwards, turn where you are, turn left/right, face the front/back.* Ask the children to go in front of another child, stop behind a child…

When the children are confident with movement and direction words, ask them to work in a group of four. They answer questions about what you have asked them to do. For example: *Stand in a line. Who is in front / at the back?*

You may like to finish the session with a Follow-my-leader game. Here the children line up behind you and follow your movements. This can be great fun!

GROUP ACTIVITIES

Where is it?

ADULT SUPPORTED

Learning objectives
Green Stepping Stones:
● Find items from positional/directional clues.
ELGs/NNS:
● **Use everyday words to describe position** and direction: for example, follow and give instructions about positions and directions in PE and other activities.

Activity
This activity is provided in detail on CD page 'Where is it?' for the LSA's reference and so they can record the children's achievements and difficulties for use during feedback. Ask the LSA to work with a group of about six to eight children. The LSA explains that they will describe something and the children have to listen carefully and then move to where the object is in the room, or outdoors.

Say, for example: *Go and stand next to the bookcase. Now, look around the room. Who can see the water tray? Where is it?* Encourage the children to describe where things are using position words. Ask for more than 'It is over there' accompanied by a point. For example: *It is next to the dolls' house, on top of the cupboard…*

Repeat this, including both the children moving to new positions and for searching for items and describing their position.

Plenary & assessment
Ask the children to listen carefully then to answer your questions. Say, for example:
● *Where is the…?*
● *What is next to… beside… on top of… underneath the…?*
Ask the children to respond by using positional language.

Include opportunities for the children to follow instructions, such as: *Go and sit inside the home area…*

Find the kittens' mothers

Learning objectives
Green Stepping Stones:
● Describe a simple journey.
ELGs/NNS:
● **Use everyday words to describe position**, direction and movement: for example, follow and give instructions about positions, directions and movements in PE and other activities.

Activity
The children will enjoy carrying out this activity in pairs. They will each need a copy of CD page 'Find the kittens' mothers'. Ask the children to decide which kitten belongs to which mother, then to draw a line along the paths to help the kitten get home. They may like to use a different coloured crayon for each of the four kittens.

Plenary & assessment
Review the children's responses to the activity sheet with them. Ask questions like:
● *How does the kitten get home?*
● *Which way does she/he have to go?*
● *Is there another way?*

Ice cream van

Learning objectives
Green Stepping Stones:
● Instruct a programmable toy.
ELGs/NNS:
● **Use everyday words to describe position**, direction and movement: for example, follow and give instructions about positions, directions and movements in PE and other activities.

Activity
Work with a group of six to eight children to set up the activity. If only one Roamer is available, then children will need to undertake the paired activity over time.

Show the children the prepared floor space and explain that Roamer's job is to deliver ice creams to the people waiting. If necessary, remind the children of how to move Roamer: forward, back, turn left, turn right. When the children understand what to do, they can work in pairs to programme Roamer to deliver the ice creams. As they work, ask questions such as: *Which way will Roamer go now? How will he do that?*

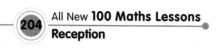

Plenary & assessment

Children may like to show how they made Roamer move. As Roamer moves around the course, ask, for example:

- *What do you think Roamer should do now?*
- *How can we help him to do that?*
- *Which way should he turn/move next?*

2 Sessions

Preparation

Put the shapes into the feely box. Make labels for 'circle', 'rectangle', 'square' and 'triangle' and put each label by one of the sorting circles.

Learning objectives

Main teaching activity
Green Stepping Stones
- Choose suitable components to make a particular model.
- Select a particular named shape.

ELGs/NNS
- Sort and match objects, pictures or children themselves, justifying the decisions made.

Vocabulary

sort, match, count

You will need
Equipment
2-D shape tiles of squares, rectangles, triangles and circles (enough for each child to be able to hold one of each shape at the same time); feely box or opaque bag; sorting circles and labels; beads of different shapes and colours and sorting trays; 3-D shapes such as those from a box of bricks, or a construction set; paper for labels.

WHOLE CLASS TEACHING

Main teaching activity

Ask the children to sit in a circle. Pass the feely box around the circle and ask each child to feel in the box for a shape. As each child finds their shape and, before they take it out of the box, ask the children to describe what they can feel. They might say, for example, that the shape has corners, has straight or curved sides. Say to the other children: *What shape do you think this is?* Invite the child holding the shape to agree or disagree when they take it out of the box. When everyone has a shape, invite the children to hold up their shapes when you say, for example: *Hold up all the squares… all the shapes with three sides… four corners….*

Now ask the children to come out, one at a time, and to put their shape into the correct sorting circle. Invite a child to count how many squares there are and to write the number onto the label.

GROUP ACTIVITIES

Bead sort

Learning objectives
Green Stepping Stones:
- Choose suitable components to make a particular model.
- Select a particular named shape.

ELGs/NNS:
- Sort and match objects, pictures or children themselves, justifying the decisions made.

Activity
Children can work individually or in pairs. Ask the children to take a large handful of beads and place these into a sorting tray. They decide how to sort their beads. Ask: *How did you sort these?*

Plenary & assessment
Ask individual children to show how they sorted the beads. Ask questions such as:
- *How did you sort these? Who chose a different way?*

Shape sort

Learning objectives
Green Stepping Stones:
- Select a particular named shape.

ELGs/NNS:
- Sort and match objects, pictures or children themselves, justifying the decisions made.

Activity
Work with a group of six to eight children. Show the children the 3-D shapes and ask: *How could we sort these?* Choose a suggestion, such as: *shapes with curves, shapes with flat faces.* Write a label and invite the children to pick out shapes that can go into that labelled set circle. Repeat this for other criteria, until all of the shapes have been sorted.

Plenary & assessment
Ask the children to sort six of the shapes that you put in front of them. Ask:
- *How could we sort these?*
- *Who has another idea?*
- *So, where will this shape go? Why is that?*

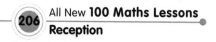

Where is it?

Work with a group of about six to eight children.

Explain that you will describe something. Ask the children to listen carefully and then move to where the object is in the room, or outdoors.

Say, for example: *Go and stand next to the bookcase. Now, look around the room. Who can see the water tray? Where is it?*

Encourage the children to describe where things are using position words. For example, 'It is over there' accompanied by a point. For example: *It is next to the dolls' house, on top of the cupboard...*

Repeat this, including both the children moving to new positions, and for searching for items and describing their position.

Record the children's achievements. It would be helpful to record how confident children are with using the vocabulary of position, direction and movement.

Child's name	What happened	What to do next time

Name   Date

Find the kittens' mothers

Help the kittens to find their mothers.

Draw a line to show each kitten the way home.

Reading and writing numbers, estimating and o'clock times

Children estimate how many in a given set, count to check and write the numeral for the set. They use a clock face and set the hands to given o'clock times. They say the time and relate various o'clock times to everyday events.

LEARNING OBJECTIVES

Topics	Stepping Stones	Early Learning Goals & NNS Learning Objectives
	Green	
Reading and writing numbers	• Begin to represent numbers, using fingers, marks on paper or pictures.	• Begin to record numbers, initially by making marks, progressing to simple tallying and writing numerals.
Counting	• Select the correct numeral to represent 1 to 5, then 1 to 9, objects.	• Estimate a number in the range that can be counted reliably, then check by counting. • Begin to read o'clock time.
Comparing and ordering measures		

4 Sessions

Preparation

Count out the toys into the tubs, so that the tubs have one to ten items in them. Prepare the tray with, say, six toys on it and another four toys to hand, and then cover the tray with the cloth.

Learning objectives

Starter
ELGs/NNS
● **Begin to use the vocabulary involved in adding and subtracting.**
● **Find one more or one less than a number from 1 to 10.**

Main teaching activity
Green Stepping Stones
● Begin to represent numbers, using fingers, marks on paper or pictures.
● Select the correct numeral to represent 1 to 5, then 1 to 9, objects.
ELGs/NNS
● Begin to record numbers, initially by making marks, progressing to simply tallying and writing numerals.
● Estimate a number in the range that can be counted reliably, then check by counting.

Vocabulary

guess, how many, estimate, nearly, close to, about the same as, just over, just under, too many, too few, enough, not enough

You will need:
Photocopiable pages
'Count and write' and 'Make a guess', one for each child, see pages 214–215.

CD pages
'Work mat', one for each child (see General resources).

Equipment
A tray with ten toys available, with a cloth to cover it; ten transparent plastic tubs with lids on with counting toys inside; Post-it notes; for each child ten counting toys in a tub; paper and crayons; flip chart or board and pens.

WHOLE CLASS TEACHING

Starter bank

These Starter bank ideas can be used throughout the unit.

Adding

Explain that you will ask some number problems. Encourage the children to listen carefully to the words that you use. Remind the children that they know how to put one of the numbers in their heads and to count on. Review each word problem and ask the children to explain how they worked out the answer. Ask, for example:

- *Tom has four kittens and Peter has two kittens. How many kittens is that altogether?*
- *Karen has collected four stickers. She wants to have six stickers. How many more does she need?*
- *Shari makes five cakes. Petra makes four cakes. How many cakes are there in total?*

Subtraction

Explain that you will ask some number problems. Encourage the children to listen carefully to the words that you use. Remind the children that they know how to put one of the numbers in their heads and to count on. Review each word problem and ask the children to explain how they worked out the answer. Say, for example:

- *David has four pens. He has two more than John. How many pens has John?*
- *There are six biscuits. Tess eats two biscuits. How many biscuits are left?*
- *Felip has seven marbles. Gosha has five marbles. How many fewer marbles has Gosha than Felip?*

One more and one less

Explain that you will say a number between one and nine. Ask the children to listen carefully and then put up their hands to give you the new number. Say, for example: *What is one more than five? What is one less than six?*

Main teaching activity

Show the children the covered tray. Explain that in a moment you will take the cover off the tray and you would like them to guess how many things are on the tray. Say: *Are you ready? Then look!* Quickly uncover the tray, then cover it up again before the children have had time to count the items. Ask: *How many do you think are there?* Write the estimates on the flip chart, then invite a child to remove the cloth and count how many there are. Write this number on the flip chart too. Discuss the children's original estimates. Ask: *Did you guess: about right… too many… too few?* Out of sight of the children, remove or add items to the tray, move them around, then cover with the cloth. Alternatively, ask the LSA to do this for you. Repeat the activity several times so that the children become confident in making estimates, and also so that they begin to understand that this is not about 'right' answers, but about making a good guess.

GROUP ACTIVITIES

Count and write

Learning objectives

Green Stepping Stones:

- Begin to represent numbers, using fingers, marks on paper or pictures.
- Select the correct numeral to represent 1 to 5, then 1 to 9, objects.

ELGs/NNS:

- Begin to record numbers, initially by making marks, progressing to simply tallying and writing numerals.

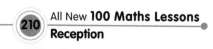

Activity

Ask a group of six to eight children to work with the LSA. Provide each child with a copy of CD page 'Count and write'. The LSA explains to the children that they have to count how many are in the first picture and write the number. Children then repeat this for the other pictures. Children who cannot yet write numerals can draw the appropriate number of spots or lines. While the children work, the LSA can ask: *How many are there? How do you know you have counted them all? What number is that?*

Plenary & assessment

Review the sheet together. Ask the children to draw the numeral in the air for each picture to show that they can draw it correctly. Ask questions such as:

- *How many are there?*
- *So what number shall we write?*
- *Who would like to write the number on the flip chart?*

Guess how many

STRUCTURED PLAY

Learning objectives
Green Stepping Stones:
- Begin to represent numbers, using fingers marks on paper or pictures.
- Select the correct numeral to represent 1 to 5, then 1 to 9, objects.

ELGs/NNS:
- Begin to record numbers, initially by making marks, progressing to simply tallying and writing numerals.
- Estimate a number in the range that can be counted reliably, then check by counting.

Activity

This is an activity for pairs of children. Put out the tubs with the counting toys in and the Post-it notes. Ask the children to make a good guess of how many are in each tub and to write that onto a Post-it note and stick that onto the lid of each tub. When they have made all of their estimates, ask the children to line up the tubs in their number order. Then they can check how close their estimates were by taking off each lid, one at a time, counting the objects, and writing the count onto the Post-it note.

Check how the children are getting on with this, from time to time. Ask questions such as: *How many do you think there are? Did you make a good guess? Were you close… just over… under?*

Plenary & assessment

Talk with the children about the estimates and counts that they made. Invite a group of children to decide how many are in each tub by estimating, write their estimate on a Post-it note, and place this on the lid. Then ask the children to order the tubs. If time, invite children to count how many are in each tub and write this on the Post-it note. Say:

- *Did you make a good guess?*
- *Which guess was too much… too few… not enough… just under… over?*

Take a handful

TEACHER DIRECTED

Learning objectives
Green Stepping Stones:
- Begin to represent numbers, using fingers, marks on paper or pictures.
- Select the correct numeral to represent 1 to 5, then 1 to 9, objects.

ELGs/NNS:
- Begin to record numbers, initially by making marks, progressing to simply tallying and writing numerals.
- Estimate a number in the range that can be counted reliably, then check by counting.

Activity

Work with a group of six to eight children. Each child will need a copy of CD page 'Work mat' and about ten counting toys in a pot. Provide the children with crayons and paper. Explain: *Take a handful of toys. Put them on the mat. No counting now! Make a guess: how many do you think there are? Write your number on the paper. Now check by counting.* Invite the children to check and to say if they have made a good guess. *Now I want you to take a handful that you think is about six toys. No counting! Put the toys onto the mat. Check how many you have. Write that number. Did you make a good guess?*

Repeat this for other quantities between three and ten. Ask the children to use the vocabulary of estimation to describe their estimate.

Plenary & assessment

Repeat the estimating once more. Ask the children about their estimates. Say:
- *Were your estimates/guesses close?*
- *Did you guess just right?*
- *How near was your guess?*

Encourage the children to talk about their estimate and to use the vocabulary of estimation in their responses.

Make a guess

ADULT SUPPORTED

Learning objectives
Green Stepping Stones:
- Begin to represent numbers, using fingers, marks on paper or pictures.
- Select the correct numeral to represent 1 to 5, then 1 to 9, objects.

ELGs/NNS:
- Begin to record numbers, initially by making marks, progressing to simply tallying and writing numerals.
- Estimate a number in the range that can be counted reliably, then check by counting.

Activity

Ask a group of six to eight children to work with the LSA. Each child will need a copy of CD page 'Make a guess' and a crayon. The LSA explains that the children should look at each picture and write how many they think there are in it. Then the children have to count and write how many they counted. While the children work, the LSA can ask questions such as: *Did you make a good guess? How do you know that you have counted all of them?*

Plenary & assessment

Review the sheet with the children. Ask questions about their estimates. Say, for example:
- *Was that a good guess?*
- *How close do you think your guess is?*

Encourage the children to use the vocabulary of estimation in their responses. If any child has difficulty with writing the numerals, practise writing these in the air.

1 Session

Preparation

Photocopy 'Clock face' onto thin card, cut out the clock face and hands, and make up the clocks with a paper fastener. Set up an interactive clocks display, using old analogue clocks and watches. The children should have access to this display, as part of their play, and have the opportunity to turn the hands, and set the hands as they wish.

Learning objectives

Main teaching activity
ELGs/NNS
- Begin to read o'clock time.

Vocabulary

time, o'clock, clock, watch, hands, hour, takes longer, takes less time, slow, slower, slowest, slowly, quick, quicker, quickest, quickly, now, soon, early, late

You will need:

CD pages
'Clock face', photocopied onto card for each child (see General resources).

Equipment
Teaching clock; old analogue clocks and watches.

WHOLE CLASS TEACHING

Main teaching activity

Show the children the teaching clock. Set the hands for 9 o'clock and say: *The clock shows 9 o'clock. This is when we come into school.* Talk with the children about where the hands of the clock are. (Follow the school policy on how to name the hands: big or hour hand; little or minute hand.) *The minute hand is pointing to the 12. The hour hand is pointing to the nine.* Explain that when the minute hand is straight up, pointing to the 12, the time is always an o'clock time. Repeat this for other o'clock times. Relate the times to things that the children do.

GROUP ACTIVITIES

What time is it?

Learning objective
ELGs/NNS:
- Begin to read o'clock time.

Activity

Work with a group of six to eight children. Provide each child with a clock face from CD page **G0.32** 'Clock face', and give them time to try moving the hands. When the children are confident with this, explain that you will say an o'clock time and that you would like them to set their clocks. Check that the children remember that the minute hand must point straight up, to the 12, for o'clock times. When the children have set their clocks, show them the time on the teaching clock each time.

Plenary & assessment

Use the teaching clock and set it to various o'clock times for the children to say the times. Say:
- *What is the time on the clock?*
- *Where is the minute/hour hand pointing?*
- *What does that tell us?*

Name	Date

Count and write

Count the flowers.

Write how many.

Name	Date

Make a guess

Make a guess of how many insects in each picture there are.
Write your guess.

Count how many insects.
Write your count.

Did you make a good guess?

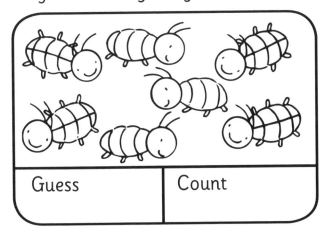

Guess	Count

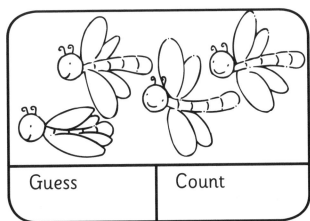

Guess	Count

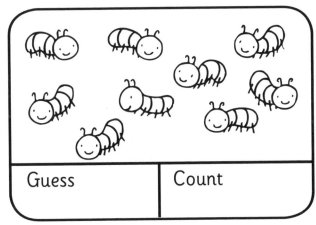

Guess	Count

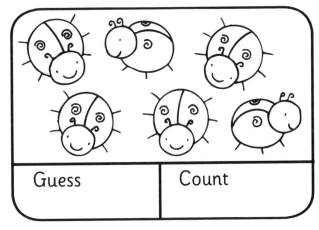

Guess	Count

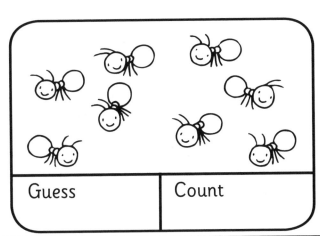

Guess	Count

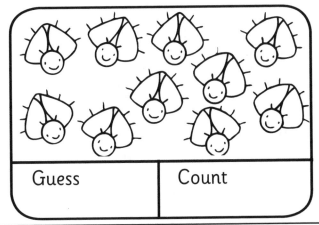

Guess	Count

Children count in tens from 0 to 100 and back again, keeping the pace sharp. They count in twos from zero to 20, then from one to 19. They solve word problems, counting up from the lower number. They say the addition sentence. They solve money problems using coins to help them. They find equivalences using coins.

LEARNING OBJECTIVES

Topics	Stepping Stones Green	Early Learning Goals & NNS Learning Objectives
Counting		● Count in tens. ● Count in twos.
Reading and writing numbers	● Begin to represent numbers, using fingers marks on paper or pictures. ● Select the correct numeral to represent 1 to 5, then 1 to 9, objects.	● Begin to record numbers, initially by making marks, progressing to simple tallying and writing numerals.
Adding and subtracting		● Work out by counting how many more are needed to make a larger number.
Problems involving real-life and money		● Sort coins, including the £1 and £2 coins and use them in role-play to pay and give change. **Use developing mathematical ideas and methods to solve practical problems** involving counting and comparing in a real or role-play context.

1 Session

Learning objectives

Starter
ELGs/NNS
● Begin to read o'clock time.
● **Begin to relate addition to combining two groups of objects, and subtraction to 'taking away'.**

Main teaching activity
ELGs/NNS
● Count in tens.
● Count in twos.

Vocabulary

count in twos… tens…, odd, even, every other, zero, ten, twenty… one hundred

You will need:
Equipment
Teaching clock face.

WHOLE CLASS TEACHING

Starter bank

These Starter bank ideas can be used throughout the unit.

O'clock times

Show the children the teaching clock. Point to each number on the clock face and ask the children to say the number: *One, two, three… twelve.* Now set the clock to different o'clock times which the children recognise, such as 9 o'clock coming into school, or 12 o'clock lunchtime, and ask: *What time does the clock show? Where is the minute (big) hand pointing? Where is the hour (little) hand pointing? What do we do when it is … o'clock?*

Adding

Tell the children that they can count on in their heads or use their fingers to help them. Say: *What is three add two? So three and four, five. So three add two is five.* Repeat this for other additions, keeping the totals to up to about seven to begin with, then extending to up to ten over time.

Subtracting

Tell the children that they can count on or back in their heads or use their fingers to help them. Say: *What is five take away two? Start on five, then four, three. So five take away two is three.* Repeat this for other subtractions, keeping the largest number to up to about seven to begin with, then extending to ten over time.

Main teaching activity

Ask the children to sit in a circle. Explain that you would like them to count with you in tens from zero to 100. Keep the pace of this sharp. The children can swing their arms, gently, in time to the count. Repeat this several times. Now ask the children to count around the group, in tens, one at a time. If a child falters, provide the number word in order to keep the pace snappy. Repeat this several times and ensure that a different child starts on zero each time. Repeat this for counting back in tens.

Now ask the children to begin on one tens number and stop on another: *Count on in tens from 30… to 60…; count back in tens from 80… to 20…; Count round the circle starting with Sara with 20; who do you think will say 70?*

Repeat the activity for counting in twos. Here the children can count from zero to 20, then from one to 19. Discuss how, when counting in twos we say 'every other number'.

GROUP ACTIVITIES

Tens and twos

Learning objectives
ELGs/NNS:
- Count in tens.
- Count in twos.

Activity

Work with a group of eight to ten children. Ask them to sit in a circle. Ask the children to count around the circle, individually, starting with the tens number you say, and stopping with the one you say. For example: *Count on in tens from 20… to 60…; count back in tens from 90… to 20…; count round the circle starting with Sara at 30; who do you think will say 80?* Repeat this for counting in twos, both starting from zero, and from one.

Plenary & assessment

Ask the children to think about:

● *If Paul starts counting on in tens from 20, who will say 90…?*
● *How did you work that out?*
● *If we count in twos starting on zero/one…, what numbers will we say?*

2 Sessions

Learning objectives

Main teaching activity
Green Stepping Stones
● Begin to represent numbers, using finger marks on paper or pictures.
● Select the correct numeral to represent 1 to 5, then 1 to 9, objects.
ELGs/NNS
● Begin to record numbers, initially by making marks, progressing to simple tallying and writing numerals.
● Work out by counting how many more are needed to make a larger number.

Vocabulary

add, more, and, make, sum, total, altogether, left/left over, difference between

You will need:
Photocopiable pages
'Handfuls' and 'Dice and spinner numbers', one for each pair, see pages 222–223.

CD pages
'Partitioned work mat', one for each pair (see General resources).

Equipment
Ten counting toys in a tub for each child; 1–6 numeral dice and paperclip for each child; flip chart or board and pens.

WHOLE CLASS TEACHING

Main teaching activity

Explain to the children that you will be asking them some word problems. Suggest to them that they solve them by counting up. Begin with a simple one, and model the problem with the children. Those who find this difficult to do mentally can use their fingers to help them to keep track of counting up. Say, for example: *There are two sweets. Five children would like a sweet. How many more sweets do we need?* On the flip chart write '2 sweets and 5 children', so that the children see the numbers as a reminder. Say together: *Two, then three, four, five. We need three more sweets. Two add three is five.* Repeat this for other examples.

Now use a difference example. For example: *There are eight cats at the farm and five dogs. How many more cats than dogs are there?* Write '8 cats and 5 dogs' on the flip chart. Say together: *Five, then six, seven, eight. There are three more cats. Five add three is eight.* Repeat this for some more examples, and include *difference*, such as: *There are six sheep and four goats on the farm. What is the number difference between the sheep and the goats?*

Give a different example: *There are eight sweets. Marcie eats six sweets. How many are left?* Again, write '8' and '6' on the flip chart. Say together: *Six, then seven, eight. There are two sweets left. So six add two is eight.* Repeat this for some more examples.

GROUP ACTIVITIES

Handfuls

Learning objectives
Green Stepping Stones:

● Begin to represent numbers, using fingers, marks on paper or pictures.
● Select the correct numeral to represent 1 to 5, then 1 to 9, objects.

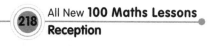

ELGs/NNS:
● Begin to record numbers, initially by making marks, progressing to simply tallying and writing numerals.
● Work out by counting how many more are needed to make a larger number.

Activity

Work with a group of six to eight children, and ask them to work in pairs. They will need a copy of CD page 'Partitioned work mat' for each pair. Ask the children to each take some of the counting toys and place these onto their work mat. Each child counts their own. They write their totals onto CD page 'Handfuls'. Then by counting up from the smaller to the larger number they find the difference, or how many more, and write this in the space provided. When you try this activity for the first time with a group, ask each pair to say their two numbers and to demonstrate how they counted up to find how many more.

If children working towards the Green Stepping Stones find this hard, suggest that they make two lines of the counting toys, and match these. Then they can see how many more toys one of the lines has than the other. Reinforce this by encouraging the children to say with you the number sentence. The children repeat the activity three times.

Plenary & assessment

Review some of the pairs of numbers and differences that children had. Encourage a pair of children to give one of their pairs of numbers and ask the other children to work out how many more by counting up. Say:
● *How many more is eight than five?*
● *What is the difference between nine and three?*
● *How did you work that out?*

Dice and spinner numbers

ADULT SUPPORTED

Learning objectives

ELGs/NNS
● Begin to record numbers, initially by making marks, progressing to simply tallying and writing numerals.
● Work out by counting how many more are needed to make a larger number.

Activity

Ask a group of six to eight children, in pairs, to work with the LSA. This activity works in the same way as 'Handfuls' except that instead of counting toys children use a 1–6 number dice, and the spinner and paperclip on CD page 'Dice and spinner numbers'. The children record their dice number and spinner number each time and find the difference between the two numbers. They do this four times in all.

Plenary & assessment

Review some of the pairs of numbers and the differences that children had. Encourage a pair of children to give one of their pairs of numbers and ask the other children to work out how many more by counting up. Say:
● *Which is the smaller/bigger number?*
● *How many more is seven than two?*
● *What is the difference between eight and one?*
● *How did you work that out?*

2 Sessions

Learning objectives

Main teaching activity

ELGs/NNS

● Sort coins, including the £1 and £2 coins and use them in role-play to pay and give change.

● **Use developing mathematical ideas and methods to solve practical problems** involving counting and comparing in a real or role-play context.

Vocabulary

compare, double, half, halve, count out, share out, left, left over, penny, pence, pound, price, cost, dear, costs more, cheap, costs less, cheaper, costs the same as, how much…? how many…? total

You will need:

CD pages
'Work mat' for each child (see General resources).

Equipment
A tub of mixed coins for each child; play food, plates and teddies in the home area; flip chart or board and pens.

WHOLE CLASS TEACHING

Main teaching activity

Explain to the children that you will be saying some problems for them to work out. Begin with a doubling problem: *Toffee apples cost 3p each. How much would two cost?* Discuss with the children how they could work this out. For example: *Let's count on: Three, then four, five, six. So three add three is six. Two toffee apples cost 6p.* Repeat this for another example such as: *Apples costs 4p each. Sapan buys two apples. How much does he spend?* This time invite two children to model the problem with money once the mental calculation has been carried out. Give one child a 10p and ask the children to work out the change. They can count up from 6p: *7p, 8p, 9p, 10p.* Invite the second child to count out the change. Repeat this for another example, such as: *Dristi buys two lollies. Each lolly costs 5p. How much do the two lollies cost?*

GROUP ACTIVITIES

Find the coins

TEACHER DIRECTED

Learning objectives

ELGs/NNS:

● Sort coins, including the £1 and £2 coins and use them in role-play to pay and give change.

● **Use developing mathematical ideas and methods to solve practical problems** involving counting and comparing in a real or role-play context.

Activity

Work with a group of six to eight children. Each child needs a copy of CD page 'Work mat' and a tub of mixed coins. Explain that you will say a problem for the children to work out with the coins. Begin with: *An orange costs 6p. Which two coins would pay for it?* Invite the children to choose coins from their pot, such as 5p and 1p. Say together: *5p add 1p is 6p.* Write '5p' and '1p' on the flip chart. Now say: *Can you find me some different ways to make 6p? How many different ways can you find?* Ask the children to use their coins to help them and to place their solutions in straight lines of coins on the work mat.

This activity can be repeated for a different total, up to 10p.

Plenary & assessment

Use the flip chart to write up the coins that the children suggest, such as 2p, 2p and 2p. Ask the children to say different ways of making 6p. (5p + 1p; 1p + 1p + 1p + 1p + 1p + 1p; 2p + 1p + 1p +

1p + 1p; 2p + 2p + 1p + 1p: 2p + 2p + 2p).

Invite the children to take turns to write the coins as pence, such as 2p, onto the flip chart. Ask:

- *Tell me how you totalled the coins.*
- *How else could we add these coins?*
- *Who has another way to make 6p?*

Sharing

STRUCTURED PLAY

Learning objective

ELGs/NNS:

- **Use developing mathematical ideas and methods to solve practical problems** involving counting and comparing in a real or role-play context.

Activity

This activity can be set up in the home area. Put out some plates of play food. Suggest to the children that they set the table for a teddies' tea party. Then ask the children to share the food between the teddies. As the children work, ask questions such as: *Is there enough for all the teddies? How many can the teddies have each? Take half the cakes off the plate? How many are left?*

Plenary & assessment

Discuss with the children how many teddies there are and how many cakes, biscuits and so on. Say:

- *Can all the teddies have some? How do you know?*
- *How many can the teddies have each?*
- *Take half the cakes away. How many are there now?*
- *Share the cakes out between you. How many times will the plate go round? Are there any left?*

Name	Date

Handfuls

Work with a partner.
You will each need ten counting toys.
You will need a copy of 'Partitioned work mat' between you.

Each take a handful of toys.
Put them onto your part of the mat.
Count the toys.

Write how many toys in the box.
Write how many more in the other box.

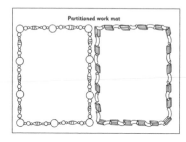   How many more?

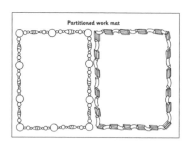   How many more?

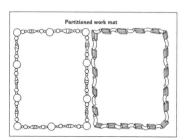   How many more?

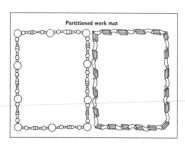   How many more?

Name	Date

Dice and spinner numbers

Work with a partner.
You will need a 1–6 dice and a paperclip.

Take turns to spin the paperclip on the spinner.
Write the spinner number.

Roll the dice.
Write the dice number.

Write the number difference.

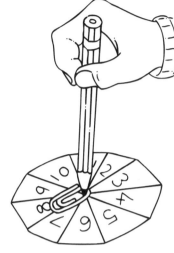

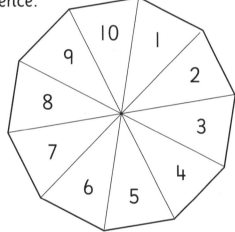

Spinner number	Dice number	Difference

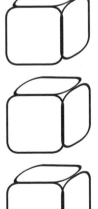